The Pocket Guide to Plays and Playwrights

For My Husband

Gwyn

The Pocket Guide to Plays and Playwrights

Maureen Hughes

REMEMBER WHEN

First published in Great Britain in 2009 by
REMEMBER WHEN
An imprint of
Pen & Sword Books Ltd
47 Church Street
Barnsley
South Yorkshire
S70 2AS

ISBN 978 1 84468 043 6

Typeset by Mac Style, Beverley, East Yorkshire
Printed and bound in the UK by CPI

Pen & Sword Books Ltd incorporates the Imprints of Pen & Sword Aviation,
Pen & Sword Family History, Pen & Sword Maritime, Pen & Sword Military,
Wharncliffe Local History, Pen & Sword Select, Pen & Sword Military Classics,
Leo Cooper, Remember When, Seaforth Publishing and Frontline Publishing.

For a complete list of Pen & Sword titles please contact
PEN & SWORD BOOKS LIMITED
47 Church Street, Barnsley, South Yorkshire, S70 2AS, England
E-mail: enquiries@pen-and-sword.co.uk
Website: www.pen-and-sword.co.uk

Contents

Acknowledgements

MY THANKS to my ever patient and supportive family and friends, my husband, Gwyn, and my children, Kieran and Vicky, who put up with me glued to my laptop, surrounded by reference books and forbidding all forms of speech for weeks on end; to my grandchildren and my new great-grandson, Jaiden, whom I am sure would be supportive were he older than just a few weeks! Thanks too to Paula and Aisha who have always been, and I know always will be, there for me in times of stress. To Marian and Tom, the greatest in-laws anyone could ever wish to have, my adorable cousin, Michael, my school friend Jo and friend Carol – my personal walking dictionary – thanks to all of you for patiently putting up with weeks of silence when I am chasing deadlines. And finally to Hilary who is both my agent and my friend – yes some agents are so good that they can become a friend too! Without all of you, my life would be empty and no book would be worth writing.

So many people have helped me out with this book that to name them all would be an impossibility, but some have been 'extra' helpful so to them I am indeed indebted; Simon Murgatroyd, Alan Ayckbourn's archivist, who went to a great deal of trouble to assist me when writing the piece on the great man himself; Vivyan Ellacott who searched his own personal archives for information when I came unstuck; Chris 'Willy' Wilson, the expert on Brendan Behan and Charlotte Elston, Straight Line Management's research assistant, who laboriously checked through the more tedious research facts and Ian Sanders who solved all of my computing problems. And last, but not least, I would like to thank Fiona Shoop, the Commissioning Editor of Remember When, for all of her help. To all of you, I would like to say a big 'Thank You'.

Foreword

MAUREEN HUGHES has done a remarkable job. She has packed a vast amount of information into a confined space. As a writer myself, I know just how difficult that is. I also learned a lot from reading her book: to my shame, I knew nothing about Seventeenth Century Italian Green Theatre or about Houdini's death from a blow to the abdomen or about the superstition concerning knitting either on stage or in the wings. But what really cheers me is that this book is a celebration of plays and playwrights: something that seems to me vitally necessary in the current cultural climate.

As Maureen Hughes constantly reminds us, there is a two-and-a-half-thousand year tradition of Western drama. Yet I believe our awareness of that tradition is under threat from several quarters. In many colleges and universities, 'performance' has become divorced from 'text'. The separation of theatre studies from literature means that generations of students are emerging who may know a good deal about impro and devised drama but who couldn't tell you the plot of *Oedipus Rex*, *Hamlet* or *Ghosts*. But this is only one of many factors militating against written drama. I could cite many others: BBC TV's abnegation of its public-service responsibility to present the best of the past, an Arts Council drama department enthralled by spectacles, circuses and street-theatre, the decline of high-quality touring groups such as Prospect, the Actors' Company or Compass which took the core canon around the country. Plays, however, are resilient objects. They offer an emotional and intellectual satisfaction that you rarely find in even the most ingenious piece of physical theatre: a first-rate production of *Twelfth Night*, *Uncle Vanya* or *Death of a Salesman* can actually change your life. All the evidence also suggests that, if plays are made available to young audiences at the right price, they can still be immensely popular. 'The future of the theatre,' Peter Brook once said, 'is cheap seats.' You only have to look at the audiences taking advantage of The National Theatre's £10 ticket scheme or the low-price standing-room at Shakespeare's Globe to realise the profound truth of Brook's remark. Make plays affordable and people will come. But the great thing about Maureen Hughes' book is that it reminds us what a wealth of world drama there is available. Her book itemises the classic canon. It also whetted my appetite for plays we rarely, if ever, see. Has anyone revived Dryden's exquisite comedy, *Marriage à la Mode*, since John Clements at the St James's in 1946? Why does no-one take a new look at Middleton's *A Game of Chess* which I saw beautifully staged in an Oxford college garden circa 1960? And how come Pinero's *The Second Mrs Tanqueray*, one of the most popular woman-with-a-past dramas of the Victorian age, has been allowed to fall into disuse?

Maureen Hughes also pays proper attention to modern drama. I'm delighted by her focus on four grand masters in Ayckbourn, Bennett, Pinter and Stoppard and her ingenuity in discovering their often hidden links to her native Yorkshire. But, in reading her book, I was struck by how much work from the recent past clamours for revival. Look at the lists of plays which won Olivier or *Evening Standard* awards and you see what I mean. Peter Nichols' *The National Health* and Peter Barnes' *The Ruling Class* are both fantastic state-of-the-nation comedies. Timberlake Wertenbaker's *Our Country's Good* is a deeply moving tribute to the transformative power of theatre. And Michael Frayn's *Alphabetical Order*, set in a newspaper cuttings-library, vividly conveys mankind's desperate attempt to impose order on prevailing chaos. I hope this book reaches not just theatre-goers and students but the people who run our theatres; it might remind them of the endless diversity of drama and the abundance of unfamiliar plays. But what I also welcome is the emphasis on youth. Maureen pays due tribute to Wimbledon's excellent Polka Theatre and to a writer like David Wood, who has specialised in creating plays for young people. The author's own recollection of being exposed as a teenager to the D'Oyly Carte company's touring Gilbert and Sullivan productions also brought back happy memories. I too saw those productions at the Birmingham Hippodrome, or what was then the Shakespeare Memorial Theatre. By today's standards, they were probably a bit dowdy. But they were part of that induction into theatre's delights that begins, if you are lucky, when you are young.

This book, in short, is a reminder of theatre's cornucopian pleasures, its historical oddities and ongoing eccentricities. But, above all, it is testament to the power of written drama. 'Do you think the play is dead?' I was recently asked by a high-ranking Arts Council bureaucrat. Staggered by the audacity of the question, coming from someone who was meant to be nurturing the form, I replied that the play was still a vibrant, living entity and that, in the words of Shakespeare's Antony, 'there's sap in't yet.' And, by way of proof, I would suggest close study of Maureen Hughes' invaluable pocket guide, which takes you on a roller-coaster ride through over two millennia of theatrical history.

Michael Billington

Chapter One

Welcome to the World of Plays, Playwrights and Theatre

Introduction

A RATHER famous playwright once wrote:

> All the world's a stage,
> And all the men and women merely players
>
> *As You Like It* – William Shakespeare

And he was right too, for we are all a part of one huge play – in many acts and scenes of course – but a huge play nevertheless! Think about it, when you go to the theatre exactly what are you going to see? I'll tell you what, you are going to see a reflection of **real life** upon a stage, life which has been trapped and recorded by a playwright for you to watch, for you to enjoy, to criticise and from which you can perhaps learn or be educated – and yes they are two different things. Theatre, you see, is as colourful and as diverse as life itself – **because, of course, it *is* life itself**.

Many of us had our initiation into the world of theatre with our involvement in the annual production of the school Nativity play. You remember this don't you? This was the time when the teacher became the playwright as he/she penned the story of the Nativity to suit the capabilities of her current charges; it was when the mothers became wardrobe mistresses as they furiously sewed together the obligatory tea towel into headdresses for the shepherds; when fathers were drafted in to make the cribs and strange looking donkeys, whilst grandparents attempted to wrap tinsel around the heads of little – and to be honest, anything but angelic – five-year-old angels. The total family and community involvement went on until, finally, the reception class trooped onto the stage, all peering into the audience to catch a glimpse of their family … and then dutifully wave to them! After that followed 10 nerve-wracking minutes as the teachers wondered whether any of the children would remember their lines and, if they did, then whether Sally would actually say the correct words, 'My eyes are wide open' as opposed to, 'My Y's are eyed open'.

Then of course there was the threat from little Tommy's mother that Santa wouldn't visit naughty boys, and the silent prayers from the teachers that this threat would pay off and, on this one occasion, stop Tommy from pulling the head off Baby Jesus and throwing it at the Angel Gabriel – again! All of this was rounded off by an out of tune rendition of 'Away in a Manger', the flashing of cameras and the general whisper of 'Ah, weren't they wonderful'. Well, frankly no, they probably weren't wonderful; in fact, the chances are that they were embarrassingly … cute! So, did it ring a bell? I'm sure it did because it is a ritual in which most 'play a part' to a lesser or greater degree. And, for some, this is the start of a lifelong love affair with the theatre.

For others the affair begins with the annual trip to the pantomime. You know, that wonderful Christmas tradition where boys play girls and girls play boys, where mice turn into horses and pull along a pumpkin – oops, I mean a coach! Then of course, there is the all-singing, all-dancing cow and the constant audience involvement as they excitedly try to warn the goodie that the baddie is around with cries of: 'He's behind you!' This too can be the springboard for many a child's future interest in the theatre, particularly when one considers the fact that local dance and theatre schools generally provide a troop of children – traditionally called 'Babes' – as singing/dancing chorus members.

And if the Nativity didn't get you, or the pantomime, then maybe your interest was captured by your involvement in school plays, or watching friends and relatives in the local amateur dramatic society; but whichever, one way or another, many peoples' interest is captured early on and it becomes a lifelong passion.

But you know what? Interest is good, but knowledge is oh so satisfying, especially when it backs up and supports a hobby or interest. And so I hope that this book will give those of you who 'love theatre' in the way that I do, a deeper insight into this fascinating and magical world of make believe – except that it's not is it, it's … a reflection of real life upon a stage, life which has been trapped and recorded by a playwright for you to enjoy.

Different types of Theatre

Theatre is as diverse as life itself and as a reflection of life, so it should be, where to begin is as confusing as any theatrical who dunnit because there are so many different types of theatre. There's …

ACADEMIC THEATRE
This is generally theatre played on a university/college campus by university/ college students for a university/college audience and can be one of the springboards to a lifetime of theatre-going. It is quite often idealistic, because it

is written and played by the young who still believe that the world can be improved!

ALTERNATIVE THEATRE

Alternative Theatre surfaced in the 1960s as a reaction against mainstream theatre and is often played in alternative venues too, such as: the back rooms of pubs, cellars and converted warehouses and frequently has a young, and thus idealistic, following.

AMATEUR THEATRE

Theatre produced and played by non-professionals for love and not for payment is called Amateur Theatre. Many local Amateur Dramatic Societies will allow anyone who wants to join their society to do so – they might, of course, be damned to a walk-on part forever more, though a genuine love of theatre is generally considered more important than talent. Some societies, however, do audition for new members just as a professional company would.

AUTO SACRAMENTAL

This is a Spanish Morality play ('Auto Sacramental' translates as 'sacramental act') to accompany the Corpus Christi Day procession, which reached its peak in the Seventeenth Century. The plays were short, in verse and dealt with some aspect of the Holy Eucharist – which the feast of Corpus Christi celebrated.

BROADWAY THEATRE

Broadway is the US equivalent of the West End and where, supposedly, only the best theatre plays. To have a production 'on' Broadway or 'in' the West End usually means you have 'made it', as they say.

BURLESQUE THEATRE

This form of theatre pokes fun at contemporary theatrical practice and the social habits of the upper classes, through the medium of comedy and music; it was a form of theatre popular from the mid-Nineteenth Century to mid-Twentieth Century – it also had a reputation for being somewhat bawdy, with scantily clad women frequently on show.

CHILDREN'S THEATRE

This type of theatre is designed to attract, stimulate and interest the next generation of theatre-goers and so plays a very important part in the world of theatre. It is a specialist form of theatre and, as in the case of the wonderful Polka Theatre in Wimbledon, reaches out beyond the action on the stage itself with the entire building, which has been designed to capture the theatrical imagination of children.

THE COMMEDIA DELL'ARTE

A form of traditionally improvised theatre which was very popular in Sixteenth and Seventeenth Century Italian theatre and in which, over a period of time, 'stock' characters and situations developed and the use of masks became commonplace.

COMMEDIA ERUDITA

This was an Italian Renaissance genre of theatre which was distinguished from Commedia dell'Arte by its literary elements and, unlike the latter used actual scripts rather than improvisation techniques. Because the scripts (which were generally in Latin or Italian and included the comedies of Plautus and Terence) were not exactly accessible to the common man, the plays tended to be performed for the nobility.

COMMERCIAL THEATRE

Commercial Theatre is theatre which is produced and performed by working, paid and full-time professional companies for and to make money – for themselves – some say by forfeiting any thought or respect for the art of theatre.

COMMUNITY THEATRE

This is generally site-specific and is played for a certain 'type' of person peculiar to that particular place; it is often theatre with a message but can actually be any sort of play or any kind of performance given for the community. Frequently, though not always, Community Theatre is performed in a community-owned venue too.

DIDACTIC THEATRE

Didactic Theatre is a form of drama intent on instructing or teaching the audience rather than entertaining them. The Medieval Mystery and Morality plays were didactic in their telling of the Bible stories and instructions about morality; today the theatre of Brecht, with its political slant, is considered to be didactic theatre.

ELIZABETHAN THEATRE

This is the theatre of the Elizabethan age, when Queen Elizabeth I reigned (1558–1603). The first playhouse was built in 1576 by one James Burbage and was called, quite simply, 'The Theatre'.

FRINGE THEATRE

Similar to Alternative Theatre in that it is frequently played in smaller venues and is often where new playwrights try out their work for the first time. A city famous for its Fringe Theatre is Edinburgh, home of the world-renowned 'Edinburgh Fringe Festival'. Theatre lovers from all over the world make an annual theatrical pilgrimage up to Edinburgh each August to see as many new works as possible in a variety of venues, which, in fact, can be as wild and as exciting as any of the new work itself! Many commercially and artistically successful works started their life at the Edinburgh Fringe Festival and part of the fun is to see whether you can spot a potential winner or future blockbuster.

GREEK THEATRE

Just as the name implies, this is theatre which was played in ancient Greece and is acknowledged by most as the father of theatre – even though, in fact, the true origins of theatre can be traced way back to primitive man.

GREEN THEATRE

Seventeenth Century Italian gardens were often planted with evergreens and designed for outdoor theatrical entertainment, with various hedges acting as concealed entrances for the actors. The best examples of Green Theatre can be found at the Imperial Hill (*Poggio Imperiale*) and at the Villa Marlia in Tuscany (near Lucca), Italy, and also Villa Garzoni at Collodi.

KABUKI PLAY

Almost four centuries old, this is traditional Japanese drama where singing and dancing is performed in a stylised manner. Traditionally, during Kabuki Theatre there is constant interplay between the actors and audience – the actors frequently interrupt the play to speak directly to the audience, who, in return, respond with praise or by clapping their hands.

KYŌGEN PLAY

This is another, but less serious, form of Japanese Theatre which consists of more than 200 one act comedies, generally acted out by just two or three actors and with very little practical help in the terms of sets and lighting. The movement is often exaggerated which makes the plays easier to understand.

MORALITY PLAYS

A Morality play is Medieval and a companion to the Mystery plays. Whereas Mystery plays depict biblical stories, Morality plays depict moral lessons.

MUSICAL THEATRE

In this type of theatre, music supports and plays an integral part in the production. It became increasingly popular during the Twentieth Century and in the transition to the Twenty-First Century. It is thought, by some, to have little dramatic depth and to be merely a way of making money from theatre through exorbitant ticket prices.

MYSTERY PLAY

These are a Medieval cycle of plays based on biblical stories and were a popular form of entertainment until the Reformation, when they were banned. In the cities of York and Chester, the Mystery plays were reintroduced in the early 1950s.

NOH THEATRE

This is traditional Japanese Theatre where, rather than acting, the performers tell the story using their appearance and movements. In consequence, little actually 'happens' in Noh Theatre, which can also be spelt 'No' and means 'talent' or 'skill'.

OUTDOOR THEATRE

As the name would suggest, this is theatre played outside – often in parkland or in the grounds of large houses and is usually called '**Open Air Theatre**'. The most famous example can be found in Regents Park, London where the Open Air Theatre has flourished since 1932. Here too, I must mention the unique and wonderful open air theatre in Scarborough, once the largest in Europe and now left to rot and decay. It was special because the stage was on an island on a lake. Restore it I say!

PROFESSIONAL THEATRE

Professional Theatre is theatre in which the actors are paid to perform in a production; once paid the actor in question can then be called a 'professional' performer in 'professional' theatre. In Professional Theatre for all involved, from the producer through to the designers, the director and actors it is their 'job', it is how they make a living and not a hobby as with amateur theatre.

PROVINCIAL THEATRE

This is theatre outside of The West End and in the provinces of the United Kingdom. Some touring companies often try out a show in the Provinces before taking it into The West End, testing audience reaction and undertaking rewrites to make it perfect before bringing it to town; other companies opt to take a successful West End show out into the Provinces and to a wider audience.

PUPPET THEATRE

Puppet Theatre is exactly what it says it is, and one of the most famous Puppet Theatres of all time is Punch and Judy, a puppet show which traditionally, though not exclusively, takes place on British beaches during the summer months in a portable hut, which can trace its origins back to the Sixteenth Century.

REPERTORY THEATRE

Commonly known as **'Rep' Theatre**, this form of theatre is the cornerstone of professional theatre and generally exists in the provinces where a resident company of actors prepare and perform a variety of productions, usually a different one each week or two, occasionally every three weeks. During 'Rep Seasons' an actor/actress is often expected to 'back to back'. This is when they will rehearse one play – the next in the season – during the day, whilst performing in the current play each night.

SATIRE

This is theatre which ridicules something specific by the use of irony, sarcasm and wit; the audience is generally familiar with the subject matter making the material even funnier. Satire has tended, in the latter half of the last century at least, to be more popular on the television than in the theatre.

SATYR PLAY

A Satyr Play is a play which is performed as comic relief at the end of a cycle of Greek tragedies. Euripides' *Cyclops* is the only complete Satyr play remaining today.

SUBSIDISED THEATRE

Often called 'non-profit making theatre', though this is not actually the intent! The aim is to provide theatre for everyone and for which the funding is derived from official sources and where the profit is not the reason for the production.

THEATRE IN EDUCATION

Theatre in Education is theatre in an educational environment; theatre which educates the audience on a variety of topics and issues, including those which are considered to be social, economic and educational.

THEATRE IN THE ROUND

This type of theatre is also called **Arena Stage, Central Stage** or **Island Stage**, and is identified by the fact that the stage is surrounded by the audience. The playwright Alan Ayckbourn writes almost exclusively for Theatre in the Round.

THEATRE OF CRUELTY

Devised by French dramatist Antonin Artaud, this type of theatre attacks the audiences' subconscious in an attempt to release generally deep-rooted and suppressed fears and anxieties.

THEATRE OF THE ABSURD

This type of theatre deals with works which attempt to convey to the audience a sense of bewilderment and anxiety as well as stimulating them to wonder about, and question, the inexplicable existence of the universe.

WEST END THEATRE

The mere name West End, without even a mention of the word 'theatre', generally conjures up visions of some of the best theatres in the world showing some of the best productions in the world.

ZAJU PLAY

Classical Chinese plays which tell a simple story accompanied by songs. In which the beautifully poetic lyrics are considered of more importance then the plot. Of the thousands of original Zaju Plays only about two hundred are in existence today.

I could go on but, as I said, theatre is as diverse as life itself – and as never ending.

Chapter Two

The History of Theatre

THROUGHOUT the centuries, theatre has grown, changed and developed as one would expect of an art that is a part of our human existence. Each era or century has been documented both in books and upon the stage, in order that future generations may study and understand their cultural ancestry.

Timeline

PRIMITIVE THEATRE …
From the beginning of time, man entertains man

ANCIENT GREEK THEATRE …
Thought by some to be the real 'father' of modern theatre

ANCIENT ROMAN THEATRE …
BC Roman debauchery led to the decline of theatre

MEDIEVAL THEATRE …
The rebirth of theatre, encouraged by the Church

RENAISSANCE THEATRE …
First theatres built; in 1642 they were closed down

RESTORATION THEATRE …
Theatres reopen; recognition for female playwrights

EIGHTEENTH CENTURY THEATRE …
The first playhouses are opened in the Provinces

NINETEENTH CENTURY THEATRE …
The influence of Stanislavski is felt as realism arrives

TWENTIETH CENTURY THEATRE …
Technology aids advancement and becomes an integral part of theatre

TWENTY-FIRST CENTURY THEATRE …
Theatre and screen become intrinsically entwined

The Beginning of Time = The Beginning of Theatre

Theatre does not and cannot exist in isolation: history, theatre and literature are a part of the social and artistic infrastructure of the world in which we live. History happens – and is recorded, monitored and commented upon in the great works of literature, bringing world facts and events to the masses, whilst theatre allows us to 'see' social and political events in action, so to speak. Even literature and theatre, which is written purely for enjoyment and not to educate, is still a part of this social and artistic infrastructure for, in contemporary writing, there is still the subconscious recording of the time in which we live and so, like it or not, we each 'play a part' in the making and recording of history.

In years to come, future generations will look at our theatre-going habits and analyse the success – or failure – of our playwrights. They will probably ponder on and discuss the 'quaint' use of live music and wonder about the lack of training in the arts! Plays which are heralded as forward thinking and groundbreaking works of art now, will, in future years, possibly be looked upon as tame and boring, perhaps even quaint.

We are often led to believe that there is 'good theatre' and there is 'bad theatre'; this is not a theory to which I subscribe. As far as I am concerned, there is 'a' theatre for each and every one of us; it is surely just a matter of preference. I abhor the so-called intellectual who looks down his nose at those who would prefer to watch and enjoy a farce or a pantomime rather than a Shakespearean production. So what? They are at the theatre and enjoying the experience and, as far as I am concerned, that is all that matters. Of course, I acknowledge that some productions are badly written, produced and directed, but let's not treat those who prefer the less intellectual productions as devoid of any theatrical sense at all. I am convinced that, once in a theatre, a love for it will only grow and, with it, a discernment for well-crafted work, surely that can only be a good thing?

So, whilst we think about and continue with the task of making theatrical history let us take a brief look back at how past theatrical history was made, thus bringing us to this point in time, and so we start with:

Primitive Theatre

There came man and there came theatre, for where there is man there is theatre. Of course long ago it was very primitive, no lights or hydraulic scenery. In fact, no stage at all (at least not that we'd recognise today) but it was nevertheless theatre, for theatre is one or more persons 'performing' a contrived piece of life for others to watch, whatever the reason and wherever the place.

Early man was a hunter/gatherer; there were no corner shops or hypermarkets for his convenience and only the strongest survived. He had no understanding of natural phenomena either and explained the existence of such by making up stories, more or less as a small child might even today. A child without the skills of literacy uses his/her imagination to explain what to them is inexplicable. That is how we have stories such as 'The Anger of God' to explain the sound of thunder.

It is natural for man to 'show-off' and, so it follows, that theatre is natural; when one person decides on the storyline of what he wants to perform for another, then he becomes a **playwright** – even if he doesn't write it down – and the person(s) watching become the **audience** – even if they don't pay or sit in a conventional theatre. So primitive theatre began with primitive man and as man has evolved, changed and developed, so has his theatre.

Earliest theatre often took the form of movement – dance – and was used for reasons other than just to entertain its audience. It is thought that these theatrical dances were used to pay homage to supernatural powers and to deter evil spirits; such 'theatre' is still in evidence in under-developed parts of the world today.

Greek Theatre – From the Sixth Century BC

Although Greek Theatre was actually the first recorded form of theatre in history, and so often thought to be the father of theatre, the true facts are still rather sketchy and open to doubt, to the point that we cannot, in fact, be certain of anything. What we do know, however, is that many modern words associated with theatre today have their roots in the Greek language. For example, the word theatre itself comes from the word *theatron* meaning 'viewing place' and the word drama comes from the word *dran* meaning 'to do'. It is generally believed though that in ancient Greece, plays were performed on special occasions, such as festivals, with the theme of the play being closely associated with religion. It was, at this time, a very competitive art form; then, of course, there was the Chorus – a group of men who supported, narrated and commented upon the action of the play and the central themes and issues. This is a technique still used today, even in very modern pieces. For example, in the musical *Little Shop of Horrors*, three girls, in the style of a Greek Chorus, comment upon the action of the man-eating plant.

In the Sixth Century BC, a priest, by the name of Thespis, introduced an element into theatre that has been seen by many as the birth of theatre as we know it today when he became the first actor to 'speak' to the Chorus. And, from that momentous moment in the history of the theatre, actors have been proud to call themselves 'thespians'.

Playwrights were then thought to be multi-talented and it was generally believed that they probably not only wrote the plays but also directed and initially acted in them too, even sometimes writing the music and choreographing the movements, making our own current triple-threat phenomena seem rather simplistic by comparison.

Women did not act in the plays and all of the parts were played by men who wore masks to depict the character they were playing. Initially, there was only one actor in each play but, as time passed, a second and then a third actor was introduced.

LAYOUT OF A GREEK THEATRE

The theatres themselves were often built in the hillsides, and once 'at the theatre' there were specified places where certain classes of people would sit. The front rows were reserved for the priests and behind them sat the important local people. The ordinary citizens sat much farther away from the stage and point of action which, at this period in time, was a raised wooden platform with a hut behind it where the actors could change.

The **Orchestra** – the literal meaning of which is 'dancing space' – was generally level and circular in shape and was where the Chorus would sing, dance and tell the audience what was happening. This space was actually just hard earth but, later on, orchestras were more sophisticated and were paved, some even with marble.

Theatron – the 'viewing place' was where the audience sat around the orchestra in a semi-circular shape, the seats were often a part of the hillside and, in the beginning, the audience would have to take something soft to sit on, for there were no 'proper' seats. As time progressed, however, seats were crafted, sometimes out of marble which was no softer, but it was a seat, and quite an impressive one too.

The **Skene** – this was a sort of hut which was furthest away from the audience and behind the orchestra. It was used as a set, as well as a hut, in which the actors could change; so here we have one of the first dressing rooms. In front of the skene, there was sometimes a wooden platform which was, in fact, an early stage. Exits and entrances were made through a door in the skene.

Mekhane – this is a crane-like contraption which hoisted the actors into the air, suspending them above the stage. This was used when an actor was playing the part of a god or a mythological creature; a little more obvious than the 'flying' mechanisms we use today for *Peter Pan* and other such plays which require an actor to fly.

Then came the decline of the Greek government and Greek society, whilst at the same time, came the rise of the Roman Empire.

Roman Theatre – 0BC–500AD

So, with the conquering Romans we come to Roman Theatre, which borrowed a lot of its 'ideas' from Greek Theatre, but actually was not as successful as the Greek theatre and was less religious too. In fact, by comparison, it was somewhat crude and could not compete with its predecessor in terms of popularity, for the populace were disinterested. Unlike the Greeks, the Romans did not structure their buildings into hillsides but built them upon their own foundations, though the basic layout was almost the same. The orchestra, however, evolved into a semi-circular area and, with Roman theatre, we began to edge a little further towards the modern theatre.

The Roman 'theatres' were enormous and the audience itself was actually more of a gathering of noise and confusion, for the Romans seemed to care little for what was going on before them and were more interested in spectacle than in theatrical content. In fact, the Romans loved bloodthirsty spectacles and, when the action of a play called for an actor to die on stage, a condemned man would often be brought on at the last moment to replace the actor. He would then actually be killed on stage as and when the plot required! Theatre in Roman times could actually be quite a dangerous pastime; when an audience did not enjoy a performance, they would jeer and shout for the actor to get off, or even throw things at him. Strangely though, the most popular of the Roman entertainments were the mimes but, as a whole, theatre at this time was really just an excuse for debauched behaviour, and so it was that the Roman theatre died.

Medieval Theatre

After the fall of the Roman Empire, theatre seemed to have no place in life and was, in fact, banned at the beginning of the Middle Ages by the Roman Catholic Church in an attempt to halt the excesses and debauchery of the Roman theatre.

Ironically, in the Tenth Century, it was the Church itself that brought a form of theatre back to the masses when it introduced drama into the Easter Liturgy to portray the religious story of the Resurrection; this was the beginning of one of the greatest forms of theatre which has, in fact, survived through to modern times, the **Mystery Plays**. The plays grew from depicting the Resurrection to eventually encompassing the entire Bible from Creation to the Last Judgement. In addition, the lives of the saints entered into this mode of performance and became known as the **Miracle Plays**; then along came the **Morality Plays** in which moral lessons were taught.

YORK MYSTERY PLAYS

The famous York **Mystery Plays** take place in a four-year cycle in the wonderfully historic, Medieval city of York.

The first recorded playing of the York **Mystery Plays** was in 1376. They continued to be played on the festival of Corpus Christi until the 1548 abolition of this festival. Sadly, it was inevitable that this would happen, as any tradition which was associated with the old religion was systematically removed from the calendar.

Eventually, and for the 1951 York Festival of the Arts, the York **Mystery Plays** were reinstated and performed in the beautifully atmospheric Museum Gardens in the city centre, amidst the legendary free roaming peacocks, often showing off far more than the actors. Here, the **Mystery Plays** were performed on a fixed stage against a Medieval backdrop; it was not until 1954, however, that travelling wagons of actors could be seen in the streets and, until 1988, it was just one or two wagons. But they continued to roll onwards until, eventually, in 2006, twelve wagons of performing actors could be seen in the streets of York. All this makes for a very special atmosphere which should be experienced at least once by all theatre lovers.

INTERESTING FACTS ABOUT THE YORK MYSTERY PLAYS

- 48 pageants illustrate the Christian history of the world from the Creation up until the Last Judgement
- The Plays are traditionally played on the feast day of Corpus Christi, a movable feast which occurs on the first Thursday after Trinity Sunday
- The word '**mystery**' in Middle English meant 'trade' or 'craft' and the Guilds of the various trades and crafts were responsible for the Plays
- The only surviving manuscript of the York plays (c. 1463–77) is in the British Library

York Mystery Plays

CHESTER MYSTERY PLAYS

On the other side of the Pennines, we find the Chester **Mystery Plays**, which are performed every five years in the 2000-year-old city of Chester, England.

The plays were originally performed at the Abbey of St. Werburgh (now Chester Cathedral), where the monks acted out the Bible stories for those who wouldn't otherwise be able to follow or understand the church services which were, at this time, all conducted in Latin. Eventually, the plays were moved outside the church and onto the streets of Chester, where they were played on decorated wagons which were trundled through the streets, stopping at appointed stations where an audience would gather to watch.

When a national ban was placed on the performance of **Mystery Plays** in the Sixteenth Century, Chester became the last to concede in 1578, thus becoming the longest running play cycle in Medieval England. As with the York Mystery Plays, the plays were revived for the Festival of Britain in 1951.

INTERESTING FACTS ABOUT THE CHESTER MYSTERY PLAYS

- In 1997, 200 people performed in the play *Noah's Flood*, making it the largest cast ever assembled for one play in the history of the Chester cycle
- Of the few surviving **Mystery Plays** in England, Chester's original texts are the most complete in existence today

Chester Mystery
Plays

- Members of the Royal family who have attended the plays are:
  1. Princess Margaret in 1962 and 1977
  2. Prince Edward in 2003
- In 1997, Finnish students staged the Resurrection, directed by Kirsi Huotari, as part of a cultural exchange programme

Renaissance Theatre/Elizabethan Theatre

Until this time, the seat of education and learning had its primary roots in the monasteries but now the resulting, and ever growing, branches of learning were spreading beyond these confines with the Latin texts of Terence, Plautus and Seneca being more widely read.

Early Renaissance theatre – which actually started in Italy – was really more about spectacle than actual dramatic content. With the passage of time the principles of Renaissance Theatre, which included Elizabethan Theatre, became more clear-cut and quite straightforward; to a point one could say almost idealistic in that theatre came to be a vehicle for portraying the correct moral message with good triumphing over evil.

One must remember that many scholars believed at this time that comedy and tragedy were not combined and that they existed in dramatic isolation; not true. Even the early playwrights appreciated and realised the power of comic relief to intensify tragedy and, as the term suggests, give the audience momentary relief from the emotional trauma of watching a tragedy unfold before their eyes whilst, of course, remaining powerless to stop it.

Until the Sixteenth Century, there were no 'proper' theatres in London. Instead, playwrights presented their plays in the inner courtyards of inns, to an audience who stood around in the yards or on the balconies overlooking the courtyards.

It was in 1576, during the reign of Elizabeth I that the first real theatre was built by James Burbage and was called quite simply 'The Theatre', heralding the birth of many more theatres which were to follow. In 1587, James Burbage died and, two years later, his two sons dismantled the building and carried the timber over the river where they used it to build a new theatre called 'The Globe', a theatre whose name was later to become synonymous with both theatre itself and with the playwright William Shakespeare, many of whose plays first saw the boards at The Globe.

We owe the layout of modern theatre to the influence of Elizabethan theatres. These venues catered for such a cross section of Londoners at the time and, pro rata, more Londoners went to the theatre on a regular basis than today – and yet we are supposedly better educated and more artistically aware.

In an Elizabethan theatre, the 'ordinary' folk stood in an open pit, open to the elements that is, and were called 'groundlings' and allowed to watch plays for a penny. Those with more money to spare could sit in the upper gallery where the seats were hard, but they were still seats! Those with even more money could sit in the two lower galleries, this time on a cushion. There were even more luxurious and expensive places to sit too, and these were to the left and right of the stage. Elizabethan theatres were pretty much the forerunners of today's theatre, although the stalls today – the positioning of the old groundlings pit – are now, of course, covered by a roof. They are also said to be the best seats in the house by some, me being one of them, and so quite expensive. In today's theatre the next level up is the Dress Circle, comfortable and equally expensive. Then in terms of comfort, I'm afraid, it is all *downhill* from there the *higher up* one sits. The next level is the Upper Circle, cheaper but with less leg-room, followed by, higher up still in some theatres, the Gallery or Gods, so named for obvious reasons; in fact, there is more chance of seeing a celestial body if you sit in the Gods than there is of seeing any action on the stage! In some theatres, seating in the Gods consists of cushioned bench seating, and is therefore much favoured by impoverished students. To the left and right of the modern stage are the boxes reserved for wealthier members of the audience. Some would say these are seats for those who wish 'to be seen' rather than 'to see', for they are in fact on view to the entire audience – though they cannot see the entire stage.

Theatres in Elizabethan times were feared by many, especially by the Church and City Officials and, as a consequence, the presentation of plays and theatre was banned within the city limits. What was the basis for these fears? Well, to be honest, it was quite a rational fear really, for where masses were gathered, and in a theatre of this time this could be in excess of 3,000 people, then there was a very real fear that the Bubonic Plague – one of the greatest and most feared killers of the time – would spread. Theatres were also used for other less savoury forms of entertainment such as bear baiting, gambling and other immoral pastimes frowned upon by the strict Puritans of the time. However, theatre was still extremely popular and audiences were always keen to see new plays, often presented by the two most famous theatrical companies: the Admiral's Men and the Lord Chamberlain's Men – in fact William Shakespeare himself was a principal writer with the Lord Chamberlain's Men. And so it was that theatre flourished.

It was fear of the earlier mentioned plague that actually gave birth to one of the most famous drama festivals in the world today, the Oberammergau Passion Plays, which have survived throughout time to the present day, and which are still performed every 10 years at Oberammergau in the Bavarian Alps.

The history of the Oberammergau Passion Plays begins in the year 1633 when, after much suffering during the Thirty Years' War and the many deaths caused by the Bubonic Plague, the inhabitants of Oberammergau made a vow that they would perform '**plays of the suffering, death and resurrection of our Lord Jesus Christ**' every 10 years if they were spared extinction.

It was during Whitsun 1634 that the inhabitants of Oberammergau kept their promise for the first time when they erected a stage above the newly dug graves of plague victims and, by the middle of the Eighteenth Century, people were travelling from all over Germany to be a part of the atmosphere in Oberammergau and to soak up the mystique of the play and the town.

This tradition has continued and, every 10 years, more than 2,000 Oberammergauers gather together to create the central core of life and hope, to delight and enchant over six hours, a thanksgiving entertainment which runs through from May to September.

In 1642, Civil War broke out in England and, as a consequence of this, theatres were closed to stave off public disorder in a society where the Puritans and Oliver Cromwell were against theatrical performances, as opposed to King Charles I who actually promoted theatre in his court.

The Passion Plays of Oberammergau

Restoration Theatre

The bleak Puritan age came to an end and the theatres reopened; Restoration dramatists then entertained their audiences with comedies which poked fun at Puritan values. The most prominent theatres in London at that time were The Dukes Theatre and The Theatre Royal, Drury Lane, but what really moved theatre forward was the introduction of actresses, the most famous being Nell Gwynne. Until 1660, all professional actors had been men but, when Charles II came to the throne, he changed all of that by insisting that women's roles be played by women instead of by young men. (Think about it, how many of Shakespeare's plays have the female characters dressing up as a young man; a convenient part of the plot, don't you think, as this made it so much easier for the young actor who was then able to play his own gender.)

The audiences of the Seventeenth Century were made up of fashionable young wits and so it was that the bawdy **Comedy of Manners** became exceedingly popular as a form of theatre, with its glittering and somewhat affected way of speaking and where a satirical look at London life became the pastime of many a young person of the day, but sadly only for the chosen few, for it was the aristocrats who poked fun at the aristocrats; meaning that the ordinary person was, in fact, excluded from the theatrical experiences of this exclusive club.

Eighteenth Century Theatre

Sadly, the Eighteenth Century saw a great decline in the level of playwriting, *but* it did see the emergence of some great actors and the building of some splendid theatres and, let's face it, each needs the other in order survive and thrive. One of the greatest actors this century gave to us was David Garrick, who reputedly stopped the practice of spectators sitting on the stage alongside the actors and was probably the first ever theatrical star. But Garrick wasn't just an enormously successful actor, he was also a producer, theatre manager and playwright, (he wrote more than 20 plays). As an actor, he used the more 'modern' realistic form of acting.

It was at this time that pantomime was introduced to England by the actor John Rich who worked under the stage name of Lun. These pantomimes had their roots in Commedia dell'Arte and began in verse with well known stories or even classical legends before the characters were transformed into Commedia dell'Arte figures, when their tricks and adventures were mimed to music in the harlequinade.

Sadly, though, middle class support waned for a while as actors were considered to be, well not very pleasant people – rogues even! In addition, the audiences were often rowdy during performances, thus giving theatre a somewhat bad reputation. Add to this the fact that production standards were often shabby, with sets and costumes giving the feel of something thrown together with neither thought nor care. Not an artistic genre for the educated and artistic middle classes.

This was also the century which witnessed The Licensing Act of 1737, an act which was to have a huge impact on the development of theatre in Britain as it stated that the Lord Chamberlain must vet any script before a performance could be staged.

Nineteenth Century Theatre

After the poor reputation theatre had acquired in the last century, the advent of the Nineteenth Century saw a concerted effort to win the approval of the masses and across all social classes with its move towards Romanticism and Melodrama. Sadly though, depth of characterisation was often forfeited in favour of creating spectacles upon the stage, spectacles which often involved live animals.

Pantomime, however, continued to thrive in England with Joseph Grimaldi creating the much-loved clown character in the harlequinade section when he appeared annually at Covent Garden, which he did until his retirement in 1823.

In England, the actual number of theatre buildings increased and whereas at the beginning of the century, there were only 10 operating theatres, towards the end of the century there were 30. The theatres themselves developed extensively during this century in terms of auditorium layout, lighting and seating. Smaller theatres, known as **Penny Theatres**, sprang up for the poorer sections of society – there were more than 30 of these theatres in London alone during the 1830s – this gave individuals the opportunity to exploit their hidden talents such as singing, dancing, etc, with the result that theatres spread and, in England, **The Music Hall** was born. Theatre for the masses had arrived and along with it, a choice of what to see and enjoy; entertainment was now big business.

The realist dramas of the final decades came from Northern Europe with the works of Norwegian dramatist Henrik Ibsen, Russian playwright, Anton Chekhov, and the Russian actor, Constantin Stanislavski, who influenced the course of writing and acting to such an extent that it has survived through to the present day, and there are, in fact, few who even now have not heard of the naturalistic form of acting known as *Method Acting*. Over the pond, it was much the same story as theatre grew in popularity through specifically built houses, as well as through the medium of showboats on the Mississippi, Wild West Shows and Minstrel Shows etc.

Twentieth Century Theatre

The realist movement of the previous century continued to reverberate around the Twentieth Century too, as the world as a whole, and with it the theatrical world, hurtled forward making unprecedented progress and breaking hitherto social barriers at an alarming rate. The advancement of technology which, as well as affecting the world and mankind, also played a huge part in the progress of theatre by opening doors and allowing representation and experimentation never before seen on the stage. Add to this the growing freedom of choice, the lifting of social barriers and restrictions and the Twentieth Century became a century of truly spectacular theatre.

Of course, not one but two World Wars dominated the first fifty years of this century and even contributed to the progress of theatre. As a relief from the on-going tensions of war and the fear each and every one felt living under the threatening cloud of death, there was a surge of interest in the arts. The man in the street escaped reality by going to the theatre whilst theatre folk entertained the troops, a practice which became very popular with the military and has continued through to this day, for wherever there is a military base – be it peacekeeping or fighting – there are always entertainers ready to fly out and 'do their bit'. It was, in part, as a result of this interest in the arts during the Second World War that we saw the first government subsidy of the arts in Britain with the founding of the Arts Council in 1946.

During the Twentieth Century, we saw the growth of serious theatre, emanating in the first instance from the pens of great playwrights such as Noël Coward, Somerset Maugham, J.B. Priestley, Terence Rattigan and George Bernard Shaw, and, in later years, through the pens of Alan Ayckbourn, Alan Bennett, Harold Pinter and Tom Stoppard.

During the Twentieth Century, we were also able to experience social drama and political drama; we saw the 'angry young men' movement; Rep Theatre thrived and the West End grew; in fact, as the century progressed, we saw virtually every type of theatre possible. Theatre was no longer banned as it had been; it was no longer elitist as it had been; neither was it bawdy nor for the lower classes. Theatre had no social, intellectual and political barriers because, if you didn't like one particular type of theatre, then you could quite easily go off and find the type of theatre that you did like.

And so, with virtually a free reign, we left behind the Twentieth Century and travelled on into the Twenty-First Century, where who knows what will happen, for man is now more in control of his theatrical destiny than ever before, and *'the world is his oyster and the stage is his world'* (Anon).

Chapter Three

Looking for Information

What, where, when, why, who, how

THESE SIX simple words dominate the English language; they support all we know and stimulate all we wish we knew – for without questions there can be no answers and without answers there can be no progress. By seeking out information, we are not only expanding our knowledge but we are also driving ourselves forward to a different place.

Hopefully, in this chapter you may find the answers to some of your own questions, or maybe the answers to questions you weren't even asking – which, arguably, is even more exciting and stimulating.

So let's start by looking at playwrights, of which there are literally thousands in the world today – of all nationalities and all ages, writing all manner of plays for all manner of people. There are playwrights at the start of their writing career, there are those at the end – though, in my experience, a playwright never puts down his pen; instead, as he ages, he becomes more selective about what he wants to write, and maybe a little slower, but he rarely stops altogether. Of course, there are excellent playwrights, there are good playwrights and there are some … well, not so good. Then there are the unique playwrights, those who transcend classification and that is where we will begin, with those I have chosen to call: '*A Quartet of Grand Master Playwrights*'.

Selecting the '*Grand Masters of British Playwrights*' was a daunting task to say the least, given the vast international subject peopled by so many talented individuals both past and present. How was I ever going to do this? There had to be basic criteria and, after much thought, this is what I came up with:

1. The playwright must be Twentieth/Twenty-First Century; my reason for this being that time can make a Master, but time can also deny a Master the joy of recognition – if only from my readers
2. The playwright must come top of my own personal market research. Yes, I did go out and poll people, over 1,000 individuals in fact and from all walks of life too. (As a result of this I now vow that when I am stopped in the street to answer questions as part of a market research poll, I will do so, and with good grace too because it is a thankless job – and people can be so rude!). The questions I asked those I polled were:

REMEMBER WHEN

Remember When
Pen & Sword Books
FREEPOST SF5
47 Church Street
BARNSLEY
South Yorkshire
S70 2BR

2

DISCOVER MORE ABOUT REMEMBER WHEN

Pen & Sword Books have over 1500 titles in print covering all aspects of history and have recently launched the *Remember When* imprint. This new imprint will cover all aspects of nostalgia, from guides to collecting antiques and classic toys to social history and celebrity biographies. If you would like to receive more information and special offers on your preferred interests from time to time along with our standard catalogue, please complete your areas of interest below and return this card (no stamp required in the UK). Alternatively, register online at www.rememberwhenbooks.co.uk. Thank you.

PLEASE NOTE: We do not sell data information to any third party companies

Mr/Mrs/Ms/Other................... Name...

Address...

.... Postcode...................................

Email address...

NOSTALGIA	☐	Animals/Pets	☐	SOCIAL HISTORY	☐
Food & Recipes	☐	Literature	☐	Biographies	☐
Fashion	☐	COLLECTABLES	☐	Women's History	☐
Music/Theatre	☐	Antiques	☐	Decades	☐
Transport	☐	Classic Toys & Games	☐	ALL THE ABOVE	☐

Website: www.rememberwhenbooks.co.uk • Email: enquiries@pen-and-sword.co.uk
Telephone: 01226 734555 • Fax: 01226 734438

i) with which of my 350 selected playwrights were they most familiar

ii) which of these they preferred

The results – in no particular order as they say – were overwhelmingly *Alan Ayckbourn • Alan Bennett • Harold Pinter • Tom Stoppard*. So, based on this outcome and for the purposes of this book only, these gentlemen are now called:

The Grand Masters of British Playwrights

So who exactly are these Grand Masters and what is it about their particular style of writing that sets them apart from other writers? What is it that made each of them top my poll?

To begin with let's take an overview of each writer by taking a brief look at their individual style, a style which, in each case, draws in so many of the theatre-going public, followed by a timeline for each and a list – though not exhaustive, I hasten to point out – of their own particular works.

Alan Ayckbourn, 1939–

Exactly what can one say about this genius that hasn't already been said? Much is written about him and many stories abound, especially within the thespian fraternity; he has written so many plays that anyone directly involved in theatre knows of someone who has been in at least one of his plays. And even outside our own closed thespian world, interest in him and his works seems to be never ending.

Alan's style of writing is to take the very ordinary situations in which we all find ourselves and add extraordinary elements, making the audience perhaps think and reflect upon their own lives and the predicaments in which they find themselves embroiled in. His plays are often described as black comedies, and comedy does have a huge part to play in an Ayckbourn play, but it is only a part and not the whole. His works are often more of a social document representing the middle classes over the past fifty years, often dominated by Alan's interest in the relationships between men and women, how they invariably do not understand each other and, in fact, are unable to communicate to any extent either. Interestingly, Alan has been described as a political writer – of sexual politics!

As a Yorkshire lass myself, I have to say that, when researching this book, I was disappointed to find that Alan is not of true Yorkshire blood as I had previously assumed – his base and home is actually in the quaint North Yorkshire seaside town of Scarborough. However, my faith was restored when I learned that he has apparently adopted Yorkshire as his permanent home; now that to me shows Alan Ayckbourn to be a man of outstanding integrity!

THE LIFE AND WORKS OF ALAN AYCKBOURN

1939   Alan Ayckbourn was born in Hampstead, England to Irene Maud Worley (Lolly) and Horace Ayckbourn.

1946   He attended Wisborough Lodge as a boarder.

1951   He won a scholarship to attend Haileybury, just 20 miles north of London.

1956   Ayckbourn left Haileybury to take his first professional job as acting stage manager with Sir Donald Wolfitt's company in *The Strong Are Lonely* at the Edinburgh Festival.

1957   Ayckbourn joined the Studio Theatre, Scarborough.

1958   Stephen Joseph challenged him to write his first play.

Stephen Joseph was a theatrical pioneer who, having seen 'theatre in the round' in the US brought the concept back to the UK where, in 1955, he established a 'theatre in the round' in the Yorkshire seaside town of Scarborough. This theatre – having since moved location – is still thriving to this day.

1959   Alan married Christine Roland and *The Square Cat*, Alan's first play, premiered at the Library Theatre, Scarborough. *Love After All*, Alan's second play, also premiered in this year.

1960   He was called up for his National Service.

1961   Ayckbourn made his directorial debut with *Gaslight* at the Library Theatre.

1962   He became a founder member and associate director of Victoria Theatre, Stoke on Trent.

1964   He left the Victoria Theatre; this was also the year of his final professional acting job and the year in which he joined the BBC in Leeds as a radio drama presenter.

1967   This year saw the death of Stephen Joseph, one of the great influences on Alan Ayckbourn's life.

1970   Ayckbourn decided that the time had come for him to concentrate on his playwriting and resigned from the BBC.

1972   He became Artistic Director of the Library Theatre, Scarborough, which had initially been created by Stephen Joseph in 1955.

1975   Alan Ayckbourn broke the record for the most productions running simultaneously in the West End of London; he also broke the same record in the same year on Broadway.

1977   Ayckbourn made his debut at The National Theatre with *Bedroom Farce*. He also became chair of the Drama Panel of Yorkshire Arts Association.

1979   He stepped down from the Yorkshire Arts Association due to ever increasing pressure of work.

1981–3 Statistically speaking, Alan Ayckbourn became the most watched and performed playwright in the UK.

1986 He took a sabbatical from Scarborough when he was appointed visiting director at the National Theatre; in the same year, he was also made Freeman of the Borough of Scarborough.

1987 Alan Ayckbourn was awarded a CBE.

1988 He returned to Scarborough.

1989 A film version of *A Chorus of Disapproval* was released.

1990 Ayckbourn directed his first Shakespearean play, *Othello*.

1992 He was appointed as the Cameron Mackintosh Visiting Professor of Contemporary Theatre at the University of Oxford.

1996 Ayckbourn's company moved from the Stephen Joseph Theatre In The Round to the Stephen Joseph Theatre – which is its first purpose-built home in an extensive conversion of Scarborough's former Odeon cinema.

1997 Alan Ayckbourn was knighted for 'Services to Theatre' and, now divorced from Christine Roland, he married Heather Stoney.

1999 He announced that he would no longer direct plays by other writers; in the same year, a survey by the National Theatre of 800 theatre professionals, placed Alan as the 14th most influential playwright of the century and *The Norman Conquests* (1973) as one of the 100 greatest plays of the century.

2001 Ayckbourn made his Broadway directorial debut with *By Jeeves* the musical, written in collaboration with Andrew Lloyd Webber.

2002 His book, *The Crafty Art of Playmaking* was published.

2003 Ayckbourn announced a suspension on the production of his plays in the West End, which wasn't lifted until November 2007.

2006 In February of this year, Alan Ayckbourn suffered a stroke; in September he returned to work to direct his play, *If I Were You*.

2009 The end of an era dawned when Alan Ayckbourn stepped down as the Artistic Director of the Stephen Joseph Theatre.

PLAYS BY ALAN AYCKBOURN

There are prolific playwrights and there are playwrights in the ilk of Alan Ayckbourn, for whom a word has yet to be invented. They write so much that eventually one gives up counting, as I did!

Below you will find a list of not all Ayckbourn's work but the bulk of his plays. To add to this list are the plays which have enjoyed a public performance, but have yet to be published; then there is his book, *The Crafty Art of Playmaking*. And, of course, who knows what he will have penned in the interim period between me writing this book and it appearing on the shelves?

For want of a better word I have called the right hand column the 'Synopsis'. However, to all of you familiar with

The Master 'In Action'

Ayckbourn's writings you will appreciate that it is not actually possible to write such a short synopsis of an Ayckbourn play because his plays are so complex and intricate in structure. So, what I have in truth done – I hope – is to whet your appetite and either make you want to read further or, at the very least, make a theatre trip to see one of these theatrical masterpieces in action.

* Name of the composer of music, where relevant, is in parenthesis *

DATE	PLAYS	SYNOPSIS
A		
1974	*Absent Friends*	Colin's fiancée has died in a drowning accident and his friends have organised a tea party to cheer him up, but it turns out that he is the only happy one among them!
1972	*Absurd Person Singular*	Set over three Christmas celebrations, past, present and future, in the kitchens of three separate couples, the end of the play sees an interesting reversal in the fortunes of all three couples.
1982	*Affairs in a Tent*	A variant of *Intimate Exchanges*.
B		
1975	*Bedroom Farce*	Set over the course of one night, but in three separate bedrooms which are all present on the stage throughout, we become voyeurs on the dissatisfactions of the three couples involved.
1990	*Body Language*	Hravic Zyergefoovc is an unethical surgeon of questionable origin who, after the accidental decapitation of two women, transplants their heads onto the other's body.
1998	*Boy Who Fell into a Book (The)*	A story for the family, about a boy who finds himself and a fictional detective looking through the different worlds

DATE	PLAYS	SYNOPSIS
		found within the books on the boy's bookshelf. They look at different genres demonstrating to children the diversity of literature.
1996	By Jeeves (Andrew Lloyd-Webber)	The story of Bertram Wooster's missing banjo, this is a musical co-written with Andrew Lloyd Webber and is essentially the same as *Jeeves* – the original version (1975) – but with fewer sub plots.

C

DATE	PLAYS	SYNOPSIS
1990	Callisto 5	A science fiction tale set on the moon of Callisto where a previous disaster had separated two children from their parents; the children are now being cared for by a computer called Iris.
1999	Callisto # 7	This is an extensively revised version of *Callisto 5* with the introduction of a second protagonist, the older sister Jodi.
1996	Champion of Paribanou (The)	As an adaptation of one of the *Arabian Nights* tales and more of an epic adventure than anything else, this is a very different play for Alan.
1984	Chorus of Disapproval (A)	Guy Jones joins Pendon Light Amateur Dramatic Society (PALOS) and quickly works his way up through the ranks to play the title role. Unable ever to say no to anyone, it is then wrongly assumed that he, therefore, 'bought' his way to the top.
1962	Christmas v Mastermind	Here we find that Father Christmas is not actually a nice man when his fairy is kidnapped and there is a plot to take over Christmas; none of this is helped by two bungling policemen.
1998	Comic Potential	A play exploring the theory that humans are the only creatures with a sense of humour and who fall in love for reasons other than procreation, so further exploring what would happen if a robot developed the ability to laugh and love, would it be construed as a malfunction?
1994	Communicating Doors	A time-travelling thriller inspired by the question of exactly where hotel communicating doors actually lead, which, in this case, is back in time to the same room. This play for Ayckbourn anyway, has a rare happy ending!
1974	Confusions	A selection of one act plays looking at the confusion that we call life.
1982	Cricket Match (A)	A variant of *Intimate Exchanges*.

D–E

DATE	PLAYS	SYNOPSIS
1960	Dad's Tale	A far-fetched story of a Christmas that can't happen for a cockney family because the bailiffs have taken everything,

DATE	PLAYS	SYNOPSIS
		including the turkey. The release is to escape into a world of make believe which culminates in Dad being turned into a budgie!
2001	*Damsels in Distress*	*Damsels in Distress* comprises of three separate plays: *GamePlan*, *FlatSpin* and *RolePlay*.
1992	*Dreams From a Summer House (John Pattison)*	A play with music, this is also a fairytale as we see when a painting comes to life and the character from the painting reveals that she can only communicate through song. Like all fairytales though, the ending is happy!
2004	*Drowning on Dry Land*	*Drowning on Dry Land* explores the concept of people who become celebrities despite having achieved nothing in their lives and looks at how celebrity status can be taken away as quickly as it is given. It also looks at the ruthlessness of the media in moving from one hot property to the next.
1982	*Events on a Hotel Terrace*	A variant of *Intimate Exchanges*.

F

DATE	PLAYS	SYNOPSIS
1985	*Family Circles*	A hypothetical question is acted out in front of our eyes: 'What would have happened had I married someone else and what would have happened to them?' Three couples come together for a wedding anniversary. At the end of each act, the partners change while retaining their original characters. The final scene sees all variants of the relationships mixed together and on stage.
2001	*FlatSpin*	This is a part of the *Damsels in Distress* series. Working as a temporary cleaner, Rosie finds herself caught up in a world of drug rings and police surveillance teams.

G

DATE	PLAYS	SYNOPSIS
2001	*GamePlan*	Another part of the *Damsels in Distress* series, 16-year-old Sorrell lives with her single mother, Lynette, who tells her that they may have to move away from London. Sorrell and her friend, Kelly cook up a plan which involves Sorrell earning money as a call girl and results in the death of a 'client'. But Sorrell's relationship with her mother survives ... because of?
1982	*Game of Golf (A)*	A variant of *Intimate Exchanges*.
1982	*Garden Fête (A)*	A variant of *Intimate Exchanges*.

H

DATE	PLAYS	SYNOPSIS
1999	*Haunting Julia*	Julia, a musical prodigy, committed suicide 12 years previously and those left behind are consumed with guilt when they consult with a psychic.

DATE	PLAYS	SYNOPSIS
1987	*Henceforward*	Suffering from writer's block, composer Jerome lives alone, his only company being his music technology and a malfunctioning robot called NAN 300F. He records and uses events from his own life to create the perfect piece, but at what cost?
1999	*House & Garden*	This play looks at the fact that we may be centre-stage to some people but to others we're less important. In 'Garden', Trish makes a brief, angry appearance and Gavin comes across well. In 'House', we sympathise with Trish and understand her behaviour whilst despising the manipulative and devious Gavin.
1969	*How the Other Half Loves*	Two sets and three couples run concurrently allowing us to see how time and space interact in relationships, denying us a definitive outcome.

I

DATE	PLAYS	SYNOPSIS
2006	*If I Were You*	Mal and Jill's marriage is on the rocks until the day they each inhabit the other's body and are able to see things from another perspective. After this experience they agree to talk about their marriage.
2005	*Improbable Fiction*	It is the usual boring meeting of the Pendon Writers' Circle when the very ordinary Isla arrives to make the tea and frees the generally unfertile minds of the circle's members.
1982	*Intimate Exchanges*	This is probably one of the most complicated of all Ayckbourn's works as it is based on a simple decision: 'To smoke or not to smoke, that is the question'. There are eight variants on the play, each with an alternative ending.
1989	*Invisible Friends*	'The grass is always greener', or so they say. But when Lucy's invisible friend takes on a 'real' life, things go horribly wrong, especially when an entire 'invisible' family appear too. The lingering question upon conclusion of the play is whether these friends were in her imagination or whether they were actually real.
1983	*It Could Be Any One of Us*	A dilapidated country house and murder set the scene for a cluedo, whodunnit style drama.

J

DATE	PLAYS	SYNOPSIS
1975	*Jeeves*	The story of Bertram Wooster's missing banjo, this is a musical co-written with Andrew Lloyd-Webber and is the original version of *By Jeeves* (1996), but with more sub-plots.
1978	*Joking Apart*	Set in the garden of Richard and Anthea over a 12-year period, we see a 'perfect couple' to whom everything comes easily and how their seemingly charmed life affects and destroys the lives of those they touch.

DATE	PLAYS	SYNOPSIS
2002	*Jollies (The)*	A birthday treat goes horribly wrong when, after entering a 'magic' cabinet, a young boy ages 25 years and then, when his mother goes into the cabinet, she returns 20 years younger! Eventually, after a lot of strange 'happenings', both are returned to their own age.
1976	*Just Between Ourselves*	Set in a garage and garden over four consecutive birthdays, we see relationships fall apart as the men look through their own personal blind spots where relationships are concerned.

L

DATE	PLAYS	SYNOPSIS
1973	*Living Together*	The events of one weekend as seen from the sitting room. Part of *The Norman Conquests*.
1959	*Love After All*	A farce in which a man attempts to marry his reluctant daughter off to the man he has chosen for her – and succeeds.
1982	*Love in the Mist*	A variant of *Intimate Exchanges*.

M

DATE	PLAYS	SYNOPSIS
1981	*Making Tracks* (Paul Todd)	Stan runs a recording studio which is facing ruin. As his latest recording star cannot actually sing, he persuades his ex-wife secretly to put down the vocals whilst his unsuspecting 'star' sings into a dead mic!
1988	*Man of the Moment*	A celebrity criminal comes face to face on a TV chat show with the man who foiled his last robbery and, as a consequence, had him sent down. The interviewer is disappointed when the sparks don't fly and her career is in jeopardy, until a twist at the end makes her the greater criminal.
2005	*Miss Yesterday*	At some point, we have all wished that we could go back in time and behave differently. In this play, which moves backwards and forwards in time, we come to realise that perhaps it would not be such a good idea after all.
1988	*Mr A's Amazing Maze Plays*	A play for children in which a character by the name of Mr Acoustics steals sounds and in which the hero of the piece sets off in search of the stolen noises.
1963	*Mr Whatnot*	*Mr Whatnot*, a silent piano tuner, engineers a way to be with the woman he loves by engineering a series of surreal encounters.
1994	*Musical Jigsaw Play (The)* (John Pattison)	A group of musicians have plunged from the charts into a strange world where all the bad pop-groups go. Their only way out is to create a hit song – and the only way they can do that is with a little help from the audience.

DATE	PLAYS	SYNOPSIS
2003	My Sister Sadie	A military helicopter crashes on a hillside and the sole survivor, Sadie, seeks refuge at a nearby farm. Sadie, however, is not human; she is a robot. But interestingly, Sadie is programmed with basic emotions which lead to an internal conflict in which her compassionate programming overrides her aggressive programming, eventually wiping the latter from her system.
1991	My Very Own Story	Due to a triple booking, three storytellers arrive at a given place at the same time each to tell their own stories and find that they are inexplicably linked – but with a happy ending for all.

N

1973	Norman Conquests (The)	A trilogy where three separate plays make up *The Norman's Conquests*: *Table Manners*, *Living Together* and *Round and Round the Garden*.

O

1982	One Man Protest (A)	A variant of *Intimate Exchanges*.
2003	Orvin – Champion of Champions (Denis King)	A musical play written initially for the NYMT, *Orvin* – which can be described as eclectic, historic and a fantasy tale as its genre states – is supported by a 'Greek Chorus' and begins with a fight, concludes with a coronation and the obligatory happy ending expected of fantasy-land drama.

P

1982	Pageant (A)	A variant of *Intimate Exchanges*.
2004	Private Fears in Public Places	This is an unusual play in that it has four stories told in 54 scenes and with no interval. The scenes cross-cut and fade in and out of each quickly and almost cinematically; all inspired by Ayckbourn's love of film, it is intended as a film for the stage.

R

1967	Relatively Speaking	A classic tale of mistaken identity where everyone believes everyone else to be someone else. Added to that there is the mystery of the slippers, which is never solved.
1989	Revengers' Comedies – Part 1 & Part 2 (The)	Two strangers, intent on suicide, meet and, instead of carrying out their act, make a pact to exact revenge on behalf of the other. Simple at the outset, but thwarted by complications, one of the pair has a total breakdown and still commits suicide at the end.
2001	RolePlay	This is a part of the *Damsels in Distress* series. Meeting the future in-laws is never easy, when everyone and the situation is 'normal' but, in a household where a missing fork is a major

DATE	PLAYS	SYNOPSIS
		catastrophe and girls drop onto the balcony from the flat above, then anything can happen and it does.
1973	*Round and Round the Garden*	The events of one weekend as seen from the garden. Part of *The Norman Conquests*.

S

DATE	PLAYS	SYNOPSIS
1980	*Season's Greetings*	Dealing with traditional Christmas celebrations at the Bunker's home, we hear the children, who are supposedly the heart of any Christmas celebration, but we never see them as Ayckbourn demonstrates through the insecurities and tensions of the adults that they are really the children of this piece.
1979	*Sisterly Feelings*	This is a play about two sisters and the choices they make, (or have made for them), over the course of a few months. Unusually, the decisions as to how the evening proceeds are actually made on stage, partly by chance and partly by the performers during the course of the action.
1987	*Small Family Business (A)*	Tackling morality and the perils of capitalism, this play shows us how one small misdemeanour can suck in all those around and can have far-reaching consequences.
2002	*Snake in the Grass*	*Snake in the Grass*, like *Haunting Julia*, is another ghost story but this time, the sisters are haunted by their dead father. The central theme of this play is domestic abuse, both past and present.
1967	*Sparrow (The)*	Ed and Evie meet at a dance hall, but any hope of a relationship developing is ruined by Ed's cold and calculating flatmate until, one night, they escape his clutches and are no longer his pawns.
1959	*Square Cat (The)*	Alice is obsessed with rock star Jerry Wattis and secretly arranges to meet him. But Jerry is only the alter ego of Arthur, a shy young man. Throughout the play, he switches between Jerry and Arthur so as not to disappoint Alice or Alice's daughter, Susan, with whom Arthur has fallen in love. Each woman seeing him as a different person.
1961	*Standing Room Only*	The country is gridlocked by traffic and one family find themselves living in a double decker bus. The arrival of a stranger and the announcement of a pregnancy causes more problems and the top deck becomes an unlikely maternity ward.
1980	*Suburban Strains* (Paul Todd)	The central figure of this piece is Caroline who struggles to make two relationships work whilst she lives in fear of all the women by whom she feels intimidated, and all the women she fears she may become.

DATE	PLAYS	SYNOPSIS
2003	*Sugar Daddies*	This play is about a young woman who finds herself in a potentially dangerous situation, and about how we change ourselves to suit those around us yet, ultimately returning to who we really are.

T

DATE	PLAYS	SYNOPSIS
1973	*Table Manners*	The events of one weekend as seen from the dining room. Part of *The Norman Conquests*.
1979	*Taking Steps*	Elizabeth plans to leave her husband but we are left wondering whether she will ever do so following a series of farcical events.
1977	*Ten Times Table*	In this play, the characters are brought together supposedly to organise a local pageant but as the play develops, so it turns into a politically driven piece which, in consequence, results in chaos for the pageant itself.
1997	*Things We Do For Love*	Centering on the love triangle between two women and one man the play is set over two weeks and the ingenious staging shows three flats. But this aside, it is a straight forward play showing love in all its glory and with all its warts.
1990	*This is Where We Came in*	A group of players (actors) are controlled by some evil, ancient storytellers and are forced to act out twisted versions of well know tales until the cycle is broken by Flavius, and the players are freed to live happily ever after.
1971	*Time and Time Again*	*Time and Time Again* revolves around one woman and how she wants one man, has been with another and does not want a third! The setting is the back of a house where the audience can hear everything that is said but the characters cannot always hear each other.
1992	*Time of My Life*	'I am not who I am but who I was and who I will be', a theory brought to life in this play as we see three couples having dinner in a restaurant. We witness the events in one couple's life before this day, one in present time, and we see what happens after another of the couples leave the restaurant. The play concludes with a toast, all blissfully unaware of what is about to happen, of course.

V

DATE	PLAYS	SYNOPSIS
2000	*Virtual Reality*	*Virtual Reality* is a play which deals with the patchwork of Twenty-First Century problems such as the difficulties encountered in relationships, with generation gaps and the different expectations and experiences each person brings to the relationship; it also explores the problem of declining personal communications within the shadow of technology – a favourite theme of later Ayckbourn plays.

DATE	PLAYS	SYNOPSIS
	w	
1981	*Way Upstream*	A play about ordinary people and how they respond to extraordinary situations, this play is set on a cabin cruiser as two couples embark on a 'water holiday', demonstrating too how people in relationships are inextricably connected.
2000	*Whenever* (Denis King)	This is a time-travelling musical play with a very definite feel of *The Wizard of Oz* to it as the character, Emily, goes on an adventure in order to return home and right a wrong.
1991	*Wildest Dreams*	A group of individuals, each with their own issues, indulge in a role play game, the result being that, at the climax of the play, each of the group has actually adopted the character of their role play character.
1985	*Woman in Mind*	Susan, trapped in a loveless marriage and mundane world, retreats to enjoy the pleasures of a fictitious family perfect in every way. The two families become intertwined and she suffers a complete breakdown.
1995	*Word From Our Sponsor (A)* (John Pattison)	A musical Faustian tale in which the devil offers a vicar the opportunity to stage a community nativity play, but with certain compromising provisos.

FURTHER WORKS BY ALAN AYCKBOURN INCLUDE:

Revues
1985   *Boy Meets Girl* (Paul Todd)
1998   *Cheap and Cheerful* (Denis King)
1980   *First Course* (Paul Todd)
1985   *Girl Meets Boy* (Paul Todd)
1983   *Incidental Music* (Paul Todd)
1981   *Me, Myself and I* (Paul Todd)
1978   *Men on Women on Men* (Paul Todd)
1986   *Mere Soup Songs* (Paul Todd)
1980   *Second Helping* (Paul Todd)
1984   *Seven Deadly Virtues (The)* (Paul Todd)
1984   *Westwoods (The)* (Paul Todd)

Adaptations
1999   *Forest (The)* (Vera Liber) [ADAPTATION: *The Forest of Ostrovsky*]
1986   *Tons of Money* [ADAPTATION: *Tons of Money* by Will Evans & Valentine]

1982   *Trip to Scarborough (A)* [ADAPTATION: *A Trip to Scarborough* by R.B. Sheridan]

1982   *Wolf at the Door* (David Walker)[ADAPTATION: *Les Corbeaux* by Henry Becque]

Plays for Television
1974   *Service Not Included*

Plays for Children & Young People
1969   *Ernie's Incredible Illucinations*
2005   *Girl Who Lost Her Voice (The)*
1999   *Gizmo*
1989   *Inside Outside Slide Show (The)*
2004   *Miranda's Magic Mirror*
2002   *Princess and the Mouse (The)*
2003   *Ten Magic Bridges*

One Act Plays
1962   *Countdown*
1984   *Cut in the Rates (A)*

Alan Bennett, 1934–

Alan Bennett is a true born and bred Yorkshire man. It is difficult to 'label' Alan Bennett for, at first glance, he would seem to be a social writer looking, as he so frequently does, at the North/South divide and the world of the ordinary man. However, his work is far more than the mutterings of old age or the mundane conversations of the working classes as they take their annual seaside holiday. Bennett has extraordinarily keen sensory observational skills and, not only can he pick up the nuances of conversational and regional speech, but his eye for detail is quite exceptional. He explores a depth and purpose behind these often seemingly inane conversations that elude even the character from whom the words emanate, to give us a social and historic insight into the working classes. Although he is probably more well known for his plays about 'ordinary folk', his writing skills are diverse and envelop many dramatic forms including biographical, historical, the comic, the tragic and the satirical, to name but a few.

THE LIFE AND WORKS OF ALAN BENNETT

1934   Alan Bennett was born on May 9th in Leeds, Yorkshire, the son of a butcher and Yorkshire housewife.

1946   He attended Leeds Modern School.

1954   He went up to Exeter College, Oxford, to study History, from where he was later awarded a First Class Honours degree.

1957   Bennett was called up to do his National Service, which during time he learned Russian.

1960   In this year, he wrote and appeared in the now legendary programme, *Beyond the Fringe.*

1960   He was appointed as a temporary Junior Lecturer in History at Magdalen College, Oxford.

1968   His first stage play, *Forty Years On,* was produced.

1985   Alan Bennett's first feature film, *A Private Function* was released.

1987   He was made an Honorary Fellow of Exeter College.

1988   Bennett's first series of *Talking Heads* was broadcast by the BBC.

1990   He was awarded a D. Lit. from the University of Leeds.

1990   Bennett's adaptation of Kenneth Grahame's *Wind in the Willows* marked the beginning of his collaboration with director Nicholas Hytner.

1991   Nicholas Hytner directed Bennett's *The Madness of George III.*

1994   He was made a Trustee of The National Gallery.

1998   His second series of *Talking Heads* was broadcast by the BBC.

1994   Nicholas Hytner directed the film adaptation of *The Madness of George III.*

2004   Nicholas Hytner directed Alan Bennett's multi-award winning *The History Boys.*

PLAYS BY ALAN BENNETT

At one point, Alan Bennet was travelling along the road to an academic career but was obviously never intended to reach his destination and thankfully, it did not take much to tempt him along another route, a route which was to result in him writing some of the most outstanding plays of the Twentieth Century and beyond.

As with Ayckbourn, you will find here not an exhaustive list of Bennett's work but certainly most of his well-known works which I hope will whet your appetite for further reading or viewing.

DATE	PLAYS	SYNOPSIS
B		
1960	*Beyond the Fringe*	A comedy stage revue co-written with Peter Cook, Dudley Moore and Jonathan Miller.
E		
1980	*Enjoy*	An ageing working-class couple living in the North of England are paid a visit by a female social worker – who is actually their son in drag; add to this is the fact that their daughter is a prostitute and you have a recipe for humour and dry wit.
F		
1968	*Forty Years On*	Set in a decaying English public school and a metaphor for the decline of the Empire, this play is a satire which analyses Britain in the Twentieth Century.
H		
1973	*Habeas Corpus*	A farce which deals with sexual liberation and the sexual excesses of the middle classes in the 1960s.
2004	*History Boys (The)*	A play inspired by Bennett's own experience of preparing for the Oxford entrance, it takes place in a grammar school in the North of England and ultimately raises a number of questions such as, 'Is education to teach life skills or to teach the pupil how to pass exams?' or 'Is History a way of establishing the truth or is it merely the telling of a good story?'
K		
1986	*Kafka's Dick*	Kafka, his parents and his publisher materialise in the suburban home of his would-be biographer.
L		
1999	*Lady in the Van (The)*	Bennett narrates the true story of an eccentric old lady, Mary Shepherd, who lived in a van in his own garden for over ten years.
M		
1991	*Madness of George III (The)*	The story of King George III's slide into insanity and the resulting political and royal backlash.
O		
1977	*Old Country (The)*	A story of spies, espionage and a British defector living in the USSR.

DATE	PLAYS	SYNOPSIS
S		
1988	*Single Spies*	This is actually a double bill incorporating *An Englishman Abroad* and *A Question of Attribution*. *An Englishman Abroad* focuses on the spy Guy Burgess whilst *A Question of Attribution* focuses on Anthony Blunt, whose identity as a spy was only made public years later.
1969	*Sing a Rude Song*	A musical about the famous, well known music hall star, Marie Lloyd. Written by Caryl Brahms and Ned Sherrin, for which Alan wrote additional material.
T		
1992	*Talking Heads*	Includes: *Bed Among the Lentils* *Chip in the Sugar (A)* *Cream Cracker Under the Settee (A)* *Her Big Chance* *Lady of Letters (A)* *Soldiering On*
V		
1987	*Visit from Miss Prothero (A)*	Retired office worker Arthur Dodsworth lives alone – apart from his budgie – when one day, his relative peace is destroyed by a vindictive ex-colleague who calls on him to impart the news that things have changed since his retirement from the office – for the better.

FURTHER WORKS BY ALAN BENNETT INCLUDE

For Television
1979 *Afternoon Off*
1979 *All Day on the Sands*
1972 *Day Out (A)*
1978 *Doris and Doreen*
1983 *Englishman Abroad (An)*
1987 *Fortunes of War*
1978 *Insurance Man (The)*
1982 *Intensive Care*
1975 *Little Outing (A)*
1982 *Marks*
1978 *Me! I'm Afraid of Virginia Woolf*
1965 *My Father Knew Lloyd George*

1982	*Objects of Affection (Our Winnie, A Woman of No Importance, Rolling Home, Marks, Say Something Happened, Intensive Care)*
1979	*Old Crowd (The)*
1966/7	*On the Margin*
1979	*One Fine Day*
1982	*Our Winnie*
1991	*Question of Attribution (A)*
1982	*Rolling Home*
1982	*Say Something Happened*
1975	*Sunset Across the Bay*
1988	*Talking Heads (A Chip in the Sugar, Bed Among the Lentils, A Lady of Letters, Her Big Chance, Soldiering On, A Cream Cracker Under the Settee)*
1998	*Talking Heads 2*
1978	*Visit from Miss Prothero (A)*
1982	*Woman of No Importance*
1990	*102 Boulevard Haussmann*

For Film

2006	*History Boys (The)*
1995	*Madness of King George (The)*
1987	*Parson's Pleasure*
1982	*Pleasure at Her Majesty's*
1982	*Prick Up Your Ears*
1984	*Private Function (A)*
1982	*Secret Policeman's Other Ball (The)*

For Radio

1990	*Lady in the Van (The)*
1986	*Uncle Clarence*

Adaptations

1990	*Wind in the Willows*

Harold Pinter, 1930–2008

Harold Pinter, known to students the world over as the master of the 'silent word', could work a piece of unspoken text like no other writer. I was once told that the strength of an argument is in what is *not* said, rather than in the spoken word itself; for in those silences the imagination creates its own scenario, outcome and result. Does that mean then that we are all co-writers with Pinter? An interesting thought but, sadly not true, for he was truly unique, and to share his page would be a travesty.

One interesting fact has come to light and that is that Pinter had an obsessional interest in cricket. I find this fascinating for it seems to be the love of many 'artistic' people – Tim Rice and Richard Stilgoe, to name but two – perhaps as polo is the sport of Kings, then cricket is the sport of thespians? Pinter was Chairman of the Gaieties Cricket Club and a lifelong supporter of the Yorkshire Cricket Club.

As Shakespeare was responsible for the invention of words, Pinter has had a word invented to describe work that has his own unique stamp upon it and that word is 'Pinteresque', and is frequently used by teachers of drama and literature to describe the power of the pause.

Harold Pinter, playwright, screenwriter, actor, director, poet and political activist was a playwright whose works have been noted for their use of the understatement – *though he, as a man, was anything but understated*; as a playwright he often made use of the 'small talk' style of dialogue – *whereas he actually had a great deal to say on matters of international importance, for he cared passionately.* His characters are, however, frequently reticent and silent – **Harold Pinter, the great political activist, reticent and silent? NEVER!**

THE LIFE AND WORKS OF HAROLD PINTER

1930   Harold Pinter was born in North-East London, the only child of Jewish parents; his father was a tailor.

1944   He received his secondary education at Hackney Downs Grammar School, where he wrote for the school magazine and discovered a love for acting.

1948   Pinter began a course at The Royal Academy of Dramatic Art but, unhappy, he soon dropped out.

1949   In this year, he was fined twice for refusing to be called up for National Service on the grounds of conscientious objection.

1951   He began work with a touring company in Ireland.

1953   He joined Donald Wolfitt's company, Kings Theatre Hammersmith.

1956   Harold married Vivian Merchant, with whom he was to have one son.

1957   His first play, *The Room*, was produced at the Bristol University Drama Dept.

1958   Vivian and Harold's son, Daniel, was born.

1958   *The Birthday Party* opened in London.

1959   The first production of Harold Pinter's play *The Dumb Waiter*.

1960	His play, *The Caretaker*, was produced: the start of this decade saw the acceleration of his career.	
1973	Harold Pinter was appointed Associate Director of The National Theatre.	
1980	Pinter married his second wife, Lady Antonia Fraser, becoming stepfather to her six children.	
2001	He was diagnosed with cancer of the oesophagus, for which he was successfully treated.	
2005	Harold Pinter was awarded the Nobel Prize for Literature, the highest honour available to any writer in the world.	
2007	The British Museum announced that it had purchased Harold Pinter's literary archive.	
2008	Harold Pinter's fight against the ill health he had so stoically endured since the year 2000 came to an end with his death on Christmas Eve.	

PLAYS BY HAROLD PINTER

The seemingly endless list of Pinter's work makes me wonder how he found the time to do anything else. Looking at the style of this Master, we find that, as in the case of Ayckbourn and Bennett, he often took a commonplace situation as a starting point but then came the creative roundabout off which he took a completely different exit and subsequent journey. Into this initially commonplace situation, Pinter gradually introduces a feeling of mystery and menace – without giving any reasonable explanation. This gives many of his pieces a deep and sinister feel; add to this the fact that whatever you then expect to happen – won't! And so you sit on the edge of your seat waiting for the Master Playwright to tell you what is going to happen – but he doesn't.

DATE	*PLAYS*	*SYNOPSIS*
A		
1996	*Ashes to Ashes*	Set in the ground floor room of a house somewhere in Britain, Devlin is desperate to hear the truth from his wife, Rebecca, about her past life.
B		
1966	*Basement (The)*	A fussy old man is living meticulously alone when his world is turned upside down by the visit of his ex room-mate who arrives with a young girl in tow; she in turn manipulates both men.

DATE	PLAYS	SYNOPSIS
1978	*Betrayal*	A time-hopping drama about a secret affair that was never a secret at all for it would appear that the husband knew all along, but seemingly didn't care.
1957	*Birthday Party (The)*	Stanley is the only guest at a seaside boarding house until two strangers come to take him away. But who are 'they'?

C

1959	*Caretaker (The)*	A down and out is given shelter in an abandoned house. At first, we feel pity for him for him, even find him amusing, but this turns into annoyance as we see a man who trusts no-one, dislikes everyone and alienates the two brothers who offered him the caretaker's job.
1999	*Celebration*	We are afforded the opportunity to laugh at the middle-classes during this play. Set in a restaurant, we see two couples bantering over material consumptions.
1961	*Collection (The)*	Two stage sets – a flat and a house – two sets of lives run concurrently and intertwined. Stella from the flat tells her husband, James, that she had a one night stand with Bill from the house. James goes to the house and despite turning the lives of Bill and Harry the older man with whom Bill lives – upside down, nothing is resolved.

D

1957	*Dumb Waiter (The)*	Pinter creates an eerie tension in the basement of an abandoned restaurant where two hired killers talk and bicker about nothing at all, and where an ancient dumb waiter inexplicably comes to life.
1960	*Dwarfs (The)*	This play concerns three young men; they talk, they interact and yet they are alone in their existence.

F

1980	*Family Voices*	What seems to be a happy family disintegrates through a series of parallel monologues as a mother and son read out letters to each other – letters which have possibly never been sent.

H

1964	*Homecoming (The)*	It would seem that although this is not Ruth's true family home, it may indeed be her that is returning home to this male-dominated house of lust, greed, fear, envy and anger. The question is what place will Ruth take and who will she be?

DATE	PLAYS	SYNOPSIS
1958	*Hothouse (The)*	The scene is a government institution where the inmates are kept behind locked doors and are referred to by a number rather than by a name. The place is full of misfits, including the staff, and there are so many questions to answer, not least whom fathered a child. But, at the end of the play, there is only one person left to answer the questions.

K

1982	*Kind of Alaska (A)*	A middle-aged woman wakes up after 30 years in a coma. However, in her mind she is only 16 years old and in a state of turmoil and confusion about the world in which she finds herself.

L

1967	*Landscape*	A Pinteresque observation and study, through the medium of conversation, of a middle-aged couple, their housekeeper and chauffeur.
1962	*Lover (The)*	The only thing keeping a marriage alive is the fact that a wife pretends her husband is her lover, whilst he pretends that she is a prostitute, but soon even that doesn't work and the two lives merge in disinterest and dissatisfaction.

M

1972	*Monologue*	A seedy room, an empty chair and a man conversing with whom? These Pinteresque qualities make up a 'typical' Pinter play.
1993	*Moonlight*	A man lies on his deathbed, his family, who have been called home, are with him; his sons are distant from him and incapable of closing this distance, even now, whereas the daughter behaves quite differently.
1988	*Mountain Language*	A political play set in the prison of an anonymous country where the inmates have been stripped of all civil liberties, including the freedom to speak in their own language.

N

1991	*New World Order (The)*	Two men threaten a third, helpless and blindfolded, in a play in which Pinter reminds us that the way of the world is not right and we need to change direction.
1959	*Night Out (A)*	Albert lives at home with his domineering mother. For once, he goes out to the office party but his social inadequacies and the intolerances of others release in him a violence hitherto unseen.

DATE	PLAYS	SYNOPSIS
1960	*Night School*	A man is released from jail but, when he returns home, he finds that his two aunts have let out his room.
1974	*No Man's Land*	Two elderly writers meet up – one has enjoyed success and the other has not – the successful writer now inhabits an emotionally barren world into which he will allow no man to enter.

O

1970	*Old Times*	A wealthy couple are entertaining the wife's former roommate and friend whom they haven't seen for many years; reveries and time hopping hint at happenings long gone but which still obviously matter.
1984	*One for the Road*	Another play about the abuse of human rights in which we see a 'civilised' interrogator humiliating a family who have supposedly become enemies of the state.

P

1991	*Party Time*	A party is in full flow in an elegant flat, whilst on the streets below, a military presence is in evidence.

R

2000	*Remembrance of Things Past*	Proust remembers his childhood in the 1870s, his move to Paris and the subsequent story as France goes to war.
1957	*Room (The)*	Set 'somewhere' in a room inhabited by Bert and Rose. Rose is worried about the strange tenant who lives in the windowless basement below her. He, it turns out, has been waiting for her!

S

1968	*Silence*	Three characters, each at a different stage in their lives, reminisce – not to and with each other but in a more solitary manner.
1958	*Slight Ache (A)*	A couple have been unnerved by the presence of a matchseller who has been standing by their back gate for weeks. They invite him in and find his 'silent' presence loosens their inner frustrations and terrors.

T

1964	*Tea Party*	Sisson, a businessman, seems to be at the centre of a series of mysterious events.

DATE	PLAYS	SYNOPSIS
√		
1982	*Victoria Station*	A questionably sane taxi driver who, much to the exasperation of his controller, doesn't even know the location of Victoria Street Station. Add to this a mysterious passenger and you have another mysterious Pinteresque work.

FURTHER WORKS BY HAROLD PINTER INCLUDE:

Sketches
1959 *Applicant*
1959 *Black and White (The)*
1959 *Dialogue Three*
1959 *Interview*
1959 *Last to Go*
1969 *Night*
1983 *Precisely*
2002 *Press Conference*
1959 *Request Stop*
1959 *Special Offer*
1959 *That's All*
1959 *That's Your Trouble*
1959 *Trouble in the Works*

Films
1966 *Accident*
1981 *Betrayal*
1967 *Birthday Party (The)*
1963 *Caretaker (The)*
1989 *Comfort of Strangers*
1997 *Dreaming Child (The)*
1980 *French Lieutenant's Woman (The)*
1969 *Go Between (The)*
1987 *Handmaid's Tale (The)*
1988 *Heat of the day*
1969 *Homecoming*
1970 *Langrishe Go Down*
1974 *Last Tycoon (The)*
1972 *Proust Screenplay (The)*

1963	*Pumpkin Eater (The)*
1965	*Quiller Memorandum*
1988	*Reunion*
1963	*Servant (The)*
2000	*Tragedy of King Lear*
1989	*Trial (The)*
1984	*Turtle Diary*
1982	*Victory*

Books Include
Collected Poems and Prose
The Dwarfs (a novel)
Various Voices: Prose, Poetry, Politics 1948–1998
War

Tom Stoppard, 1937–

Like Harold Pinter, Tom Stoppard has also given birth to a 'new' word, a word which is now commonly used to describe work displaying verbal wit and intellectual games, as one would expect to find in his works, and that word is 'Stoppardian'.

Tom Stoppard is often wrongly described as, 'the intellectual one.' Of course he is intellectual, but this statement implies that the other are not and nothing could be further from the truth; all are possessors of great minds, each unique in their literary output. I think the best description to afford to the writings of Tom Stoppard would be to say that they frequently, though not exclusively, have a political and humanist slant. Whereas Ayckbourn, Bennett and Pinter tend to write about everyday folk, Stoppard does quite the opposite. He tends to look at the world of espionage, of Shakespeare and literature, for example, and his plays are quite verbally acrobatic – which I suppose is one of the reasons he is called the intelligent one – as well as being a haven for his literary jokes. One could rarely imagine a Stoppard play as being a reflection of the life of the man in the street, as one conceivably could with the other Three Masters.

THE LIFE AND WORKS OF TOM STOPPARD

1937	Stoppard was born on July 3rd as Tom Straussler in Zlin, Czechoslovakia, the son of a Jewish doctor.
1939	His family fled Czechoslovakia, ahead of the Nazi invasion, and made for Singapore.

1941 They were not safe in Singapore either, so Tom, together with his mother and brother, fled again, this time to Darjeeling, India, and escaping just before the Japanese invaded. His father, Eugene Straussler, however, stayed behind only, to be killed in the invasion.

1946 Stoppard's family arrived on British soil, his mother having married Kenneth Stoppard, a Major in the British Army who gave Tom his surname, followed by an English education.

1954 He left school not wanting to go to university and began work as a journalist for *The Western Daily Press*.

1958 He started work as a journalist for *The Bristol Evening World*, where he stayed for two years.

1962 Stoppard dipped his toe into the thespian pool when he became a freelance drama critic for *Scene*, a British literary magazine. About this time, he also started writing plays for radio and television.

1965 He married Josie Ingle, with whom he was to have two sons.

1972 Divorced from Josie, Stoppard married Miriam, née Moore-Robinson, (Dr Miriam Stoppard), with whom he was to have another two sons.

1978 He wrote the piece *Professional Foul* for Amnesty International's Prisoner of Conscience Year.

1978 Tom was awarded a CBE.

1981 *On the Razzle*, adapted from Johann Nestroy's *Einen Jux will er sich machen*, was staged at The National Theatre.

1989 Stoppard was appointed to the Board of The National Theatre where he remained until 2003.

1997 Tom Stoppard was knighted by the Queen for his contributions to English literature and became 'Sir' Tom Stoppard.

2002 *The Coast of Utopia*, a play about the Russian philosopher and politician Alexander Hertzen, was staged at The National Theatre.

2005 *Heroes*, Tom Stoppard's translation of Gerald Sibleyras' play *Le Vent de Peupliers*, opened in the West End.

2006 *Rock 'n' Roll* opened in the West End, and is a play in which Tom took a backward glance at his native Czechoslovakia.

PLAYS BY TOM STOPPARD

Stoppard's work has a philosophical edge, political leanings and humanist concerns; he has a mind overcrowded by a million questions and a desire to create ever more of his own to evoke further questions and a social conscience among the masses. He is a man of wit, irony and a master of juxtaposition.

DATE	PLAYS	SYNOPSIS
A		
1970	*After Magritte*	Based on a Magritte painting in a suburban household, this is a surreal play in which the characters behave in an increasingly bizarre way, worthy of any Magritte painting.
1993	*Arcadia*	Two researchers investigate past and present events.
1972	*Artist Descending a Staircase*	Three artists who, although now old, were previously members of the avant-garde movement in their youth and are still in that mind-set when tragedy befalls one of them.
C		
2002	*Coast of Utopia (The)*	A trilogy which gives us an epic account of the revolutionary, political and artistic movements of the mid-Nineteenth Century.
D		
1976	*Dirty Linen*	A farce in which a special committee investigates the story that a significant number of MPs have all been having sex with the same woman.
1979	*Dogg's Hamlet, Cahoot's Macbeth*	Two one act plays often performed together. *Dogg's Hamlet*: explores how people use language to communicate through an alternative language called 'Dogg', in which English words have different meanings. *Cahoot's Macbeth*: deals with political censorship where public theatrical productions are forbidden and 'living room productions' are also now under threat. Then a character turns up from the first play and teaches the actors 'Dogg', with the result that, as authorities cannot understand the actors, they cannot arrest them either.
E		
1977	*Every Good Boy Deserves Favour*	Inspired by a meeting with the Russian exile Viktor Fainberg, this is a play about Soviet dissidents – and features an orchestra upon the stage too.

DATE	PLAYS	SYNOPSIS
1968	*Enter a Free Man*	Adapted for the stage from Stoppard's own screenplay, *A Walk on the Water*.

F

DATE	PLAYS	SYNOPSIS
1979	*15 Minute Hamlet*	The entire play of Hamlet – but in just 15 mins.

H

DATE	PLAYS	SYNOPSIS
1988	*Hapgood*	Another politically-influenced play, this time about spying and double agents.

I

DATE	PLAYS	SYNOPSIS
1995	*Indian Ink*	This play looks at two contrasting worlds, India in the 1930s and India in the 1980s, from the perspective of an Anglo-Indian relationship. It is based on Stoppard's own radio play, *The Native State*.
1997	*Invention of Love (The)*	*The Invention of Love* looks at the life and death of the poet A.E. Housman, including his repressed homosexuality and love for Moses Jackson.

J

DATE	PLAYS	SYNOPSIS
1972	*Jumpers*	A play which looks at the world of academic philosophy, pondering the imponderable.

N

DATE	PLAYS	SYNOPSIS
1976	*Newfoundland*	Two government officials try to reach a decision on whether to award British citizenship to an eccentric American.
1978	*Night and Day*	This is the story of the difficult lives journalists face when stationed in foreign war zones.

R

DATE	PLAYS	SYNOPSIS
1968	*Real Inspector Hound (The)*	A play within a play, where two theatre critics are watching *A Country House Murder Mystery* when they accidentally become involved in the action.
1982	*Real Thing (The)*	A farce which focuses on the relationship between Henry, a playwright, and Annie, an actress, this is another of Stoppard's plays which uses the technique of a 'play within a play'.
2006	*Rock 'n' Roll*	A backward glance at Tom Stoppard's birth-land of Czechoslovakia and an analytical look at the power of a nation being in the hands of its people, and not in the hands of its government.

DATE	PLAYS	SYNOPSIS
1966	*Rosencrantz and Guildenstern Are Dead*	A retelling of Shakespeare's *Hamlet* from the perspective of two of the play's most insignificant characters.

T

DATE	PLAYS	SYNOPSIS
1974	*Travesties*	A parody of Oscar Wilde's *The Importance of Being Earnest*, this play is based on the strange and historical improbability that James Joyce, Lenin and the Dadist poet, Tristan Tzara, must have been in Geneva at the same point in time. The events of the play and the imagined meeting of the three are related by a minor British consular official and become very mixed up in Wilde's play.

Many of Stoppard's works cross back and forth over the bridge between one artistic medium and another and so a play might start its life on the stage only to be heard at a later date on the radio and vice versa; for that reason not all 'visitations' to each medium are recorded as it would involve excessive doubling up.

FURTHER WORKS BY TOM STOPPARD INCLUDE:

Adaptations and Translations

1986 *Dalliance* [ADAPTED FROM: *Liebelei* by Arthur Schnitzler]

2004 *Henry IV* [TRANSLATED FROM: *Henry IV* by Italian writer Luigi Pirandello]

1972 *House of Bernarda Alba* (The)[ADAPTED FROM: *The House of Bernarda Alba* by F. G. Lorca]

1982 *On the Razzle* [ADAPTED FROM: *Einen Jux will er sich machen* by Johann Nestroy]

1979 *Undiscovered Country* [ADAPTED FROM: *Das Weite Land* by Arthur Schnitzler]

Plays for Radio and Television

1967 *Albert's Bridge*

1967 *Another Moon Called Earth*

1991 *Billy Bathgate*

1985 *Brazil*

1965 *Dales (The)* – series for which he wrote five episodes

1964 *Dissolution of Dominic Boot (The)*

1988 *Dog It Was That Died (The)*

1987 *Empire of the Sun*

2001	*Enigma*
1980	*Human Factor (The)*
1966	*If You're Glad I'll Be Frank*
1991	*In the Native State*
1964	*'M' is for Moon Among Other Things*
1978	*Neutral Ground*
1983	*On the Razzle*
1998	*Poodle Springs*
1977	*Professional Foul*
1990	*Russian House (The)*
1966	*Separate Peace*
1998	*Shakespeare in Love*
1984	*Squaring the Circle*
1966/7	*Student's Diary (A): An Arab in London* – series for which he wrote 70 episodes
1967	*Teeth*
1975	*Three Men in a Boat*
1963	*Walk on the Water*
1970	*Where Are They Now*

Novels

1966	*Lord Malquist and Mr Moon*

A FIFTH AND FINAL MASTER

I know I said there were four Grand Masters but there is actually one more gentleman I would like to add to this list – one gentleman I *need* to add to this list – and that is David Wood, the playwright hailed as the 'National Children's Dramatist'. He wasn't included on the list for my poll quite simply because I knew that few would recognise his name, which is a sad reflection of the credibility given to the skill required in writing for children.

Writing for children is not only a skill but it is a necessary skill so few possess, and yet the future of theatre is very much in the hands of our children. Entice a child into the theatre and you may well ignite a spark which in turn could turn into an artistic fire in adulthood; David Wood does just that.

Children are notoriously difficult to write for; they don't care who writes the play, just that they enjoy it. An adult would say: 'Have you seen the new Ayckbourn play?' A child would say: 'Have you seen *The BFG*?' Children will also tell you if they don't like something: 'That was rubbish' or 'That was boring'. Adults dress up the truth with words such as: 'I prefer his/her previous work', children do not – and let's face it, who in their right mind wants to expose themselves to such brutal honesty?

A children's playwright has to have the most vivid and continually active imagination. Children are not interested in 'stories' about a man at a bus stop; they don't want to listen to a conversation between four people which lasts for over two hours. They want action, they want excitement and colour; and I mean colour in the widest sense of the word, not just colourful clothes. A child expects exciting and colourful names and exciting and colourful sets for, remember, a child's view of theatre is far more visual than an adult's; a child expects to 'see' things happen and not just hear about them. Dramatic references may work for an adult, but they certainly don't work for children.

I believe also that children's dramatists must be more versatile than those who write for adults, for the mind of a child is like a butterfly constantly flitting from one thing to another. You will also notice in the list of works below just how many are musical plays, for Wood incorporates music and lyrics into his works, just as he often incorporates magic too, (he is a member of the Magic Circle). Children's drama is very much a sensory field; David Wood recognises this and encourages his audience of children to use their imagination to explore new ideas, as well as giving them a reason to laugh, and to think, as he introduces them to our wonderful world of theatre. David Wood is the greatest living playwright of children's theatre, if not the greatest playwright of children's theatre ever – and so deserves to be the fifth Grand Master.

David Wood, 1944–

Photo of David Wood

THE LIFE AND WORKS OF DAVID WOOD

1944 David Wood was born on 21st February in Sutton, Surrey, the son of Richard Edwin and Audrey Adele (Fincham) Wood. His early education was at Chichester High School.

1966 He graduated from Worcester College, Oxford, with a B.A. Honours Degree in English.

1966	He married Sheila Ruskin; the marriage was dissolved in 1970.
1967	Wood wrote his first play for children, *The Tinderbox*.
1969	*The Owl and the Pussycat Went to See …* (co-written with Sheila Ruskin) became his first children's play to be produced in London.
1975	Wood married Jacqueline Stanbury and they were to have two daughters, Katherine and Rebecca.
1978	He was made a member of the drama advisory panel of the Arts Council of Great Britain, a position he held until 1980.
1979	Together with John Gould, David Wood ran Whirligig Theatre (a touring theatre company for children) and continued to do so until 2003.

David Wood understands the complexities and expectations of a child's mind

1979 In this year, David Wood became a board member for Polka Theatre – the children's theatre in Wimbledon.

1983 He was co-founder and director of Verronmead Limited (a television production company).

1986 David co-founded and became a director of Westwood Theatre Productions.

1995 He co-founded and became a director of W2 Productions.

1996 From 1996–2003, Wood was a Trustee of Wimbledon Theatre.

1997 He became chair of Action for Children's Arts.

2002 David was promoted to membership of the Inner Magic Circle, with Gold Star, for his contribution to children's magic.

2003 David Wood became a board member for Polka Theatre, Wimbledon.

2004 It was in this year that David Wood was awarded an OBE in the Queen's Birthday Honours List for Services to Literature and Drama.

2005 He was awarded an Honorary Master of Arts Degree by Chichester University.

2006 He was appointed a Trustee of The Story Museum, Oxford.

2006 David Wood wrote *The Queen's Handbag*, a play to celebrate the Queen's 80th birthday; this was performed in Buckingham Palace Gardens and seen by 8,000,000 BBC One viewers.

PLAYS BY DAVID WOOD INCLUDE

ADAPTATIONS

DATE	TITLE	ADAPTED FROM

1977/8   *Babe, the Sheep-Pig*   From the book: *The Sheep-Pig* by Dick King-Smith.
The story of one piglet's rise to become the world famous 'sheep-pig'.

1991   *BFG (The)*   From the book of the the same name by Roald Dahl.
The 24ft tall BFG (Big Friendly Giant) and a little orphan called Sophie team up to save the
children of England from child-eating giants.

2004/5   *Danny the Champion of the World*   From the book of the the same name by Roald Dahl.
When Danny sets out to save his father from the nasty, greedy Victor Hazell, he finds himself as the
mastermind behind the most incredible and exciting plot ever attempted against this man.

2001   *Fantastic Mr Fox*   From the book of the the same name by Roald Dahl.
The farmers try to get rid of the fox who regularly steals food from their farms, only to be
outwitted by 'Fantastic Mr Fox' at every turn.

2001/2   *James and the Giant Peach*   From the book of the the same name by Roald Dahl.
This tale is related by James himself and by the insect characters. It begins at the end of the story
as James and his friends explain how they came to be living in a giant peach stone.

2000   *Lighthouse Keeper's Lunch (The)*   From the book of the the same name by: Ronda &
                                             David Armitage.
Each day, seagulls steal Mr Grinling's lunch, but Mrs Grinling has a plan.

1981   *Meg and Mog Show*   Based on the Meg and Mog books by Helen Nicoll &
                                             Jan Pieńkowski.
Meg, Mog and Owl set off on an adventure to find the ingredients for a spell to get rid of an
invading Stegosaurus.

2008   *Tiger Who Came To Tea (The)*   From the book of the same name by Judith Kerr.
Sophie and her Mummy are having tea when a tiger arrives and eats and drinks everything in the
kitchen. How will Daddy react when he comes home?

2000   *Tom's Midnight Garden*   From the book of the same name by Philippa Pearce.
Tom travels from the present to the past and meets Hatty, a 10 year old girl. Over a short period
of time, although Tom remains the same age, Hatty grows into a young woman.

1999   *Twits (The)*   From the book of the same name by Roald Dahl.
Set in a circus where, bored with playing silly tricks on one another, Mr & Mrs Twit turn their
attentions to capturing and training a family of monkeys for a circus act. The monkeys cruel
incarceration in a cage is avenged when the Birds trick the Twits into believing the world has
turned upside down. The audience help in the trick by pretending to be upside down too. (They
put their shoes on their outstretched hands).

1992   *Witches (The)*   From the book of the same name by Roald Dahl.
Boy and his Grandmother defeat the Grand High Witch and her followers, who are holding a
Conference in an English seaside hotel, but, during the struggle, Boy is turned into a mouse. The
Witches are nothing like the ones who wear pointed hats and fly on broomsticks – they look very
much like ordinary women, which helps in their deception.

MUSICAL PLAYS

(Unless otherwise stated the book is by David Wood)

DATE	TITLE	MUSIC & LYRICS
1983	*Abbacadabra*	Music by: Benny Andersson Björn Ulvaeus Lyrics by: Mike Batt Don Black & Björn Ulvaeus

Three children magically enter a computer game and help Aladdin, Cinderella, Pinnochio and the Beast escape the evil Carabosse in time to attend Sleeping Beauty's wedding.

1980	*Aladdin*	David Wood

Princess Zadia and Aladdin are childhood friends in this retelling of the original tale. Charming touches include a monkey, a baby dragon and a Genie who is the long-lost uncle of the genie of the ring.

1978	*Babes in the Magic Wood*	David Wood

It is Christmas Eve and, worryingly, the toys are still being made. A Fairy Godmother intervenes and the toys are then magically finished – but the Fairy Godmother is not all she seems.

1979	*Cinderella*	David Wood

This follows the original story but the characters have different personalities to the ones we have come to expect.

2004	*Clockwork*	Music by Stephen McNeff (Based on the novel by Philip Pullman)

An opera in which Fritz begins the story of Dr Shatzburg whose mechanical figures seem to take on a life of their own. But Fritz is horrified when, half-way through the story, the fictional Dr Kalmenius appears.

1981	*Dick Whittington and Wondercat*	David Wood

A crowd gather to greet Sir Richard Whittington on his installation as Lord Mayor of London. One young boy is not impressed until he learns, through the retelling of how Dick Whittington came to be Lord Mayor, that this Mayor is indeed a good man.

1986	*Dinosaurs and All That Rubbish*	Lyrics by David Wood Music by Peter Pontzen (based on the book by Michael Foreman)

A moral tale which tells of the earth that man has destroyed is restored to its natural beauty by dinosaurs and the animal kingdom.

1971/2	*Flibberty and the Penguin*	David Wood

Young Penguin has come from Iceland to find his Mother and Father before the spring weather becomes too warm. He is helped by Flibberty, a genial goblin, and eventually the pair discover the parent penguins in the zoo and set them free.

DATE	TITLE	MUSIC & LYRICS
1998/9	*Forest Child*	Libretto by David Wood Music by Derek Clark (based on the book by Richard Edwards)

A children's opera in which 'the Forest Child' has been raised by the animals of the forest. She is captured by a hunter and taken back to 'civilisation' where she is treated badly, before being rescued by the hunter's son.

| 1976 | *Gingerbread Man (The)* | David Wood |

The newly-baked Gingerbread Man tries to cure the sore throat of Herr Von Cuckoo, who lives in the cuckoo clock.

| 1973/4 | *Hijack over Hygenia* | David Wood |

Hygenia is the cleanest kingdom in the world and disease is unknown. But, as a result of all this cleanliness, Dr Spicknspan is always out of work and so he arranges for Measle to enter the kingdom illegally and bring everyone out in spots!

| 1982 | *Jack and the Giant* | David Wood |

The traditional tale told in the inimitable David Wood style.

| 1984 | *Jack the Lad* | Lyrics by David Wood and Dave & Toni Arthur
Music by Dave & Toni Arthur |

A musical celebration of Jack, the ubiquitous hero or everyman of English legend, myth and folklore – from 'Little Jack Horner', through 'Jack and the Beanstalk' to 'Spring-Heeled Jack', the Terror of London. The setting is a gypsy encampment, where a series of Jack tales and songs are performed by the gypsies to celebrate the 80th birthday of their senior member – affectionately known as 'Jack the Lad'.

| 1969 | *Larry the Lamb in Toytown* | Music & lyrics by David Wood
Book by David Wood & Sheila Ruskin
(based on the stories by S.G. Hulme-Beaman) |

The Toytown characters come under threat from a dragon and a villainous highwayman.

| 1995 | *More Adventures of Noddy* | Adaptation, stories & songs by David Wood
(based on the Noddy books by Enid Blyton) |

Two one act plays following the story of the much-loved character Noddy and his equally loved chums, Big Ears and Mr Plod the Policeman.

| 1977 | *Nutcracker Sweet* | David Wood |

Set in the Nutty May Fair, the play follows the struggle of the nuts against the villainous confectioner, Professor Jelly Bon Bon, who is searching for nuts with which to create a new chocolate assortment.

DATE	TITLE	MUSIC & LYRICS
1976	*Old Father Time*	David Wood

A time travelling tale which begins when Big Ben stops and Old Father Time, who lives in the clock and controls time, travels to various periods in history.

| 1986 | *Old Man of Lochnagar (The)* | David Wood (based on the book by HRH The Prince of Wales) |

The story follows the Old Man, who lives in a cave by the loch under the mountain, Lochnagar, as he sets out to save the Gorms from the menacing Giant, Gormless.

| 1975 | *Old Mother Hubbard* | David Wood |

One Christmas Eve, a lonely dog arrives at Mother Hubbard's Home for Lost Children; but her cupboard is bare and, worse still, she and her brood of nursery-rhyme children are turned out by the bailiff and the rent collector.

| 1968 | *Owl and the Pussycat Went to See … (The)* | David Wood & Sheila Ruskin / Music & Lyrics by David Wood (based on the verses and stories by Edward Lear) |

The Owl and the Pussycat must find a ring and someone to marry them; they are helped by the Quangle Wangle and the Dong with a luminous nose, and hampered by the villainous Plum Pudding Flea and the Jumblies.

| 1972 | *Papertown Paperchase (The)* | David Wood |

The Salamander, a sort of dragon, is in trouble with the Fire Flies because he is unable to create a fire by breathing on a pile of sticks! To redeem himself, he is sent on a mission to burn down Papertown.

| 1988 | *Pied Piper (The)* | Book and Lyrics by David Wood and Dave & Toni Arthur / Music by Dave & Toni Arthur |

Set in modern times, it seems that the Pied Piper has returned to claim the fee denied him all those years ago and once more spirits away the children but, this time, all ends happily.

| 1970 | *Plotters of Cabbage Patch Corner (The)* | David Wood |

The garden insects are infuriated by the constant 'spraying' and so the unattractive Slug, Greenfly and Maggot call for a rebellion. But the 'pretty' insects – Red Admiral, Ladybird and Bumble Bee – oppose this and war is declared.

| 1981 | *Robin Hood* | Book and Lyrics by David Wood and Dave & Toni Arthur / Music by Dave & Toni Arthur |

A group of villagers are celebrating May Day with a variety of pastimes – singing, dancing, acrobatics and competitive sports. The villagers take on Robin Hood roles to tell the various well-known tales of Robin Hood and his Merry Men.

DATE	TITLE	MUSIC & LYRICS
1974/5	*Rock Nativity*	Book and Lyrics by David Wood Music by Tony Hatch & Jackie Trent

The modern-day equivalent of a Medieval Mystery play – simple, yet not naïve, humorous, yet not disrespectful.

1993	*Rupert and the Green Dragon*	David Wood (Based on the Rupert stories and characters by Mary Tourtel and Alfred Bestall)

Edward Trunk wishes for a sunny day for his birthday, but Nutwood is currently experiencing only winter weather. On the advice of Wise Owl, Rupert goes to see the Clerk of the Weather. The friendly Green Dragon is a great help, but Zita, the Ice Maid, has to be foiled first.

1990	*Save the Human*	Book and Lyrics by David Wood Music by David Wood & Peter Pontzen Additional Lyrics by Tony Husband

Long ago, human beings ruled the world but they made a terrible mess and now the animals are in charge.

1986	*See-Saw Tree (The)*	David Wood

An interesting play which looks at important environmental issues. *The See-Saw Tree*, an ancient oak, stands on ground which is ear-marked for development into a children's playground. A public meeting is called to discuss this proposal, which includes cutting down the 300-year-old oak tree and so we see the effect this would have on the creatures who live in the tree.

1983	*Selfish Shellfish (The)*	Songs by David Wood Incidental Music by Peter Pontzen

Life for the rockpool dwellers is full of uncertainty. Every new tide brings fresh surprises or new problems. But they cope reasonably well, until Seagull brings them warning of a possible catastrophe – the Great (oil) Slick is coming.

2000	*Spot's Birthday Party*	David Wood (Based on the books by Eric Hill)

In this play, David Wood has created an exciting introduction to theatre for small children, using the simple plot of a birthday party where the audience is treated more like guests at the party than an audience watching a show.

1979	*There was an Old Woman …*	David Wood

Mother Shipton lives in an overcrowded shoe with her hoards of children. But the shoe actually belongs to a giant who lost it and has been looking for it – with one bare foot – ever since. This musical play calls for a lot of talented children and a not very good magician.

1972	*Tickle*	David Wood

A workman eats too much pepper. He complains of a tickle in his nose and sneezes violently. The 'tickle' is ejected – and arrives as a new-born baby on the stage who is only anxious to find a friend and a home.

1967	*Tinderbox (The)*	David Wood (Based on the story by Hans Christian Andersen)

David's first (unpublished) play for children, featuring a soldier on a quest to marry a Princess.

FURTHER WORKS BY DAVID WOOD INCLUDE:

Books Include

Baby Bears Buggy Ride: To the Shops and *To the Park* created with, and illustrated by, Richard Fowler

Bedtime Story created with, and illustrated by, Richard Fowler

BFG (The): Plays for Children adapted from the book by Roald Dahl

Chish 'n' Fips illustrated by Don Seed

Christmas Story (The): A Nativity Play illustrated by Asun Balzola

David Wood Plays (vols 1 & 2)

Discorats (The) illustrated by Geoffrey Beitz

Funny Bunny's Magic Show created with, and illustrated by, Richard Fowler

Gingerbread Man (The) illustrated by Sally Ann Lambert

Happy Birthday Mouse! created with, and illustrated by, Richard Fowler

Lady Lollipop: A Play for Children adapted from the book by Dick King-Smith

Magic Show (The) created with, and illustrated by, Richard Fowler

Meg and Mog (four plays for children) adapted from the books by Helen Nicoll and Jan Piénkowski

Mole's Bedtime Story created with, and illustrated by, Richard Fowler

Mole's Summer Story created with, and illustrated by, Richard Fowler

Mole's Winter Story created with, and illustrated by, Richard Fowler

Operats of Rodent Garden (The) illustrated by Geoffrey Beitz

Phantom Cat of the Opera (The) illustrated by Peters Day

Play Theatre: Jack and the Beanstalk created with, and illustrated by, Richard Fowler

Play Theatre: Nativity created with, and illustrated by, Richard Fowler

Playstage (plays for children) co-written with Dave & Toni Arthur

Poems in: *The Kingfisher Book of Comic Verse*

Poems in the: *Much Better Story Book*

Pop–up Theatre: Cinderella created with, and illustrated by, Richard Fowler

Save the Human created with, and illustrated by, Tony Husband

Sidney the Monster illustrated by Clive Scruton

Silly Spider created with, and illustrated by, Richard Fowler

Theatre for Children: Guide to Writing, Adapting, Directing and Acting co-written with Janet Grant

Toy Cupboard (The) created with, and illustrated by, Richard Fowler

Twits (The): Plays for Children adapted from the book by Roald Dahl

Witches (The): Plays for Children adapted from the book by Roald Dahl

Film Screenplays

Swallows and Amazons

Tide Race

TV
Back Home
Chips Comic
Chish 'n' Fips
Emu's Christmas Adventure
Gingerbread Man (The)
Old Man of Lochnagar (The)
Playaway
Seeing and Doing
Watch
Writers' Workshop

Radio
Swallows and Amazons

Recordings Include
The David Wood Song Book
The Gingerbread Man
Meg and Mog Show
The Owl and the Pussycat Went to See …
Chish 'n' Fips

Plays for Grown Ups
Four Degrees Over [with John Gould]
Hang Down Your Head and Die [with David Wright and others]
Life in Bedrooms (A) [with David Wright]
Luck of the Bodkins (The) [with John Gould – Based on the book by P.G. Wodehouse]
Maudie [with Iwan Williams – Based on the cartoons of Osbert Lancaster]
Three to One On [with John Gould]

FINAL COMMENT

David Wood is a multi-talented gentleman; he is a Playwright, Children's Author, Actor, Director, Composer and even a Magician.

Popular Playwrights Through the Ages

Well, we have seen the five contemporary giants but there are more, oh so many more, for **'There was man AND there was theatre'** (Anon).

You could say that man and play-acting was a kind of simultaneous creation/evolvement for, as we have seen since the beginning of time, man felt the need to act out his emotions and experiences for other people to watch, to ward off evil spirits or explain the inexplicable.

We are now going to look at the most popular playwrights through time, starting from Greek Theatre through to the present day. The reason for this being that it is more difficult to be exact when looking at theatre earlier than Greek Theatre for, in the ancient world, little was committed to any form of retrieval system.

As we know, theatre is a reflection of life – past, present and, indeed, even the future; it is a commentary on the world around us; it is a political tool; it is an expression of emotion; a manipulative force; it IS life. It figures that it is helpful, even necessary, to have at least a rudimentary grasp of significant parallel milestones in the development of the world. So, before each section, you will find a few significant world events in that particular period of history, and a few to get us going up and to that period too.

Greek Theatre

SIGNIFICANT EVENTS AT THIS TIME … (5500 BC–0 BC)

Cotton is used for the first time • Egyptians develop Hieroglyphics, a system of writing which tells stories through pictographs • First paper is made from the papyrus reed • First wheels are used • Flax threads are woven together to create fabric • Great Pyramids are built • Great Wall of China is built stretching over 1,000 miles along China's Northern border • Hippocrates survives a plague which kills much of the population of Athens and goes on to become the first person to say that disease is not a punishment inflicted by the gods upon man; he is, of course, also well known for the Hippocratic Oath, to which all doctors swear • Julius Caesar is assassinated • Roman Republic is founded

NAME	DATE	PLAYS
Aeschylus	c525–456 BC	Agamemnon Oresteian Trilogy (The) Persians (The)

Aeschylus wrote Greek tragedies which, up until his time, were very basic and usually involved just one actor playing all parts – helped by the use of masks and, of course, the legendary Greek Chorus. He is credited with introducing a second actor into the play, thus making interactive dialogue possible and reducing the need for, and the size of, the chorus.

Aristophanes	c450–385 BC	Birds (The) Frogs (The) Lysistrata

Aristophanes' plays are the only representatives of Greek Old Comedy. *Lysistrata* is the most regularly performed in modern times because of its slant on sexual politics and its anti-war message.

Euripides	c480–406 BC	Bacchae Medea Trojan Women

In many ways, Euripides was a misunderstood man for, in general, he didn't conform to the way of life at his time in Ancient Greece; these were violent times and Euripides was actually a pacifist and a humanitarian, qualities which were unappreciated then.

Sophocles	c495–406 BC	Antigone Electra Oedipus Rex

Like many artistic individuals, both ancient and modern, Sophocles was multi-talented. As well as writing great plays he was also a proficient actor and appeared in many of his own plays, of which he wrote more than 120.

Roman Theatre

SIGNIFICANT EVENTS AT THIS TIME ... (0 BC–500 AD)

Hadrian's Wall is built, stretching 70 miles across Northern England • Herod is deposed [as result of his cruel treatment of the Jews] • Jesus Christ is born • Jesus Christ is put to death by the Romans in Jerusalem • Mount Vesuvius erupts destroying Pompeii and Herculaneum; 20,000 people are killed • Rome burns, allegedly set fire to by Nero; legend has it that Nero fiddled as Rome burned • Rule of 'The Five Good Emperors' begins; they are – 1) Marcus Nerva, 2) Marcus Traianus, 3) Hadrian, 4) Antoninus Pius and 5) Marcus Aurelius, during which peace reigns and road systems are built • The Romans withdraw from Britain – never to return

NAME	DATE	PLAYS
Plautus (Italian)	C254–184 BC	*Amphitruo* *Braggart Soldier (The) [Miles Gloriosus]* *Menaechimi*

Although he is rated as one of the greatest of the comic Roman dramatists, little is actually known about the man himself – not even his forenames with absolute certainty. In general, his plays are based on exaggerated humour and farcical situations.

Seneca (Spanish later taken to Rome)	4 BC–65 AD	*Hercules Furens* *Troades* *Thyestes*

Although Seneca reportedly suffered from poor health, he was trained in Rhetoric and was a popular Roman philosopher of his time, as well as having a reputation as a great orator and has been credited with tutoring the young Nero. His plays are generally considered suitable for recitation rather than for performance.

Terence (Born in North Africa but taken to Rome as a slave)	C195–159 BC	*Adelphi* (or *Adelphoe; The Brothers*) *Andria* (*The Andrian Girl*) *Hecyra* (*The Mother-in-Law*)

His Roman master, impressed by his intelligence, educated Terence and later granted him his freedom. As with many of this period, little is known of the man and even less of his slave, Terence. Despite his premature death, however, Terence still managed to write six plays.

Medieval Theatre

SIGNIFICANT EVENTS AT THIS TIME ... (500 AD–1500 AD)

Botticielli Paints 'The Birth of Venus' and Da Vinci paints 'The Last Supper' • Bubonic Plague (The Black Death), starts its march through Europe, killing in excess of an estimated 25 million people • Construction begins on the Tower of London • Joan of Arc frees Orleans and is later burned to death at the stake • King John of England signs the Magna Carta giving the British aristocracy the rights to trial by jury • Printing Press is invented • Work begins on Notre Dame in Paris • Henry V defeats the French at Agincourt • The Peasants Revolt is lead by Watt Tyler and results in the beheading of the Archbishop of Canterbury and eventually the death of Tyler himself • William the Conqueror defeats Harold II at the Battle of Hastings and is crowned King of England • Universities of Oxford and Cambridge are founded

NAME	DATE	PLAYS
Chester Cycle of Mystery Plays	14th–16th C	*Various*

A five-year cycle of Medieval religious plays depicting Creation through to the Last Judgement and still played in Chester, England today.

NAME	DATE	PLAYS
Hrotsvitha of Gandersheim (German)	c935–973	*Dulcitius* *Gallicanus* *Paphnutius*

Hrotsvitha was actually a nun who styled her writings on those of Terence, though modified and with a Christian influence and, of course, written in Latin; she also wrote poetry.

NAME	DATE	PLAYS
Medwall, Henry (British)	B. 1461 died post-1501	*Fulgens and Lucrece* *Nature*

Medwall, who was born in Southall, was educated at Eton and later at Cambridge, after which he worked as a lawyer. No-one knows for certain when Medwall died because after the death of his employer, Cardinal John Morton, in 1500; nothing more was heard of Medwall himself after the year 1501.

NAME	DATE	PLAYS
York Cycle of Mystery Plays	14th–16th C	*Various*

A four-year cycle of Medieval religious plays depicting Creation through to the Last Judgement and still played in York, England today.

Sixteenth Century Plays and Playwrights

SIGNIFICANT EVENTS OF THE CENTURY ... (1500–1599)

The Reformation begins as Henry VIII is excommunicated by the Pope and makes himself the Head of the English Church • *Shakespeare is born* • On the Revolution of Heavenly Bodies *by Nicolaus Copernicus – highlights his theory that the earth revolves around the sun* • *Leonardo da Vinci paints the 'Mona Lisa'; Michelangelo sculpts 'David' and paints the Sistine Chapel* • *Nostradamus publishes* Centuries, *a book of predictions* • *St. Peter's Church is started in Rome; it is designed and decorated by such artists and architects as Bramante, Michelangelo, da Vinci, Raphael, and Bernini, though it will not be completed until 1626* • *Pope Gregory XIII implements the Gregorian calendar* • *Spanish Armada is defeated by the English*

NAME	DATE	PLAYS
Jonson, Ben (British)	1572–1637	*Alchemist (The)* *Every Man in His Humour* *Volpone*

Jonson was born into a life of poverty and yet, despite the lack of a university education, he became one of the most learned men of his time and a great and humorous playwright. His work, *Every Man in his Humour* acts as a visual representation of Elizabethan England.

| Kyd, Thomas (British) | 1558–1594 | *Cornelia* *Spanish Tragedy (The)* |

Kyd was educated at Merchant Taylors' School in London. Although we are fairly certain that Kyd had – some part – in the writing of other works we can only say with certainty that he wrote these two. In 1593, he was arrested and tortured as a suspect of treasonable activity. He died in debt in 1594.

| Lyly, John (British) | c1554–1606 | *Endimion* *Midas* *Woman in the Moon (The)* |

Lyly was born in Kent and educated at Magdalen College, Oxford; he was well known for writing comedies, the plots of which he drew from classical mythology and legends. His popularity waned though and, eventually, he died in poverty.

| Marlowe, Christopher (British) | 1564–1593 | *Dr. Faustus* *Jew of Malta (The)* *Tamburlaine the Great* |

The son of a shoemaker, Marlowe was educated at Corpus Christi College, Cambridge and is credited with introducing blank verse into English literature. Marlowe became an actor and dramatist for the Lord Admiral's Company in 1587.

| Shakespeare, William (British) | 1564–1616 | * See separate chapter on Shakespeare |

The most celebrated and performed playwright of all time.

| Webster, John (British) | c1580 | *Devil's Law Case (The)* *Duchess of Malfi (The)* *White Devil (The)* |

Webster collaborated with other playwrights, including Thomas Dekker with whom he wrote *Westward Ho* and *Northward Ho*. To a lesser degree, he collaborated with several others too.

Seventeenth Century Plays and Playwrights

SIGNIFICANT EVENTS OF THE CENTURY ... (1600–1699)

Barometer is invented by Evangelista Torricelli • Black Death kills in excess of 25,000 people; it is followed by The Great Fire of London which helps to stamp it out • Christopher Wren rebuilds St Paul's after The Great Fire of London • Dom Perignon, a French monk, invents Champagne • Guy Fawkes attempts to blow up Parliament • Habeaus Corpus Act passed ensuring there can be no imprisonment without a court appearance first • Isaac Newton describes the theory of gravity • Oliver Cromwell becomes ruler of England, Scotland and Ireland • St Peter's Basilica in Rome is completed • Taj Mahal is completed • The first illustrated book for children is published • The Pilgrim Fathers set sail in The Mayflower *landing at Plymouth Rock • William Harvey discovers the circulation of blood*

NAME	DATE	PLAYS
Behn, Aphra (British)	1640–1689	*Forc'd Marriage (The)* *Lucky Chance (The)* *Rover (The)*

Although very little is known of Behn – not even her birthplace or details of her parentage – it is widely believed that she was the first English woman to earn a living by writing and, by entering that stronghold, she was frequently hailed as an early champion of women's rights. It is also said that, before becoming a professional writer, she was a professional spy for England. Quite a woman!

NAME	DATE	PLAYS
Brome, Richard (British)	1590–1652	*Antipodes (The)* *Joviall Crew (A)* *Northern Lasse (The)*

All we really know of Brome himself is that he worked in service for Ben Jonson and that he went on to write some great works. Sadly, though, his writing career came to an end in 1642 when Parliament closed the theatres; he died a pauper in 1652.

NAME	DATE	PLAYS
Congreve, William (British)	1670–1729	*Love for Love* *Old Bachelor (The)* *Way of the World (The)*

A protégé of John Dryden, Congreve became renowned for his satirical portrayal of the war of the sexes. His last play, *The Way of the World*, was his most successful and is considered, by some, to be the wittiest play ever written.

NAME	DATE	PLAYS
Corneille, Pierre (French)	1606–1684	*Clitandre* *Mélite* *Palace Corridor (The)*

Corneille was born into a middle-class, professional family. He was educated at a Jesuit school and later became a licentiate in law. He wrote his first play – a comedy – called *Mélite* before he was 20 years old.

Davenant, Sir William (British)	1606–1668	*Love and Honour* *Platonic Lovers (The)* *Witts (The)*

Born in Oxford, Sir William Davenant was reputedly the godson of William Shakespeare (some say he might even have been his son). After the death of Ben Jonson, Davenant was appointed Poet Laureate. He was knighted by King Charles I in 1643 in recognition for his support during the Civil War and for running supplies across the Channel.

Dekker, Thomas (British)	1572–1632	*Family of Love (The)* *Honest Whore – Part Two (The)* *Shoemaker's Holiday (The)*

Dekker is well known for his graphic depictions of London life, which is ironic really as we know very little of the early life of Dekker himself and can only wonder on the speculation that he was born of Dutch immigrants. He was a great collaborator with well known dramatists of the time as well as writing on his own.

Dryden, John (British)	1631–1700	*Aureng-Zebe* *Marriage à-la-Mode* *Secret Love*

The son of a country gentleman, Dryden was educated at Westminster School where his love of classical literature began. He later went up to Trinity College, Cambridge and graduated in 1654. He is probably best known as a poet and was appointed Poet Laureate in 1668. When the theatres reopened – after closure by the Puritans in 1642 – he turned to writing for the stage too.

Farquhar, George (Irish)	1678–1707	*Beaux' Stratagem (The)* *Love and a Bottle* *Recruiting Officer (The)*

Farquhar was the son of a clergyman and studied at Trinity College, Dublin, as a sizar (this is one who received a college allowance in return for menial duties). Later, and after an unsuccessful spell as an actor, he turned his more successful hand to writing. His final play *The Beaux' Statagem* was completed on his deathbed.

Fletcher, John (British)	1579–1625	*Loyall Subject (The)* *Wife for a Month (A)* *Wild Goose Chase (The)*

Born in Sussex, the son of a minister, Fletcher became well known as a great collaborator – which is an art in itself. However, he did also write plays single-handedly. Fletcher died in the Great Plague in 1625.

NAME	DATE	PLAYS
Middleton, Thomas (British)	1580–1627	*Changeling (The)* *Game of Chess (A)* *Women Beware Women*

Born into a wealthy family of craftsmen, Middleton's father died when Thomas was just six years old. He later pulled out of his studies at Oxford, possibly due to financial problems. He was a popular playwright of his time and was often called upon to write the Lord Mayor's pageants and other civic entertainments.

Molière, Jean-Baptiste Poquelin (French)	1622–1673	*Le Malade Imaginaire* *Le Misanthrope* *Tartuffe*

A true thespian in every sense of the word, Molière was a writer, director, stage manager, actor, and generally all things to the theatre. One of the most famous stories – fact, not fiction about Molière was that he died as he lived, on the stage while performing *Le Malade Imaginaire*. In reality, he actually collapsed on stage and died at his house a few hours later.

Racine, Jean (French)	1639–1699	*Andromaque* *Bajazet* *Phèdre*

His full name was Jean-Baptiste Racine; he was orphaned by the time he was a toddler and so was taken in by his grandparents. After the death of his grandfather, he received a classical education in Latin and Greek at a convent near Paris. He later went on to study law before becoming a successful writer.

Vanbrugh, John (British)	1664–1726	*Provoked Wife (The)* *Relapse (The)*

Vanbrugh's grandfather was a Flemish merchant and his father a sugar baker in Cheshire. He was commissioned into the army – and was later arrested as a suspected British agent. Whilst in prison, he wrote the first draft of a comedy. He also designed country houses (e.g. Castle Howard in Yorkshire) and was knighted in 1714, becoming Sir John Vanbrugh.

Wycherley, William (British)	1671–1715	*Country Wife (The)* *Love in a Wood* *Plain Dealer (The)*

Wycherley was born in the small Shropshire village of Clive, the eldest of six children and was educated at Queen's College, Oxford, though he never graduated. His plays epitomised the bawdy ways of his times, through use of scintillating and witty language.

Eighteenth Century Plays and Playwrights

SIGNIFICANT EVENTS OF THE CENTURY ... (1700–1799)

American War of Independence • Arkwright patents a spinning machine – an early step in the Industrial Revolution • Boston Tea Party • Convicts are sent from Britain to Australia • Earthquake in Portugal kills thousands • French Revolution – the Paris Bastille is stormed • George Washington is elected as the first President of the United States • HMS Bounty *Mutineers settle on Pitcairn Island • Industrial Revolution • James Watt invents the steam engine • Methodist Church founded by John Wesley • Nitrogen is discovered • Robert Walpole becomes the first British Prime Minister*

NAME	DATE	PLAYS
Gay, John (British)	1685–1732	*Beggar's Opera (The)*

Born into an impoverished family, Gay travelled to London to become an apprentice to a silk mercer and and it was there that he settled. Although more of a poet than a dramatist, he will be forever remembered for his great dramatic work, *The Beggar's Opera.*

NAME	DATE	PLAYS
Garrick, David (British)	1717–1779	*Lethe* or *Aesop in the Shades* *Lying Valet (The)* *Miss in her Teens*

Garrick was one of seven children and the eldest son in the family home in Lichfield. His plans to study law changed with an inheritance he received after his father's death. He then began mixing in theatrical circles and turned his hand to writing and acting. It was a long time before he told his family that he was an actor – in those days it was frowned upon as a profession. He is hailed by many as the greatest actor who has ever lived.

NAME	DATE	PLAYS
Goethe, Johann Wolfgang von (German)	1749–1832	*Die Mitschuldigen [Partners in Guilt]* *Faust* *Lover's Caprice (The)*

Johann was the first child of lawyer Johann Casper Goethe and Katherine Elizabeth Textor, his mother being the one to encourage his literary aspirations. Like many an artistic genius, Goethe travelled in many artistic directions; he was a poet, novelist, theatre director, critic, artist, scientist, statesman and, of course, a playwright. Working for most of his life on *Faust*, he finished the second part of it just before his death.

NAME	DATE	PLAYS
Goldsmith, Oliver (Irish)	1730–1774	*Good Natur'd Man (The)* *She Stoops to Conquer*

Goldsmith was the son of an Anglo-Irish clergyman. He was educated at Trinity College, Dublin and later at medical school in Edinburgh, though it would seem that he did not take a degree in Edinburgh. Not a prolific writer for the theatre, he will be forever remembered, however, for his masterpiece, *She Stoops to Conquer.*

NAME	DATE	PLAYS
O'Keefe, John (Irish)	1747–1833	*She-Gallant (The)* *Son-in-Law (The)* *Wild Oats*

O'Keefe was known for his comic writings which were excellent commentaries of the times in which he lived. His most well known work is *Wild Oats* which is full of mistaken identities, love interests and innuendoes.

Sheridan, Richard Brinsley (Irish)	1751–1816	*Rivals (The)* *School for Scandal (The)* *St Patrick's Day*

Sheridan had three high profile careers. He was a qualified lawyer and distinguished playwright, before finally becoming an MP with a reputation as a great orator.

Voltaire (French)	1694–1778	*Candide* *Oedipe* *Zaire*

He was actually born as Francoise-Marie Arouet – the name Voltaire not evolving until about 1718 – as the son of a high-ranking civil servant. He was educated at the Jesuit Collège Louis-le-Grand, in Paris. In 1717, he was imprisoned in the Bastille for 11 months as a punishment for writing a scathing satire about the French government

Nineteenth Century Plays and Playwrights

SIGNIFICANT EVENTS OF THE CENTURY ... (1800–1899)

Britain abolishes the slave trade • Crimean War (Russia, Turkey, Britain, France, Sardinia) • Dynamite is invented • First anaesthetic – ether – is used • First tin cans are produced in Britain to preserve food • Irish Potato famine • Jack the Ripper murders in London • Marconi invents wireless telegraphy • Napoleon becomes Emperor of the French • Napoleon is defeated at the Battle of Waterloo • Postage stamps are introduced in Britain • Rear Admiral Viscount Nelson defeats Napoleon Bonaparte at the Battle of Trafalgar • Robert Peel sets up the Metropolitan Police • The world's first photograph is taken • Thomas A. Edison invents practical electric light

NAME	DATE	PLAYS
Barrie, (Sir) James (Scottish)	1860–1937	*Admiral Crichton (The)* *Peter Pan* *What Every Woman Knows*

Educated at Edinburgh University, Barrie spent two years as a journalist before becoming a freelance writer. Barrie idealised childhood, with little time for the adult way of life. In 1929, Barrie gave the copyright of his work, *Peter Pan*, to Great Ormond Street Hospital, thus providing the Hospital with a substantial income and enabling many children to do just what Peter Pan never did, and that was 'grow up'.

Chekhov, Anton (Russian)	1860–1904	*Cherry Orchard (The)* *Seagull (The)* *Uncle Vanya*

Chekhov began to support himself at just 16 years old; he then earnt the money by writing short stories to put himself through medical school. Sadly, it wasn't until after his death that the weight of his plays gained the recognition they rightly deserved.

Galsworthy, John (British)	1867–1933	*Justice* *Mob (The)* *Strife*

Galsworthy was educated at Oxford and called to the Bar in 1890 but, finding law unfulfilling, he turned to writing. He is known both for his novels and for his dramatic works, the latter of which generally dealt with ethical and social problems.

Ibsen, Henrik (Norwegian)	1828–1906	*Doll's House (A)* *Ghosts* *Hedda Gabler*

By the age of just 23 years, Ibsen was already a director and writer in residence at a theatre where he had to write a play a year. He remained a prolific writer until his death, writing plays which made audiences examine their own lives and morals.

Jerome, Jerome K. (British)	1859–1927	*Passing of the Third Floor Back (The)* *Prude's Progress (The)* *Soul of Nicholas Snyders (The)*

Jerome did not have an easy start in life as, following the death of his parents, he found himself alone in the world at just 16. He had a variety of dead end jobs before he married and found success as a writer, both within a short time of each other.

Pinero, Arthur Wing (British)	1855–1954	*Magistrate (The)* *Second Mrs Tanqueray (The)* *Trelawny of the 'Wells'*

Pinero was born into a family descended from Portuguese Jews. He began studies in law but, at 19, abandoned this route to become an actor. He became well known for his superbly crafted farces. Closely associated with The Royal Court Theatre, Pinero was knighted in 1909.

NAME	DATE	PLAYS
Shaw, George Bernard (Irish)	1856–1950	*Major Barbara* *Pygmalion* *St Joan*

Shaw is one of those playwrights who spanned two centuries and one of whom scholars have argued over for decades: 'Is he a Nineteenth or Twentieth Century dramatist?' Well, I'm not even going to attempt to answer that one; this is where I have put him – others may disagree. Despite being an intensely shy man, his self-discipline was such that he became an accomplished public speaker.

Strindberg, August (Swedish)	1849–1912	*Father (The)* *Ghost Sonata (The)* *Miss Julie*

Strindberg didn't have an easy early start in life, his childhood being marred by emotional insecurities and poverty. In fact, he was plagued by demons of varying kinds throughout his life. Despite this, he wrote more than 70 plays and was inspirational to the many writers who were to follow him.

Synge, J.M. (John Millington) (Irish)	1871–1909	*Deirdre of the Sorrows* *In the Shadow of the Glen* *Playboy of the Western World (The)*

Synge was born into a wealthy family of Protestant landowners in Rathfarnham, Ireland. Initially, he studied music at Trinity College, Dublin, followed by further studies in Germany and Paris. He was hugely influenced by W.B. Yeats whom he met in Paris. It is thought that it was Yeats who encouraged Synge to look for inspiration in his native Ireland. Sadly, Hodgkin's disease robbed us of Synge's genius at a tragically young age.

Wilde, Oscar (Irish)	1854–1900	*Ideal Husband (An)* *Importance of Being Earnest (The)* *Woman of No Importance (A)*

Wilde was born and raised in an intellectual environment; his father was a surgeon and writer and his mother was also a writer. He was educated at both Trinity College, Dublin, and Oxford, after which he became part of the fashionable aesthetic fraternity.

Twentieth Century Plays and Playwrights

SIGNIFICANT EVENTS OF THE CENTURY … (1900–1999)

Berlin Wall is built separating East Berlin from West Berlin • British scientists develop radar • Diana, Princess of Wales dies in a car crash in Paris • DNA is discovered • Easter Rising against British government in Ireland • Female oral contraceptive becomes widely available • First and Second World Wars divide the world • General Strike brings Britain to a standstill • John F. Kennedy is assassinated • John Logie Baird invents the television • Man walks on the moon • Margaret Thatcher becomes the first female Prime Minister of Great Britain • Persecution of the Jews by the Nazis • Rapid advancement of technology • Russian Revolution • Rutherford splits the atom • Terrorism becomes the new war • Yuri Gagarin becomes the first man in space

NAME	DATE	PLAYS
Albee, Edward (American)	1928–	*Delicate Balance (A)* *Three Tall Women* *Who's Afraid of Virginia Woolf?*

Albee started writing for the theatre in the 1950s and went on to write some of the most outstanding plays of the Twentieth Century. In his later years, Albee has preferred to direct his own works – thus protecting them from what he believes to be the artistic excesses of some directors.

Anouilh, Jean (French)	1910–1987	*Antigone* *Eurydice (Point of Departure)* *L'Alouette (The Lark)*

Anouilh is renowned for the perfect crafting of his works and for the way in which he used his writing to convey his own personal love of theatre. In the crafting of his plays, he often used techniques such as a play within a play, flashbacks and flashforwards.

Arden, John (British)	1930–	*Sergeant Musgrave's Dance* *Waters of Babylon* *Workhouse Donkey (The)*

Cambridge-educated Arden is a controversial writer renowned for leaving unresolved issues at the conclusion of his plays. He is one of the most influential political dramatists of his generation; he himself was greatly influenced by Margaret D'Arcy, whom he met in 1955.

Artaud, Antonin (French)	1896–1948	*Cenci (Les)* *Coquielle et le Clergyman (Le)* *Théâtre et son Double (Le)*

Artaud was a tortured artistic soul who spent his life fighting drug addiction and living in lunatic asylums. His works are difficult to comprehend but nevertheless retain the intangible touch of a genius.

Ayckbourn, Alan * (British)	1939–	* See separate entry, p33.

Ayckbourn is one of world's most renowned and prolific playwrights having written 70 plays, as well as revues and plays for children.

Barry, Philip (American)	1896–1949	*Holiday* *Philadelphia Story* *Punch for Judy (A)*

Yale and Harvard educated Barry is well known for his comedies on the life and manners of the socially privileged sections of society – of which he was actually a part.

Beckett, Samuel (Irish)	1906–1995	*Endgame* *Krapp's Last Tape* *Waiting for Godot*

Beckett is known for his solitary lifestyle, which is often mirrored in his works. He was well travelled for his time and had a life-long love affair with the city of Paris; he was a Nobel Prize winner for literature.

NAME	DATE	PLAYS
Behan, Brendan (Irish)	1923–1964	*Hostage (The)* *Quare Fellow (The)* *Richard's Cork Leg* (completed posthumously by Alan Simpson)

Born into an Irish family, Behan was politically active from a young age – he was a member of the IRA at the age of 14 years –and was jailed for political offences and attempted murder when he was 19 years old and used his experiences to feed his writings. However, his life of political involvements, imprisonments and alcoholism culminated in the early death of this great writer.

NAME	DATE	PLAYS
Bennett, Alan * (British)	1934–	*See separate entry, p45.

Oxford-educated Bennett co-wrote and starred in the cult comedy revue 'Beyond the Fringe' with Peter Cook, Jonathan Miller, and Dudley Moore. He is best recognised for translating the mundane into the special, thus appealing to everyone.

NAME	DATE	PLAYS
Berkoff, Steven (British)	1937–	*Acapulco & Brighton Beach Scumbags* *Harry's Christmas* *Secret Love Life of Ophelia (The)*

Berkoff studied drama and mime before forming the London Theatre Group. He is not only a writer for the stage but for the screen too; he is also well known for his adaptations; he acts and directs; he writes books and travels extensively.

NAME	DATE	PLAYS
Betts, Torben (British)	1968–	*Mummies and Daddies* *Swing of Things (The)* *Unconquered (The)*

Betts was educated at Liverpool University and then trained as an actor, before embarking on a career as a playwright. His writing of the tragic-comedy genre has resulted in him being hailed, by some, as the successor to Alan Ayckbourn.

NAME	DATE	PLAYS
Bleasdale, Alan (British)	1946–	*Having a Ball* *It's a Madhouse* *On the Ledge*

Bleasdale is probably better known, and more recognised, for his television dramas – *Boys from the Blackstuff* being his most famous – than he is for his theatre work.

NAME	DATE	PLAYS
Bolt, Robert (British)	1924–1995	*Flowering Cherry (The)* *Man for All Seasons (A)* *Vivat! Vivat! Regina*

Bolt taught English and history for several years and only became a full-time writer after the success of his play *The Flowering Cherry*. He then went on to achieve not only critical acclaim for his stage work but also for his screenwriting.

NAME	DATE	PLAYS
Bond, Edward (British)	1934–	*Black Mass* *Narrow Road to the Deep North* *Saved*

Bond left school at 14 and had a series of jobs in factories and offices, whilst writing plays in his spare time; he then sent these plays off to the Royal Court, the home of new and undiscovered writers. Bond became a controversial writer, dealing with often 'untouchable' subjects.

Brecht, Bertolt (German)	1898–1956	*Caucasian Chalk Circle* *Good Person of Szechwan (The)* *Mother Courage and Her Children*

Brecht is best recognised for his belief that an audience should not become too involved with the characters and the story of a play but should be encouraged to stand *outside* the action, enabling them to think and analyse the process before them. He is undoubtedly one of the most influential figures of modern theatre. His work in a military hospital inspired his lifelong commitment to pacifism.

Brenton, Howard (British)	1942–	*Epsom Downs* *Gum and Goo* *Scott of the Antarctic*

Watching Brenton's work can be an uncomfortable experience for he tends to pull out the more unsavoury parts of society and explores subjects many would rather forget.

Brighouse, Harold (British)	1882–1958	*Hobson's Choice* *Northerners (The)* *Zack*

Although Brighouse ended his formal education at 16, he went on to write more than 70 plays and was one of the first Twentieth Century playwrights to write about the working- and middle-class society.

Cartwright, Jim (British)	1958–	*Bed* *Rise and Fall of Little Voice (The)* *Road*

Bolton-born Cartwright's plays are now consistently performed around the world and have been translated into more than 27 languages; they are also frequently used as set study texts for higher level education.

Christie, Agatha (British)	1890–1976	*And Then There Were None* *Mousetrap (The)* *Witness For the Prosecution*

Christie is a writer in the extreme in that almost everyone knows her name and not only those interested in theatre and literature either. Her works have been translated into more than 100 languages and the story of her long running play, *The Mousetrap*, is legendary.

NAME	DATE	PLAYS
Churchill, Caryl (British)	1938–	*Cloud Nine* *Striker (The)* *Top Girls*

Oxford-educated Churchill began her stage writing career as Resident Dramatist at the Royal Court. She favours the workshop method of developing her plays.

NAME	DATE	PLAYS
Cooney, Ray (British)	1932–	*Caught in the Net* *Funny Money* *Run for Your Wife*

Cooney is often referred to as 'The Master of Farce'. In his early days as an actor, he worked with Sir Brian Rix in the famous Whitehall Farces and so writing farce himself was a natural next step.

NAME	DATE	PLAYS
Coward, Noël (British)	1899–1973	*Hay Fever* *Private Lives* *Vortex (The)*

Coward was the eccentric, quintessential – and flamboyant – English man; he was a genius thespian through and through working in almost every section of the theatre – producing, directing, dancing, even singing. He also wrote, acted and directed films.

NAME	DATE	PLAYS
Edgar, David (British)	1948–	*Destiny* *Life and Adventures of Nicholas Nickleby (The)* *Maydays*

Edgar was born into a theatrical family in Birmingham. He read Drama at Manchester University, after which he went into journalism before taking up writing as a full-time career in 1972, going on to write over 50 plays, becoming one of Britain's major dramatists. He is a socio-political dramatist and has written for The Royal Court, The National Theatre and The RSC.

NAME	DATE	PLAYS
Eliot, T.S. (American-English)	1888–1965	*Cocktail Party (The)* *Elder Statesman (The)* *Murder in the Cathedral*

Harvard-educated Eliot is better known as a poet than as a playwright; which is ironic as one of the great theatrical success stories of the Twentieth Century was *Cats*, a musical based on his poems from *Old Possum's Book of Practical Cats*.

NAME	DATE	PLAYS
Fo, Dario (Italian)	1926–	*Gli Arcangeli Non Giocano a flipper* [Archangels Don't Play Pinball] *Non si paga, Non si paga!* [We Can't Pay? We Won't Pay!] *Morte Accidentale di un Anarchico* [Accidental Death of an Anarchist]

Dario Fo was born on 26th March, 1926 in San Giano, a small town on Lago Maggiore in the province of Varese. As well as a playwright, Fo is also a director, set designer, costume designer and actor; he has even been known to compose the music for his plays. He studied art and architecture in Milan and works closely with his actress wife, Franca Rame.

NAME	DATE	PLAYS
Frayn, Michael (British)	1933–	*Donkey's Years* *Noises Off* *Now You Know*

Born in London, Frayn learned Russian during his two-year National Service before going up to Emmanuel College, Cambridge, to read Philosophy. He later translated and adapted several plays by Chekhov but his own plays are generally comedies, the most famous of which is *Noises Off*.

NAME	DATE	PLAYS
Friel, Brian (Irish (Northern Ireland))	1929–	*Dancing at Lughnasa* *Philadelphia, Here I Come!* *Translations*

His early career was that of a school teacher; he turned to full-time professional writing in 1959 and, through his playwriting, he was able to challenge the social and political problems in Southern and Northern Ireland.

NAME	DATE	PLAYS
Fry, Christopher (British)	1907–2005	*Boy with a Cart (The)* *Lady's Not for Burning (The)* *Yard of Sun (A)*

Fry, (his mother's surname, his real name being Harris), was a writer of verse plays and became famous for his play *The Lady's Not for Burning*. He also wrote for the big screen, TV and radio, collaborating on the screen plays for epic films such as *Ben Hur* and *Barabbas*.

NAME	DATE	PLAYS
Fugard, Athol (South African)	1932–	*Blood Knot* *Boesman and Lena* *No Good Friday*

Fugard – his full name being Athol Harold Lannigan Fugard – was born in South Africa to English/Afrikaner parents. He was educated at Cape Town University, where he read Philosophy, but left before he graduated. He is known for his powerful political writing which actually led to his passport being withdrawn.

NAME	DATE	PLAYS
Genet, Jean (French)	1910–1986	*Deathwatch* *Maids (The)* *Screens (The)*

Genet was a controversial figure. Illegitimately born to, and then abandoned by, his mother, Gabrielle Genet. He was subsequently raised by a family of peasants. He grew to be a rebel and an anarchist of the most extreme sort; his writings, however, earned him the support of many well known writers of his time.

NAME	DATE	PLAYS
Gill, Peter (British)	1939–	*Friendly Fire* *Small Change* *York Realist (The)*

Gill was raised in Cardiff, Wales and was educated at St Illtyd's College, Cardiff. He began his career as an actor both on stage and screen before becoming a renowned playwright and director, as well as the founder of The National Theatre Studio.

NAME	DATE	PLAYS
Godber, John (British)	1956–	*Bouncers* *Shakers* *Teechers*

Godber initially trained as a drama teacher and went on to become Head of Drama at his former school – Minsthorpe High School – prior to his appointment as Artistic Director of Hull Truck Theatre Company. He has also written and directed plays for television.

| Griffiths, Trevor (British and Irish) | 1935– | *All Good Men* *Comedians* *Thatcher's Children* |

Griffiths, born of Irish and Welsh descent, was the first in his family to go to University and later worked as teacher, then as a further education officer, before becoming a full-time writer.

| Hall, Willis (British) | 1929–2005 | *Children's Day* (with Keith Waterhouse) *Help Stamp Out Marriage* (with Keith Waterhouse) *Long and the Short and the Tall (The)* |

Willis was born in Leeds, Yorkshire and is probably as well known for his collaboration with lifelong friend, Keith Waterhouse, as for his plays. When he was just 18, Willis joined the British army and it was whilst he was in Asia that he started writing radio plays for Chinese children. His craft wasn't just restricted to the stage but reached out to books and musicals too.

| Hamilton, Patrick (British) | 1904–1962 | *Gaslight* *Man Upstairs (The)* *Rope* |

Patrick Hamilton was the youngest of three children; his parents were both published writers and his younger brother also became a writer. At the peak of his career, he was badly injured when he was accidentally run over by a car. One wonders whether this was the reason he spiralled into the alcoholism which would later kill him.

| Hampton, Christopher (British) | 1946– | *Les Liaisons Dangereuses* *Philanthropist (The)* *When Did You Last See My Father* |

Oxford-educated Hampton, ex-Resident Dramatist at The Royal Court Theatre, writes not only for the stage but for the screen. He also wrote the book, and co-wrote the lyrics, for Andrew Lloyd Webber's musical *Sunset Boulevard*.

| Hare, David (British) | 1947– | *Amy's View* *Plenty* *Racing Demon* |

Hare, born in Bexhill, East Sussex was educated at Lancing College and Jesus College, Cambridge. Hare was literary manager and Resident Dramatist at the Royal Court Theatre in the 1970s; he then went on to write and direct for The National. He was knighted in 1998.

NAME	DATE	PLAYS
Hellman, Lillian (American)	1905–1984	*Children's Hour (The)* *Little Foxes* *Toys in the Attic*

Lillian Florence Hellman was born in New Orleans and began her career as a book reviewer and later as a script reader before becoming a professional writer herself. The greatest influence on Hellman's career was author Dashiell Hammett who suggested some of her subject matters.

| Houghton, Stanley (British) | 1881–1913 | *Hindle Wakes* *Independent Means* *Younger Generation (The)* |

Houghton was born in Ashton-upon-Mersey. He worked in his father's office until 1912, when, after the success of *Hindle Wakes*, he was going to earn his living as a writer. Tragically, his young and promising career was brought to an abrupt end when he died in 1913, after being taken ill abroad.

| Ionesco, Eugène (Romanian) | 1909–1994 | *Journeys Among the Dead* *Killer (The)* *Rhinoceros* |

Ionesco was in his forties before he wrote his first play and quickly became a writer for Theatre of the Absurd, pointing out the insignificance of man's existence. He once said that, unlike Brecht, he did not deliver messages for he was not a postman.

| Jellicoe, Ann (British) | 1927– | *Giveaway (The)* *Knack (The)* *Sport of My Mad Mother (The)* |

Jellicoe was born in Middlesbrough, Teesside and attended Queen Margaret's School in Yorkshire before going on to study performing arts at the Central School of Speech and Drama. Over the years, she developed an interest in community theatre.

| Jones, Marie (Irish) | 1955 - | *Hamster Wheel (The)* *Somewhere Over the Balcony* *Stones in his Pocket* |

Jones was born in Belfast, Northern Ireland, into a working class family. For many years, she wanted to be an actress but when the right calibre of jobs didn't come her way, along with some other disillusioned friends, she created her own opportunities by founding the Charabanc Theatre Company.

| Kushner, Tony (American) | 1956– | *Angels in America* *Bright Room Called Day (A)* *Slavs!* |

Kushner was born into an American Jewish family and is renowned for writing epic plays tackling epic issues of political importance. He is best known for his two-part play, *Angels in America*, for which he was awarded the Pulitzer Prize and which, when performed as a whole, runs for approximately seven hours.

89

NAME	DATE	PLAYS
Lawrence D.H. (British)	1885–1930	*Collier's Friday Night (A)* *Daughter-in-Law (The)* *Widowing of Mrs Holroyd (The)*

Born David Herbert Lawrence in Nottinghamshire, he would become known only by the initials. He was the fourth child of a coal miner – who was reputedly virtually illiterate. Lawrence studied at the University of Nottingham.

Leigh, Mike (British)	1943–	*Abigail's Party* *Bleak Moments* *Smelling a Rat*

Leigh is 'artistically' highly trained, having attended not only RADA but also Camberwell and Central Art Schools, as well as the London Film School. As a writer, he is known as 'the one who improvises', meaning he develops his final script through improvisation with his actors.

Lorca, Federico Garcia (Spanish)	1898–1936	*Blood Wedding* *House of Bernarda Alba (The)* *Mariana Pineda*

As a painter, poet, dramatist, guitarist, pianist and composer, Lorca is another of the multi-talented geniuses who so liberally litter the artistic world. He was born into a wealthy family and studied at the Universities of Granada and Madrid. The Spanish Civil War brought his life to a violent end when, seen as an enemy of the right-wing forces, he was shot without a trial.

McGrath, John (Irish)	1935–2002	*Cheviot, The Stag and The Black, Black Oil (The)* *Out of Our Heads* *Random Happenings in the Hebrides*

McGrath was born in Birkenhead to an Irish Catholic family and was educated at St John's College, Oxford. A committed socialist, he believed in using his artistic skills as a writer and director to reach a mass audience. He was prolific, not only in his writings for the stage, but also for the screen, both large and small, in fact, he wrote and directed many of the early episodes of BBC TV's *Z Cars*. McGrath was renowned for being a devoted family man.

Mamet, David (American)	1947–	*Glengarry Glen Ross* *Oleanna* *Speed-the-Plow*

Mamet began his life in the theatre as an actor and director, before turning to writing. His distinct style involves the use of sparse, clipped dialogue and a lack of stage directions in plays which deal with the decline in morals.

Matura, Mustapha (Trinidadian)	1939–	*As Time Goes By* *Coup (The)* *Play Mas*

Matura was born in Trinidad as the son of a car salesman; his mother was a shop assistant. He left Trinidad in the 60s to do 'something creative' in England. In 1978, he co-founded the Black Theatre Co-operative with Charlie Hanson.

NAME	DATE	PLAYS
Maugham, Somerset W. (British)	1874–1965	*Circle (The)* *Constant Wife (The)* *Sacred Flame (The)*

Brought up by an uncle after he was orphaned at the tender age of just 10 years old, Maugham went on to qualify as a doctor but his success as a writer led him to give up his medical career. His short stories and novels were more successful than his plays though, which, because they were essentially Edwardian comedies, soon became dated.

NAME	DATE	PLAYS
Medoff, Mark (American)	1940–	*Children of a Lesser God* *Homage that Follows (The)* *Wager (The)*

Born in Illinois, Medoff is the son of a doctor and a psychologist. In 1980, he won a Tony and an Olivier for *Children of a Lesser God*. He also writes for the screen and works as a theatre and film director, as well as an actor.

NAME	DATE	PLAYS
Miller, Arthur (American)	1915–2005	*All My Sons* *Crucible (The)* *Death of a Salesman*

Arthur Miller revolutionised American theatre with his honest look at the state of the world and its people though, sadly, he is remembered by many for the more flippant reason and that is that he was, at one point, married to Marilyn Monroe.

NAME	DATE	PLAYS
Nichols, Peter (British)	1927–	*Day in the Death of Joe Egg (A)* *Passion Play* *Privates on Parade*

After completing his National Service, Nichols trained as an actor at the Bristol Old Vic. He is known for being an autobiographical writer as he draws upon his own life experiences to write his plays.

NAME	DATE	PLAYS
O'Casey, Sean (Irish)	1880–1964	*Juno and the Paycock* *Plough and the Stars (The)* *Shadow of the Gunman (The)*

Born into Irish poverty of the Dublin tenements, O' Casey was in fact uneducated and taught himself to read when he was in his teens. His lack of education meant that he wrote from the heart and with no thought of 'the rules of writing'. As with life, his plays had no rules.

NAME	DATE	PLAYS
Odets, Clifford (American)	1906–1963	*Awake and Sing* *Country Girl (The)* *Waiting for Lefty*

Odets was born to Jewish immigrant parents in Philadelphia, US. He was raised in New York City, dropping out of school aged 17 years to pursue a career in acting, turning later to writing. He wrote both for the stage and for the screen; his work was influenced by his sympathy for the working classes and not by the American Communist Party as some believed.

NAME	DATE	PLAYS
O'Neill, Eugene (American)	1888–1953	*Beyond the Horizon* *Iceman Cometh (The)* *Long Day's Journey into Night*

Born into an Irish immigrant background, O'Neill is recognised as one of the greatest and most prolific of the American dramatists, gaining international recognition and earning him no less than four Pulitzer prizes.

Orton, Joe (British)	1933–1967	*Entertaining Mr. Sloane* *Loot* *What the Butler Saw*

In the late 1950s, Orton abandoned his life as an unsuccessful actor and turned to writing. In the mid-1960s, he achieved his first success with his radio play, *The Ruffian on the Stair*. From that point, and until his untimely death in 1967, his success was enormous and we are now left wondering how he would have developed given the opportunity. Sadly however, Orton was beaten to death by his long-time companion – a less successful writer – Kenneth Halliwell, who then committed suicide.

Osborne, John (British)	1929–1994	*Entertainer (The)* *Inadmissible Evidence* *Look Back in Anger*

Like many playwrights, Osborne started his theatrical career in a different area of theatre; in his case, it was as an assistant manager and as an actor in repertory companies. His first work, *Look Back in Anger,* was an enormous success but his later works became somewhat unpredictable.

Pinter, Harold (British)	1930–2008	* See separate entry, p 49.

Pinter began his career in the theatre as a trained actor (RADA) before deciding, in the 1950s, to concentrate on writing. His use of the pause and his sparse style of writing has given birth to a new word, 'Pinteresque'.

Pirandello, Luigi (Italian)	1867–1936	*Cosí é (Se vi Pare)* [Right You Are (If You Think You Are)] *La Vita Che ti Diedi* [The Life I Gave You] *Vestire Gli Ignudi* [To Clothe the Naked]

Pirandello was born in Girgenti, Sicily. He studied philology and from 1897 to 1922 he was Professor of Aesthetics and Stylistics at the *Real Istituto di Magistere Femminile* in Rome. Pirandello was also a novelist but was best known for his stage works.

Priestley, John Boynton (J.B.) (British)	1894–1984	*An Inspector Calls* *I Have Been Here Before* *When We Are Married*

Cambridge-educated Priestley had his first play produced in 1932 and had five more plays in production before the end of the decade.

NAME	DATE	PLAYS
Rattigan, Terence (British)	1911–1977	*Browning Version (The)* *Separate Tables* *Winslow Boy (The)*

Rattigan was educated at Harrow and Oxford and was known as a great craftsman of theatre, which was seen by some as boring, unadventurous and safe. He had the last laugh though when he was knighted for his services to theatre. He also left a credit of many screenplays.

NAME	DATE	PLAYS
Ravenhill, Mark (British)	1966–	*Faust is Dead* *Mother Clap's Molly House* *Shopping and F**king*

Ravenhill grew up in Haywards Heath, West Sussex, the eldest son of Ted and Rita Ravenhill and was educated at Bristol University where he studied English and Drama before becoming a hard-hitting and controversial playwright. It was at the invitation of Max Stafford-Clark to write a full-length play for Out of Joint that *Shopping and F**king* – the play which brought his name to the front of playwriting circles – was born.

NAME	DATE	PLAYS
Rudkin (James), David (British)	1936–	*Cries from Casement as His Bones Are Brought to Dublin* *Triumph of Death (The)* *Will's Way*

Rudkin was born in London, the son of a pastor, David Jonathan Rudkin and a teacher, Anne Alice (née Martin). He was educated at St Catherine College Oxford, after which he taught Latin, Greek and Music. He also wrote for television, film and radio.

NAME	DATE	PLAYS
Russell, Willy (British)	1947–	*Educating Rita* *Shirley Valentine* *Stags and Hens*

Born in Whiston, near Liverpool, Russell spent his early years as a hairdresser. His first play, *Blind Scouse,* was taken to the Edinburgh Fringe where it was 'discovered' by a representative of Liverpool's Everyman Theatre. His plays have also been made into successful films but he remains essentially a Liverpudlian.

NAME	DATE	PLAYS
Sartre, Jean-Paul (French)	1905–1980	*Alton* *Bariona* *In Camera*

Sartre was born in Paris and studied at the *École Normale Supérieure*. In 1931, he became a Professor of Philosophy at *Le Havre*. At the end of the Second World War and after further periods of study and teaching, he became a writer. As an erudite writer of the first degree he was awarded the Nobel Prize for Literature in 1964, but it his plays for which he is most well known.

NAME	DATE	PLAYS
Shaffer, Anthony (British)	1926–2001	*Murderer* *Sleuth* *Whodunnit*

Anthony, twin brother of Sir Peter Shaffer, was born in Liverpool and educated at Cambridge where he graduated with a law degree. He also wrote screenplays and co-wrote several novels with his twin.

Shaffer, Peter (British)	1926–	*Equus* *Five Finger Exercise* *Royal Hunt of the Sun (The)*

Peter, twin brother of Anthony Shaffer, was born in Liverpool and educated at Cambridge where he studied history. He was a playwright of great versatility and able to swap easily between genres. He also wrote screenplays and co-wrote several novels with his twin.

Shepard, Sam (American)	1943–	*Buried Child* *La Turista* *States of Shock*

Born Samuel Shepard Rogers in Illinois, US, the oldest of three children. He developed an interest in acting and writing in High School. As well as writing for the stage, Shepard also writes and acts for the screen.

Sherriff, R.C (British)	1896–1975	*Journey's End* *Kicking a Dead Horse* *True West*

During the First World War, Sherriff served as a captain in the East Surrey Regiment, after which he began to write, drawing on his war time experiences to create the masterpiece *Journey's End*. He also wrote several film scripts, notably *Goodbye Mr Chips*.

Simon, Neil (American)	1927–	*Barefoot in the Park* *Odd Couple (The)* *Star-Spangled Girl (The)*

Raised in the Bronx, Simon studied at New York University before working in television as a comedy writer. He later became a successful theatrical playwright and his autobiographical play *Come Blow Your Horn* ran for two years on Broadway. He wrote the screenplays for many of his own works as well as original screenplays; he also wrote the libretto for several successful musicals.

Soyinka, Wole (Nigerian)	1934–	*Play of Giants (A)* *Requiem for a Futurologist* *Swamp Dwellers (The)*

NAME	DATE	PLAYS

Soyinka was born in Abeokuta, near Ibadan in western Nigeria. He began his studies in 1954 at the Government College in Ibadan, later continuing his studies at the University of Leeds where, in 1973, he took his doctorate. Whilst in England, he was a dramaturgist at the Royal Court Theatre in London before returning to Nigeria to study African Drama. Since 1975, he has been Professor of Comparative Literature in Nigeria whilst occasionally a visiting Professor at the Universities of Cambridge, Sheffield and Yale.

| Stoppard, Tom (Czechoslovakian) | 1937– | * See separate entry on p56 |

He was born Tom Straussler in Czechoslovakia, the son of a Jewish doctor, and was forced to flee his homeland at the outbreak of the Second World War.

| Terson, Peter (British) | 1932– | *Mooney and His Caravans* *Night to Make the Angels Weep (A)* *Zigger Zagger* |

Born as Peter Patterson in Newcastle-upon-Tyne, Terson is known as 'an amusing observer of life'. Before his first play was produced, he worked for 10 years as a teacher. His name has been much associated with The National Youth Theatre for whom he has written many plays.

| Toller, Ernst (German) | 1893–1939 | *Hoppla, We're Alive* *Machine Wreckers (The)* *Man and the Masses* |

Toller was invalided out of the forces after 13 months at the Front during World War One. A pacifist at heart, Toller launched a peace movement and, in 1933, before the accession of Hitler, he emigrated to the US where he brought out his autobiography, *Eine Jugend in Deutschland* [I Was a German]. Feeling a failure in Hollywood, he committed suicide.

| Townsend, Sue (British) | 1946– | *Bazaar and Rummage* *Secret Diary of Adrian Mole Aged 13¾* *Womberang* |

Townsend is known primarily for her humorous character Adrian Mole which tends to push her other works into the shadows. She was the one time Thames Television Writer in Residence at Leicester's Phoenix Theatre. A sufferer of diabetes for many years, she is now registered blind.

| Travers, Ben (British) | 1886–1980 | *Bed Before Yesterday (The)* *Outrageous Fortune* *Plunder* |

Travers was known first and foremost for his farces, although he did write works in other genres, as well as novels and non-fiction. A prolific writer, he wrote his final work when he was in his ninetieth year, a work which was produced in the West End.

NAME	DATE	PLAYS
Treadwell, Sophie (American)	1885–1970	*Gringo* *Le Grand Prix* *Machinal*

Sophie Anita Treadwell was born in California, the only child of Alfred and Nettie Treadwell. After graduating from university in 1906, Treadwell began her writing career with her first full-length play. She also worked as a journalist, novelist and even had a short spell as an actress.

NAME	DATE	PLAYS
Wasserstein, Wendy (American)	1950–2006	*Uncommon Women and Others* *Heidi Chronicles (The)* *Isn't It Romantic*

Wasserstein was one of the most commercially successful female dramatists in the US before her tragically early death, writing real dialogue about real and easily identifiable women, highlighting the insecurities which beset many women.

NAME	DATE	PLAYS
Waterhouse, Keith (British)	1929–	*Billy Liar* (with Willis Hall) *Jeffrey Bernard is Unwell* *Squat Betty* (with Willis Hall)

Born as Keith Spencer Waterhouse in Leeds, Yorkshire – just like his lifelong friend and collaborator Willis Hall. Waterhouse left school at the tender age of 15 to later become a newspaper columnist, a job he continued throughout his 'other' writing career.

NAME	DATE	PLAYS
Wertenbaker, Timberlake (British)	1951–	*Grace of Mary Traverse (The)* *Love of the Nightingale (The)* *Our Country's Good*

Although Wertenbaker is British she actually grew up in the Basque region of France and was educated in Europe and the US, before finally settling in London to become Writer in Residence at both Shared Experience and the Royal Court.

NAME	DATE	PLAYS
Wilder, Thornton (American)	1897–1975	*Long Christmas Dinner (The)* *Merchant of Yonkers (The)* *Our Town*

Thornton Niven Wilder was born in Madison, Wisconsin, to Amos Parker Wilder, a US diplomat and Isabella Niven Wilder; his twin brother died at birth. His was a brilliant family where all five children were high achievers. After graduating from Yale, Thorton studied archaeology in Rome and later taught Dramatic Literature and the Classics at the University of Chicago. He was a three times Pulitzer Prize winner.

NAME	DATE	PLAYS
Williams, Tennessee (Pseudonym for Thomas Lanier Williams) (American)	1911–1983	*Cat on a Hot Tin Roof* *Glass Menagerie (The)* *Streetcar Named Desire (A)*

Like many artistic people, Williams had demons which plagued his personal life and he battled with depression and addictions to prescription drugs and alcohol. Despite this, he was still a prolific writer and produced 25 full-length plays.

NAME	DATE	PLAYS
Williamson, David (Australian)	1942–	*Coming of the Stork (The)* *Removalists (The)* *Up for Grabs*

Born in Melbourne, Australia, where he was also educated, Williamson is now regarded as one of Australia's foremost playwrights. His plays are generally a dissection of Australian Society; so maybe this is why he has not received the recognition of many other playwrights, as some may feel alienated by the subjective themes.

Wilson, August (American)	1945–2005	*Fences* *Ma Rainey's Black Bottom* *Piano Lesson (The)*

Born in Pittsburgh, Pennsylvania, his early experiences in the black slums were to influence his work and to establish him as an African-American playwright and and be instrumental in achieving the Pulitzer Prize for *Fences*.

Wood, David (British)	1944–	* See separate entry p62

Known by many as 'The National Children's Dramatist', Wood has written extensively for children.

Yeats, W.B. (Irish)	1865–1939	*Countess Cathleen (The)* *King's Threshold (The)* *Land of Heart's Desire (The)*

Born William Butler Yeats in Sandymount, County Dublin, Ireland to John Butler Yeats and Susan Mary (Pollexfen); he was the eldest of four children. It was his mother who introduced him to Irish history and mythology which were to greatly influence his work. His family moved for a while to England, where he attended Godolphin School in Hammersmith, before returning to Ireland. Yeats married relatively late in life and had two children. He is remembered as a co-founder of The Abbey Theatre in Dublin and as an author and poet as well as a playwright.

Zindel, Paul (American)	1936–2003	*Amulets Against the Dragon Forces* *Effect of Gamma Rays on Man-in-the-Moon Marigolds (The)* *Secret Affairs of Mildred Wild (The)*

Zindel was born on Staten Island, New York, where he grew up and where he studied chemistry at Wagner College. After graduation, he taught chemistry in a High School for a while. His plays are influenced by the broken marriage of his parents, by the fact that he was raised by a somewhat domineering mother and by the fact that he rarely saw his father.

Twenty-First Century Plays and Playwrights

SIGNIFICANT EVENTS OF THE CENTURY ... (2000 –)

Britain joins the US to invade Iraq • Climate change wreaks havoc worldwide • Reality TV becomes an international obsession • Ten new states join the European Union • Terrorists bring down the Twin Towers in the US • Terrorists attack transport in Madrid and London

Of course, being at the start of a century dictates that there can as yet be no entries, for the label 'good' relies, in part, on comparison and, as yet, there is none. However, we can of course look down the road we are about to travel and speculate; should we be able to see in the distance a different mode of theatre? The world has changed so much that surely it follows that theatre as a reflection must follow suit. We now live in a violent and destructive society, so does that meant that plays will reflect this? Or does it mean that playwrights will use the escapist and fantasy technique? Today, through the medium of reality TV, writing schemes and initiatives, individuals and novices are afforded opportunities more readily than they were years ago? So, does that mean that there will be more young people wanting to give playwriting a try, believing that they will be given an opportunity? If so, maybe the marriage of the two will result in a modern day resurgence of the 'Angry Young Men' dramatic style of the 1950s. Interesting thought, for wasn't that style attractive as a result of the raw and rough edges? So where will the advancement in technology sit in all this – "You decide".

A–Z of Popular Plays – A Brief Synopsis

Have you ever recognised the name of a play and/or a playwright and yet had no idea whatsoever what the play is about? Well wonder no longer, for below, you will find a very brief synopsis of 138 plays to answer that very question for you, and maybe whet your appetite either to view or read the play for yourself.

PLAY	PLAYWRIGHT	BRIEF SYNOPSIS
A		
Abigail's Party	Mike Leigh	A group of neighbours have a drinks get-together whilst one of their teenage daughters has a party; the audience then see the relationships and tensions of the group develop to a dramatic conclusion.

PLAY	PLAYWRIGHT	BRIEF SYNOPSIS
Accidental Death of an Anarchist (Morte Accidentale di un Anarchico)	Dario Fo	A play based on the suspicious death of anarchist Giuseppe Pinelli when he was being held in police custody. He had been falsely arrested for planting a bomb.
Agamemnon	Aeschylus	[One in the trilogy, *Oresteia*] King Agamemnon returns home victorious from the Trojan Wars bringing with him Cassandra. His wife, who has been having an affair, murders the pair and her lover, Aegisthus, declares himself King.
Alchemist (The)	Ben Jonson	The story of how greed and lust can make a person gullible and open to ridiculous suggestions.
Amadeus	Peter Shaffer	Here we see the genius of Wolfgang Amadeus Mozart pitted against the decent, although uninspiring, court composer, Antonio Salieri, who, may – or may not – have poisoned Mozart!
Antigone	Jean Anouilh	A classic work set against background of the German occupation.
Art	Christopher Hampton	The question here is how much would you pay for a white painting and is the identity of the artist important; indeed what would make it a work of art? Serge has bought just such a very expensive painting; his two friends don't understand and so the painting becomes central to their relationships.

B

PLAY	PLAYWRIGHT	BRIEF SYNOPSIS
Barretts of Wimpole Street (The)	Rudolph Besier	Based on the true love story between poets Robert Browning and Elizabeth Barrett, this is a tale about the power of a love which enables the sick Elizabeth not only to walk for the first time in years but which also gives her the strength to escape her tyrannical father.
Bed Before Yesterday (The)	Ben Travers	A widow is put off sex on her first bridal night and then, having survived two sexless marriages, marries an impoverished widower – for company. But things change when she finally discovers the joy of sexual relationships.
Beggar's Opera	John Gay	A story of vice and wrong-doings, restricted it seems to neither the lower nor upper classes, which is later re-written by Bertolt Brecht and Elizabeth Hauptmann as *The Threepenny Opera*.
Billy Liar	Willis Hall & Keith Waterhouse	Billy is a 19-year-old Yorkshire boy living with his parents whilst inhabiting the world of his imagination in which he dreams of life in the big city.

PLAY	PLAYWRIGHT	BRIEF SYNOPSIS
Blithe Spirit	Noël Coward	Following a séance, Charles Condomine finds himself being haunted by the ghost of his dead wife, Elvira.
Blood Wedding	Federico Garcia Lorca	A bride runs away with a previous lover and is subsequently murdered by her husband.
Boeing Boeing	Marc Camoletti	A typical farce in which Bernard is 'three' timing a trio of air hostesses and keeping each ignorant of the others' existence with the help of an air traffic control timetable.
Bouncers	John Godber	Set in a nightclub called Mr Cinders, the play focuses on four doormen and their customers.
Browning Version (The)	Terence Rattigan	Disliked not only by his unfaithful wife but by his colleagues and students, Andrew Crocker-Harris is coming to the end of his teaching career.
Buried Child	Sam Shepard	A macabre story of a dysfunctional family with a dark secret; the secret being that, years ago, the eldest family member killed and buried a baby in a field behind their farmhouse; was the baby the result of incest?

C

PLAY	PLAYWRIGHT	BRIEF SYNOPSIS
Cat on a Hot Tin Roof	Tennessee Williams	Millionaire Big Daddy Pollitt is dying of cancer and his relatives want to stake their claim on his money.
Caucasian Chalk Circle (The)	Bertolt Brecht	A group of goat-herders and a group of fruit growers meet to discuss who has the greater claim to a fertile valley. A piece of Brechtian 'epic theatre' extolling the virtues of humanity being more important than possessions.
Changeling (The)	Thomas Middleton & William Rowley	Beatrice cannot marry the man she loves because her father has promised her to another, so she arranges for a servant, De Flores, whom she finds repulsive, to murder her fiancé. The plot reveals the entwinement of revulsion and sexual chemistry which ultimately leads to the death of both Beatrice and De Flores.
Cherry Orchard (The)	Anton Chekhov	Money has become more important than class privilege, a fact Madame Ranevskaya and her brother fail to acknowledge, the result being that she loses her country estate and her brother is forced to take a job.
Children of a Lesser God	Mark Medoff	The story of Sarah Norman who has been deaf since birth and who resists all attempts to learn to lip read and speak, preferring to live in her own non-hearing world.

PLAY	PLAYWRIGHT	BRIEF SYNOPSIS
Chips with Everything	Arnold Wesker	When Pip Thornton does his National Service, he wants to be treated as one of the men and not trained to be an Officer. But, as a middle-class man, he fails to become one of the proletariat. Why? Because he is an idealist and actually despises their 'chips with everything' attitude to life.
Circle (The)	W. Somerset Maugham	A young MP is witness to history repeating itself when the mother he hasn't seen since childhood, after she ran away with a married man, arrives to visit him and his wife, and his wife falls for a house guest.
Comedians	Trevor Griffiths	An old comedian trains a group of stand-up comics who, desperate to escape their mundane lives, make jokes about minority groups – all, that is, except one would-be comedian. A seemingly straightforward story told in a realistic style which makes the political undertones both accessible and enjoyable, and leaves the audience to choose between humanity and hate.
Copenhagen	Michael Frayn	Set in 1942, this is a play about the meeting between the physicists Werner Heisenberg and Niels Bohr in Copenhagen, exploring what actually occurred at the meeting and how it affected the development of World War Two, and the relationship between the two men.
Country Wife (The)	William Wycherley	Horner professes to be impotent in the belief that it will gain him easy access to other men's wives.
Crucible (The)	Arthur Miller	This play is based on the Salem Witch Trials of the 1690s with added fictional sections for dramatic effect. It is also supposedly making a political statement during the McCarthy period in American history when Americans were accusing each other of Pro-communist beliefs.

D

Dancing at Lughnasa	Brian Friel	Michael tells the story of his life in rural Ireland in the 1930s, a life with the five Mundy sisters – his mother being the youngest – his Uncle Jack and an errant father who pops in now and again.
Day in the Death of Joe Egg (A)	Peter Nichols	Bri and his wife, Sheila, cope with the problems of caring for their totally paralysed daughter, Little Joe. Comedy and wit are used to deal with this sensitive situation for which there is no conclusion, let alone a happy ending.

PLAY	PLAYWRIGHT	BRIEF SYNOPSIS
Death of a Salesman	Arthur Miller	Willy Loman loses his job at the age of 63 and, in a final desperate attempt to raise the money his family needs, he kills himself.
Deep Blue Sea (The)	Terence Rattigan	The story of events after a failed suicide attempt by a heartbroken woman who finds the strength to live with the help of another heartbroken soul.
Doll's House (A)	Henrik Ibsen	Nora is treated and kept by her husband, Torvald Helmer, as some sort of trophy doll, but Nora is by no means 'all good' and, when Helmer discovers his wife's deceit, he cares only for his own reputation. Nora sees him for what he is and selfishly leaves her children to be independent, thus there is no straight forward good versus bad.
Donkey's Years	Michael Frayn	25 years after their graduation, six former college students get together for a reunion to relive their youth and all that went with it.
Dry Rot	John Chapman	A gang of bookies stay at a country hotel, near a racecourse, which is run by a colonel, his wife and daughter. It has all the ingredients of mistaken identity and near misses essential to a successful farce.
Duchess of Malfi (The)	John Webster	Based on a true story, this is a very bloody tale with no less than nine killings on stage. The Duchess defies her malevolent brothers by secretly marrying the man she loves. But she is betrayed by a spy who informs her brothers, thus unleashing a spate of murders.
Dutchman	Amiri Baraka	A play about racism in which a white girl attacks a 'decent' young black man, killing him before moving on to another black victim.

E

PLAY	PLAYWRIGHT	BRIEF SYNOPSIS
Educating Rita	Willy Russell	Susan White wants to better herself through education; Frank needs the money and so tutors her, the result being that two different social classes meet and grow.
Endgame (The)	Samuel Beckett	Hamm is blind and can't stand up; Clov, his servant, can't sit down. They live in a tiny house devoid of all comforts except their continual fighting; also present are Hamm's legless parents, Nagg and Nell, who also argue inanely.
Entertainer (The)	John Osborne	We see the 'state of England' through the eyes of a poor and inadequate song and dance man, who also has a desperate home life.

PLAY	PLAYWRIGHT	BRIEF SYNOPSIS
Entertaining Mr Sloane	Joe Orton	A young and attractive murderer believes he has captivated a woman and her brother into giving him a cushy life but, instead, finds that he is trapped as their sexual toy.
Equus	Peter Shaffer	A stable boy blinds six horses after a frustrated sexual liaison.

F

Front Page (The)	Ben Hecht & Charles MacArthur	The story of love and passion versus a journalistic scoop as an editor attempts to lure away his star reporter from his long-suffering financée.

G

Glass Menagerie (The)	Tennessee Williams	Amanda Wingfield is a domineering mother controlling her shy daughter.
Glengarry Glen Ross	David Mamet	Four desperate real estate agents will go to any lengths – be it unethical or illegal – to sell undesirable real estate to unwilling and reluctant buyers.

H

Hard Man (The)	Tom McGrath	A play based on the life of Jimmy Boyle, the well known Scottish ex-convict.
Having a Ball	Alan Bleasdale	A story about four young men who are awaiting surgery in a vasectomy clinic.
Hay Fever	Noël Coward	The Bliss family invite guests to their home but their eccentricities drive the guests away.
Hobson's Choice	Harold Brighouse	Maggie Hobson marries the shy but skilled bootmaker Willie Mossop – he actually had little say in the matter – and together they take over the town's boot-making business from her father.
Hostage (The)	Brendan Behan	The IRA have kidnapped a British soldier and are holding him hostage in order to bargain for the release of an IRA prisoner who is to be executed the next morning.
House of Bernarda Alba (The)	Federico Garcia Lorca	The story of a tyrannical mother and her daughters, the youngest of whom commits suicide over her lover Pepe el Romano who is in fact engaged to Angustías, her elder sister.

I

Iceman Cometh (The)	Eugene O' Neill	Set in Harry Hope's Saloon in 1912, we see an evening where all pipe dreams are crushed; the emphasis being on truth telling which would become the hallmark of O' Neill's later works.

PLAY	PLAYWRIGHT	BRIEF SYNOPSIS
Ideal Husband (An)	Oscar Wilde	Sir Robert Chiltern seems to be an ideal husband in every way, but he has a secret. Attempts to expose his secret fail and the play ends with him still seeming 'ideal'.
Inspector Calls (An)	J.B. Priestley	A detective investigating a murder visits a middle-class Yorkshire household. Responsibility and guilt for the murder spread to touch everyone and, when the visit of a second 'detective' is announced, the identity of the first detective comes into question.
Importance of Being Earnest (The)	Oscar Wilde	Farce and melodrama are thrown together in this play of mistaken identities.

J

PLAY	PLAYWRIGHT	BRIEF SYNOPSIS
Jew of Malta (The)	Christopher Marlowe	Based on the failed siege of Malta by the Ottomans in 1565, the play depicts the stereotypical perception of a Jew at that time, who gets all he deserves. The Christians, however, are not idealised, instead they are portrayed as devious and hypocritical.
Journey's End	R.C. Sherriff	Set in the trenches of the First World War, this play gives an insight into the experiences of the serving British Officers of the time.
Juno and the Paycock	Sean O'Casey	A comedy, a tragedy and an observation on how individuals react when faced with events such as murder and pregnancy, and the inadequacies of personalities.

K

PLAY	PLAYWRIGHT	BRIEF SYNOPSIS
Knack (The)	Ann Jellicoe	Here we see the relationships and shifting power balances between a woman and three men who are sharing a house.

L

PLAY	PLAYWRIGHT	BRIEF SYNOPSIS
Lady's Not for Burning (The)	Christopher Fry	A romantic comedy in which the heroine is charged with being a witch.
Long Day's Journey into Night	Eugene O'Neill	Recognised as an autobiographical work for which O'Neill won the Pulitzer Prize for Drama, we see a family fighting and opening old wounds as they face problems of morphine addiction, illness and drink.
Look Back in Anger	John Osborne	This is the foundation of 'kitchen sink drama', and is set in a dingy bedsit where we see a bitter and angry Jimmy verbally lashing out at Alison, his middle-class wife, until she finally leaves – before returning.

PLAY	PLAYWRIGHT	BRIEF SYNOPSIS
Loot	Joe Orton	A pair of young male lovers have robbed a bank and hidden the loot in the coffin of one of the boys' mothers. The mother had been murdered by her nurse, who planned to marry the father before murdering him too. Included in this 'farce' are a bent detective and a body which must be kept hidden. Eventually, everyone gets a share of the loot, except the murdered woman's husband, who, although innocent, is taken off to jail.

M

PLAY	PLAYWRIGHT	BRIEF SYNOPSIS
Major Barbara	George Bernard Shaw	Barbara is a Major in the Salvation Army and committed to easing poverty, whilst her father is an arms manufacturer who funds the Salvation Army shelter. Major Barbara is forced to accept his patronage and ethical questions are left unanswered.
Man for All Seasons (A)	Robert Bolt	This play focuses on the conflict between Sir Thomas Moore and Henry VIII.
Mariana Pineda	Federico Garcia Lorca	This play is based on the true story of Mariana Pineda, the heroine from Grenada who was executed for being in possession of a Republican flag adorned with the words: LIBERTY, EQUALITY and LAW.
Matchmaker (The)	Thornton Wilder	A woman becomes engaged to the penny-pinching man she has been trying to match up with somebody else.
Miss Julie	August Strindberg	This is the first play in which sex is separated from love.
Mother Courage and Her Children	Bertolt Brecht	Set in the Thirty Years War of the 1600s, Mother Courage makes a profit from the war by selling goods to the soldiers, but there is always a price to pay and the cost to her is the loss of her three children.
Mousetrap (The)	Agatha Christie	The longest-running play in the West End incorporates all the elements which make good theatre – a little bit of farce, fear, suspense and a question running throughout, just begging to be answered by the audience.
Murder in the Cathedral	T.S. Eliot	A play which deals with the assassination of Thomas à Becket, who was later canonised.
My Mother Said I Never Should	Charlotte Keatley	A view on the lives and relationships of four generations of women from the same Manchester family – not played in chronological order.

PLAY	PLAYWRIGHT	BRIEF SYNOPSIS
N		
Night of the Iguana (The)	Tennessee Williams	The scene is a cheap Mexican hotel in which a strange collection of individuals find themselves thrown together; the final message being that one can always survive and there is life beyond despair.
Noises Off	Michael Frayn	This is a 'play within a play' showing that the 'goings on' behind the scenes are far funnier than the supposed comedy happening on the stage.
O		
Odd Couple (The)	Neil Simon	Two mismatched men, separated from their wives, become roommates. One is sloppy and one meticulously tidy, traits which probably ended their relationships and which soon creep threateningly into this new 'roommate' arrangement.
Oedipus the King	Sophocles	The story of a man who killed his father and married his mother – hence the saying, 'Oedipus complex'.
Oleanna	David Mamet	The relationship between a college professor and his student breaks down amidst a fog of misunderstanding or sexual harassment and, as a consequence, one or both face inevitable destruction.
Once a Catholic	Mary O'Malley	Set in a North London school, this is an amusing dig at Catholicism, damnation and the sexual awakenings of adolescent girls.
Once in a Lifetime	Moss Hart & George S. Kaufman	A comedic tale of a failing vaudeville trio act who decide to try their hand in the expanding film industry, setting up a school of elocution. But out of incompetence arrives success.
Oresteian	Aeschylus	The only complete trilogy to survive from the classical Greek theatre, it tells the story of crime breeding crime until the intervention of the goddess Athene.
Our Country's Good	Timberlake Wertenbaker	Set in Australia in the Eighteenth Century, a group of convicts attempts to put on a play.
Our Town	Thornton Wilder	A character in the play 'The Stage Manager' narrates and oversees the story, set over a period of years in a fictional American town. There are no sets and no props as Wilder wanted the audience to concentrate on the characters.

PLAY	PLAYWRIGHT	BRIEF SYNOPSIS
P		
Peter Pan	J.M. Barrie	The story of a boy who never grew up.
Philadelphia Story (The)	Philip Barry	Tracy Lord realises that she prefers personality to money and so leaves her fiancé for a more interesting man. (Later made into the film and stage musical, *High Society*).
Philanthropist (The)	Christopher Hampton	A witty play in which the odd and eccentric characters lead such insular lives that nothing makes an impression on them, not even the assassination of almost the entire government.
Playboy of the Western World (The)	J.M. Synge	Christy Mahon wanders into a small Irish village and declares that he has just murdered his father. He is initially applauded but the villagers soon change their opinion as the plot develops.
Plough and the Stars (The)	Sean O'Casey	Set during the Easter Rising of 1916 in a tenement house in a Dublin street, this play looks at ordinary people and their reaction to the events around them.
Private Lives	Noël Coward	A divorced husband and wife bump into one another whilst honeymooning with their second spouses. The result is that they ditch their new partners and run off to Paris together.
Provoked Wife (The)	John Vanbrugh	Lady Brute is trapped in a loveless marriage to the bad-tempered drunkard, Sir John. One man offers her love but this is at a time when divorce is not an option.
Pygmalion	George Bernard Shaw	Of course, this play is actually better known for its musical version *My Fair Lady*, and is the story of a market girl learning to become a lady.
Q		
Quare Fellow (The)	Brendan Behan	A realistic portrait of prison life, questioning the moral issues that surround capital punishment. The 'Quare Fellow' himself, a man who has been condemned to death the next day, is never actually seen.
R		
Racing Demon	David Hare	The arrival of an enthusiastic young curate only serves to magnify the problems with which a team of clergymen are struggling as they try to make sense of their mission in life.
Recruiting Officer (The)	George Farquhar	Silvia, the daughter of a local justice, wants to be near her lover and so she disguises herself as a man in order to enlist in the army.

PLAY	PLAYWRIGHT	BRIEF SYNOPSIS
Rise and Fall of Little Voice (The)	Jim Cartwright	A shy teenager has a splendid singing voice and is adept at impersonating the greats, but she lives in the shadow of her 'loud' mother until a theatrical agent comes along who sees the girl as a meal ticket.
Road	Jim Cartwright	An account of the unemployment problem in Thatcher's Britain as seen through the eyes of the narrator, Scully, and the inhabitants of a Lancashire street.
Roots	Arnold Wesker	A play exploring the theme of self-discovery, in which we never see the central and most important character, Ronnie, and yet it is he who awakens an insatiable thirst for knowledge in Beatie a simple lass, who then finds her own roots and philosophy on life.
Royal Hunt of the Sun (The)	Peter Shaffer	A play which portrays the destruction of the Inca empire.
Ruling Class (The)	Peter Barnes	A madman inherits an earldom and believes that he is God.
Run for Your Wife	Ray Cooney	Ray Cooney is widely acclaimed as the Master of Farce and in his farce, *Run for Your Wife*, he brings together all the essential ingredients as a bigamous husband attempts to keep his two wives from a catastrophic meeting.

S

PLAY	PLAYWRIGHT	BRIEF SYNOPSIS
Saved	Edward Bond	A play commissioned by the Royal Court about the effects of an act of violence (the stoning of a baby), on ordinary people, which was instrumental in bringing the argument over the laws of censorship to a head, resulting in an eventual change of the law.
School for Scandal (The)	Richard Brinsley Sheridan	Lady Teazle arrives from the country as the naïve young wife of a much older man to experience and be educated by the London society of the day.
Seagull (The)	Anton Chekhov	This play looks at the human failing of wanting what you can't have and rejecting what you can have.
Second Mrs Tanqueray (The)	Arthur Wing Pinero	The story of how one woman's past affected her new family's present and future, and how it is impossible always to bury the past because it will always come back to haunt you.

108

PLAY	PLAYWRIGHT	BRIEF SYNOPSIS
Sergeant Musgrave's Dance	John Arden	It is the 1880s and a group of army deserters, with their brutal and fanatical leader, Sergeant Musgrave, invade an army town in the North of England.
Serious Money	Caryl Churchill	Set in the world of big business, this play is an attack on the selfishness and greed of the city, where Jake Todd is found shot dead, a presumed suicide. His sister thinks differently and, initially, sets out to uncover his 'killers' but, eventually, seeks out his corrupt millions instead.
Shakers	John Godber	Four long-suffering waitresses attempt to smile and help the difficult customers whilst trying, at the same time, to cope with their own problems.
She Stoops to Conquer	Oliver Goldsmith	A comedy of manners in which the character, Kate Hardcastle, uses great skill to expose the double standards of sexual morality prevalent at the time.
Shoemaker's Holiday (The)	Thomas Dekker	The tale of a cobbler who becomes Lord Mayor of London.
Shopping and F**king	Mark Ravenhill	A play which uses the themes of sex and consumerism as it explores all previously taboo subjects.
Six Characters in Search of an Author	Luigi Pirandello	A rehearsal in a theatre is interrupted by the arrival of a strange family group who claim to be characters from an incomplete play.
Skin of Our Teeth	Thornton Wilder	The history of mankind seen as a litany of encounters with chaos.
Sleuth	Anthony Shaffer	Set in the home of the successful mystery writer, Andrew Wyke, who is also fascinated with games and game playing, but where does Wyke's imagination end and reality start?
St Joan	George Bernard Shaw	The story of a young girl, Joan, who – when just a teenager – led the French resistance against the English invasion of France and was eventually burned at the stake.
Stones in His Pockets	Marie Jones	A two-hander in which the actors concerned must play the diverse characters required by a story set in a rural Irish community upon which a film crew descends, bringing with it all the eccentricities of film-making.
Streetcar Named Desire (A)	Tennessee Williams	Blanche arrives to stay with her sister, Stella, and so starts a battle of attraction and repulsion with Stella's vile husband, Stanley; the play subsequently becomes a minefield of exhausting emotions.

109

PLAY	PLAYWRIGHT	BRIEF SYNOPSIS
Strife	John Galsworthy	A play about a long, on-going strike where an eventual agreement is reached – on the same terms as were offered at the start.

T

PLAY	PLAYWRIGHT	BRIEF SYNOPSIS
Taste of Honey (A)	Shelagh Delaney	Set in a working-class environment, this is the story of a mother-daughter relationship, of feminism and an unprejudiced approach to illegitimacy, racism, homosexuality and the strength of women to survive.
Teechers	John Godber	A new teacher arrives at a comprehensive school to face a multitude of problems from difficult caretakers to obstructive pupils. The question is will he survive in such a school or should he go elsewhere?
'Tis Pity She's a Whore	John Ford	Set in Italy, this is the tale of an incestuous love between Giovanni and his sister, Annabella, which ends in disaster and death.
Top Girls	Caryl Churchill	A play about the challenges working women face in business and society. The highlight of this play is a dinner party in the opening scene where five women from different periods in history are gathered together.
Trelawny of the 'Wells'	Arthur Wing Pinero	A Victorian comedy taking a nostalgic look at theatre in which love conquers all and all ends happily.
Two Thousand Years	Mike Leigh	Set against world events, this comedy tells the story of secular Jewish parents and their struggle to come to terms with their son's new, fiercely strong dedication to the Hebrew faith.

U

PLAY	PLAYWRIGHT	BRIEF SYNOPSIS
Uncle Vanya	Anton Chekhov	The privileged characters in this play are bored and realise their complacency has led to missed opportunities; there is little plot for there is no heroic, central figure upon which the plot can hang, Uncle Vanya himself being a simple, hard-working and blundering man with the patronising label, 'Uncle'.
Unconquered (The)	Torben Betts	A mercenary soldier intrudes on the family home of a young girl when a people's revolution breaks out.

PLAY	PLAYWRIGHT	BRIEF SYNOPSIS
V		
Victory	Howard Barker	*Victory* deals with the aftermath of the restoration of Charles II.
View from the Bridge (A)	Arthur Miller	The themes of love, honour, betrayal and self-deception are central to this story of a working man, the guardian of a niece whom he loves obsessively.
Vortex (The)	Noël Coward	The decadent 1920s are portrayed in this play about an ageing beauty, her succession of toy boy lovers and the devastating affect of this upon her drug-addled son.
W		
Waiting for Godot	Samuel Beckett	A play which portrays the resilience of man even when there is no hope shows us two tramp-like figures waiting for the arrival of Godot – who never actually arrives.
Way of the World	William Congreve	Millamant and Mirabell have a rather unconventional marriage arrangement which is based on their knowledge of the way of the world.
Weir (The)	Conor McPherson	Three regulars in a bar in a rural part of Northern Ireland try to unnerve Valerie who has recently arrived from Dublin, but the tables turn and it is she who eventually unnerves them.
What the Butler Saw	Joe Orton	The unethical behaviour of a psychiatrist and his attempts at a cover-up make this comedy a farce.
When We Are Married	J.B. Priestley	Three couples celebrating their silver wedding are faced with the news that they may not be married after all as the parson who married them was not authorised to do so.
Widowing of Mrs Holroyd (The)	D.H. Lawrence	Lizzie Holroyd lives a miserable existence with her drunken husband, wanting a better life with another man. Her husband's subsequent death in a pit accident leaves her consumed with guilt, as it was she who wished he were dead.
Winslow Boy (The)	Terence Rattigan	Based on the true story of young George Archer-Shee who was expelled from Naval College, accused of stealing a five shilling postal order.
Who's Afraid of Virginia Woolf	Edward Albee	The relationship between a professor and his wife is scrutinised in this play as they drag a young couple into their power games.

PLAY	PLAYWRIGHT	BRIEF SYNOPSIS
Woman in Black	Stephen Mallatratt	An adaptation of Susan Hill's novel and horror story, this play has a cast of only two – or could it be three? The audience also become involved in this spine-chilling theatrical experience.
Woman of No Importance (A)	Oscar Wilde	The upper classes gather for a weekend house party. When it is announced that Gerald Arbuthnot has been appointed as Lord Illingworth's secretary, his mother's secret threatens to ruin her son's success.

Y

PLAY	PLAYWRIGHT	BRIEF SYNOPSIS
You Can't Take it With You	Moss Hart & George S. Kaufman	Set in New York, this is a somewhat eccentric play with the eccentric characters of the Vanderhofs versus the money-minded individuals in the world around them and where Grandpa Vanderhof decided not to become rich because it would take too much time!

Z

PLAY	PLAYWRIGHT	BRIEF SYNOPSIS
Zigger Zagger	Peter Terson	Harry, a football mad hooligan, epitomises the futile existence of so many young people when they leave school too early and move from one dead-end job to another.
Zoo Story (The)	Edward Albee	Set on a bench in Central Park, New York where a lonely man starts up a conversation with another man, eventually forcing him to participate in an act of violence.

Biographies of 39 'Modern' Playwrights

In this section, you will find brief biographical details on just 39 of some of the most popular 'modern' playwrights – generally, though not rigidly speaking, post 1900.

This was such a difficult section to write as it was difficult to know where to draw the line (I could so easily have gone on and on). I am sure that some will wonder why, for example, I didn't include X. Well, the answer is that I probably did, but space and word count necessitated a lot of cutting!

Every playwright included in this section has either been contacted directly, or via their agent or estate, to verify the content and to assure that they are happy with the way in which they have been portrayed. Of course, it is the way of human nature that not all responded, but I did want to give each one the opportunity to be their own editorial pen.

Edward Albee, 1928–
American

PLAYS BY EDWARD ALBEE INCLUDE

All Over • American Dream (The) • Box and Quotations from Chairman Mao Tse-Tung • Counting the Ways • Death of Bessie Smith (The) • Delicate Balance (A) • Fam and Yam • Fragments • Lady from Dubuque • Listening • Man Who Had Three Arms (The) • Marriage Play (The) • Occupant • Play about the Baby (The) • Sandbox (The) • Seascape • The Goat, or Who is Sylvia • Three Tall Women • Tiny Alice • Who's Afraid of Virginia Woolf • Zoo Story (The)

THE LIFE AND WORKS OF EDWARD ALBEE

- Edward Albee was born on 12th March, 1928 in Washington DC and was adopted by Reed and Frances Albee when he was a few weeks old; they gave him the name Edward Franklin Albee III after Reed's father
- The wealthy Albees acquired their considerable wealth from a chain of Nineteenth Century vaudeville theatres
- His childhood was one of luxury, being raised in the family's mansion where his beloved grandmother also lived. It was his grandmother who left him a trust fund, enabling him to follow his dream of becoming a writer
- From the age of 11, Albee was educated at various boarding schools
- His first and major success was his stage play, *Who's Afraid of Virginia Woolf*, which opened on Broadway in 1963, making him a very wealthy man

AND FINALLY

- Although theatre was not in Albee's natural, biological blood, it was in his adoptive family's blood – thus fuelling the 'nature versus nurture' debate even further, especially when one considers his enormous successes

Samuel Beckett, 1906–1989
Irish/French Descent

PLAYS BY SAMUEL BECKETT INCLUDE

Act Without Words • All that Fall • Breath • Cascando • Catastrophe • Come and Go • Eh Joe • Embers • Endgame • Footfalls • Ghost Trio • Happy Days • Krapp's Last Tape • Nacht und Träume • Not I • Ohio Impromptu • Piece of Monologue (A) • Play • Quad • Rockaby • That Time • Waiting for Godot • What Where • Words and Music

THE LIFE AND WORKS OF SAMUEL BECKETT

- Samuel Beckett was born of Anglo-Irish parents in Dublin and educated in the North and South of Ireland
- As well as being a brilliant pupil, he also excelled at sports
- He studied French and Italian at the University of Dublin
- He wrote in both French and English
- In the late 1920s, Beckett went to Paris where he worked for a time with James Joyce
- Whilst in Paris, he worked as a lecturer in English
- He also wrote verse novels and short fiction, apparently turning to drama as a form of relaxation!
- *Waiting for Godot* brought worldwide fame to Samuel Beckett
- He is known by many as a writer of 'Theatre of the Absurd', although he despised being categorised in this way
- His work can be confusing and difficult to understand, often minimalist in staging, sometimes with verbal language replaced by sounds – but he always adamantly refused to give any explanations of his works

AND FINALLY

- Samuel Beckett was active in the French Resistance during World War Two. His underground group was discovered by the Germans – although, thankfully, he escaped

Brendan Behan, 1923–1964
Irish

PLAYS BY BRENDAN BEHAN INCLUDE

Gretna Green • Hostage (The) • Quare Fellow (The) • Richard's Cork Leg (completed posthumously by Alan Simpson)

THE LIFE AND WORKS OF BRENDAN BEHAN

- Brendan Francis Behan was born on 9th February, 1923 in Dublin, the son of Stephen Behan, a painter, and Kathleen
- His family nickname was 'Benjy'
- By tradition, the Behan family were anti-British
- His early years were spent in an overcrowded tenement block where the Behan family of nine lived in just two rooms with six boys to one bed

114

- He joined the IRA in 1937
- Working for the IRA, he was arrested in 1939 and later sentenced to three years in a Borstal detention centre
- His brushes with the law came to a head in 1942 when, following an attempt to shoot a police officer, he went on the run. The order went out that he was to be shot on sight. However, he was captured without being shot and sentenced to 14 years imprisonment, though served only four before the general IRA Amnesty of 1946
- 1947 saw him back in prison, a situation that was to be repeated many times in the future
- Despite his spells in prison, Brendan Behan still managed to write
- In February 1955 Brendan married Beatrice ffrench-Salkeld, (a botanist from The National Museum)
- In 1956, his play *The Quare Fellow* was produced by the renowned Joan Littlewood at Stratford East Theatre
- In 1956, he made a drunken appearance on the TV programme *Panorama* with Malcolm Muggeridge, which in itself made him a household name – and, in turn, sold books!
- In 1958, Behan was commissioned to write a regular column for *The People*
- He actually wrote more books than plays and yet is still recognised as a major Twentieth Century playwright
- He had one daughter with Beatrice
- Sadly, the drink got him in the end and he died on March 20th, 1964

AND FINALLY

- Brendan once described himself as – 'A drinker with a writing problem'
- Brendan volunteered to fight for the Republicans in the Spanish Civil War. However, his call-up letter was intercepted and burnt by his mother, therefore, never reaching him
- His play, *The Hostage*, was such a huge success that curtain calls would often last for over an hour
- Behan said of himself, 'I ruined my health by drinking to everyone else's'

Robert Bolt, 1924–1995
British

PLAYS BY ROBERT BOLT INCLUDE

Critic and the Heart (The) • *Flowering Cherry* • *Gentle Jack* • *Man for All Seasons (A)* • *State of Revolution* • *Thwarting of Baron Bolligrew (The)* • *Tiger and the Horse (The)* • *Vivat! Vivat! Regina*

THE LIFE AND WORKS OF ROBERT BOLT

- Robert Oxton Bolt was born on 15th August, 1924 in Manchester, the son of a shopkeeper
- He was educated at Manchester Grammar School
- He worked in an insurance office before attending Manchester University where he studied history, graduating with a BA degree in 1949
- After a postgraduate course at Exeter University, he worked as a school teacher until 1958
- During his time as a teacher, he wrote plays for radio
- It was the success of his stage play, *Flowering Cherry*, that allowed him to leave teaching
- He married four times during his lifetime and fathered four children
- Like many playwrights, or so it would seem, Robert Bolt was involved in the Campaign for Nuclear Disarmament (C.N.D.), a fact that is reflected in his work *The Tiger and the Horse*
- He wrote the screenplays to three of David Lean's epic movies, *Lawrence of Arabia*, *Dr Zhivago* and *Ryan's Daughter*
- Robert Bolt died in Hampshire on February 20th, 1995

AND FINALLY

- Robert Bolt served in the Royal Air Force and the Army during World War Two
- He married screen actress Sarah Miles – twice. So, although he married four times, in fact he only actually had three wives

Jim Cartwright, 1958–
British

PLAYS BY JIM CARTWRIGHT INCLUDE

Baths • Bed • Eight Miles High • Hard Fruit • I Licked a Slag's Deodorant • Prize Night • Rise and Fall of Little Voice (The)• Road •Two

THE LIFE AND WORKS OF JIM CARTWRIGHT

- Jim Cartwright was born on 27th June, 1958 in Farnworth, Lancashire
- He was educated at Harper Green Secondary Modern School
- His plays have been translated into more than 30 languages
- His first play, *Road*, opened at the Royal Court in 1986 and has since won numerous awards
- Cartwright is an Honourary Fellow of the University of Bolton and a Visiting Professor at Salford University
- Many of his works are used as set texts for A-level and University courses

AND FINALLY

- His old school, Harper Green, have named a building after him

Agatha Christie, 1890–1976
British

PLAYS BY AGATHA CHRISTIE INCLUDE

Appointment with Death • Black Coffee • Death on the Nile • Fiddlers Three • Go Back for Murder • Hollow (The) • Mousetrap (The) • Rule of Three (The) • Spider's Web (The) • Ten Little Niggers (Also known as Ten Little Indians or And Then There Were None) • Toward Zero • Unexpected Guest (The) • Verdict • Witness for the Prosecution

THE LIFE AND WORKS OF AGATHA CHRISTIE

- Agatha Miller was born in Torquay, England on 15th September, 1890
- In 1914, Agatha married Colonel Archibald Christie, an aviator in the Royal Flying Corps with whom she had a daughter, Rosalind

- Agatha and the Colonel divorced in 1928
- Her second husband was Sir Max Mallowan
- She wrote a total of 16 plays with the first performance of a Christie mystery being staged at the Prince of Wales Theatre on 15th May, 1928
- Agatha Christie is one of the most successful thriller writers of all time. As well as her plays, she has penned 80 novels and short story collections
- Her play, *The Mousetrap*, opened in 1952 and is, to date, the longest running play ever and now even figures as a London tourist attraction!
- Agatha Christie created the detective characters of Miss Marple and Hercule Poirot, both hugely popularised by television series
- She also wrote romantic fiction under the pseudonym, Mary Westmacott
- In 1971, she received the Order of Dame Commander of the British Empire
- Agatha Christie died peacefully at home on 12th January, 1976, after a short cold

AND FINALLY

- An Agatha Christie play, *Chimneys*, written in 1931 and originally intended for the Embassy Theatre in London, mysteriously disappeared and so never had that first performance. However, in recent years, after being rediscovered languishing in a pile of dusty scripts, *Chimneys* received its belated world premiere in Calgary, Canada, in 2003 with its UK premiere being at the Pitlochry Festival Theatre as part of their Summer 2006 season
- Two billion copies of Agatha Christie's work have been sold worldwide and her work has been translated into more than 45 foreign languages

Caryl Churchill, 1938–
British

PLAYS BY CARYL CHURCHILL INCLUDE

Blue Heart • Blue Kettle • Cloud Nine • Drunk Enough to Say I Love You • Far Away • Fen • Hearts Desire • Hot Fudge • Hotel • Icecream • Light Shining in Buckinghamshire • Mad Forest • Mouthful of Birds (A) • Number (A) • Objections to Sex and Violence • Owners • Serious Money • Softcops • Striker (The) • This is a Chair • Three More Sleepless Nights • Top Girls • Traps • Vinegar Tom

THE LIFE AND WORKS OF CARYL CHURCHILL

- Caryl Churchill was born on 3rd September, 1938, in London
- She grew up in the Lake District and in Montreal, Canada, where her family emigrated during World War Two
- She was educated at Lady Margaret Hall, Oxford, where she read English
- In 1961, Churchill married David Harter and they had three sons
- Like many writers, Churchill started her career by writing for radio
- She is known for her feminist themes
- From 1974 to 1975, Churchill was Resident Dramatist at the Royal Court, the home of new writers
- In the mid-1970s, she wrote her first play for Joint Stock Theatre Group, called *Light Shining in Buckinghamshire*
- *Top Girls*, the play for which she most well known, opened at the Royal Court in 1982, opening in New York later that same year

AND FINALLY

- While a student at Lady Margaret Hall, Caryl Churchill wrote three plays including a one-act play, *Downstairs*, which was produced by Oriel College in 1958
- She prefers to use the improvisational workshop method to develop her new works

Ray Cooney, 1932–
British

PLAYS BY RAY COONEY INCLUDE

Caught in the Net • *Chase Me Comrade* • *Funny Money* • *It Runs in the Family* • *Out of Order* • *Run for Your Wife* • *Two into One*

COLLABORATIVE WORKS INCLUDE

Charlie Girl (with Hugh and Margaret Williams Music & Lyrics by David Heneker & John Taylor) • *Come Back to My Place (with John Chapman)* • *Move Over Mrs Markham (with John Chapman)* • *My Giddy Aunt (with John Chapman)* • *Not Now Darling (with John Chapman)* • *One for the Pot (with Tony Hilton)* • *Stand by Your Bedouin (with Tony Hilton)* • *There Goes the Bride (with John Chapman)* • *Tom, Dick and Harry (with Michael Cooney)* • *Why Not Stay for Breakfast? (with Gene Stone)* • *Wife Begins at Forty (with Arne Sultan and Earl Barrett)*

THE LIFE AND WORKS OF RAY COONEY

- Ray Cooney was born Raymond George Alfred Cooney on 30th May, 1932, in London, the son of Gerald and Olive (Clarke)
- Cooney began his acting career at 14 years old; he then joined Brian Rix's farce company at the Whitehall Theatre Company in London
- In 1962, he married Linda Dixon, with whom he had two sons
- His first play was *One for the Pot* which he co-wrote with Tony Hilton
- In 1983, he created his own Theatre of Comedy at London's Shaftesbury Theatre
- In 2005, Cooney was awarded an O.B.E. for services to drama in the Queen's New Year's Honours List

AND FINALLY

- His work has been translated into more than 40 languages
- He co-wrote the play, *Tom, Dick and Harry,* with his son, Michael

Michael Frayn, 1933–
British

PLAYS BY MICHAEL FRAYN INCLUDE

Afterlife • *Alarms and Excursions* • *Alphabetical Order* • *Benefactors* • *Clouds* • *Copenhagen* • *Crimson Hotel* • *Democracy* • *Donkey's Years* • *Look Look* • *Make and Break* • *Noises Off* • *Now You Know* • *Sandboy (The)* • *Two of Us (The)* [comprising *Black and Silver, The New Quixote, Mr Foot, Chinamen*]

THE LIFE AND WORKS OF MICHAEL FRAYN

- Michael Frayn was born in Mill Hill, London on 8th September, 1933
- He learnt Russian during his two years National Service and later went on to translate many works from Russian into English, including plays by Chekhov and Tolstoy
- Frayn read philosophy at Emmanuel College, Cambridge
- In 1957, he co-scripted Cambridge University's Footlights revue 'Zounds'
- He began his career as a journalist and columnist on *The Guardian* and *The Observer*, during which time he wrote four novels
- In 1970, his first play, *The Two of Us,* was staged in the West End of London
- In addition to his plays, he also writes novels

AND FINALLY

- As well as an impressive list of plays and numerous novels, Frayn also wrote the screenplay for the hugely successful comedy film, *Clockwise*, starring John Cleese
- He has allegedly declined a knighthood

**Brian Friel, 1929–
Northern Irish**

PLAYS BY BRIAN FRIEL INCLUDE

Afterplay • Aristocrats • Communication Cord (The) • Crystal and Fox • Dancing at Lughnasa • Enemy Within (The) • Faith Healer • Freedom of the City (The) • Gentle Island (The) • Give Me Your Answer, Do! • Home Place (The) • Living Quarters • London Vertigo (The) • Lovers • Loves of Cass Maguire (The) • Making History • Molly Sweeney • Philadelphia, Here I Come • Translations • Volunteers • Wonderful Tennessee

ADAPTATIONS BY BRIAN FRIEL INCLUDE

Month in the Country (A) • Three Sisters • Uncle Vanya

THE LIFE AND WORKS OF BRIAN FRIEL

- Brian Friel was born in Omagh, County Tyrone, Northern Ireland on 9th January, 1929, to Patrick Friel, a school teacher, and Mary McLoone, a postmistress
- In 1939, he moved with his family to Derry
- A Catholic, Friel trained to become a Priest at St Patrick's College but changed his mind and, in 1950, he began teaching

- In 1954, he married Ann Morrison, with whom he had four daughters and one son
- In 1960, Friel began to write full-time
- In 1980, he co-founded (with the actor Stephen Rea), the Field Day Theatre Company in Derry
- From 1987–89, he served in the Senate
- 1990 saw the production of what many believe to be Friel's greatest work, *Dancing at Lughnasa*

AND FINALLY

- He is not just famous for his writing but also for his reclusive nature
- In addition to his plays, he has written short stories and screenplays; he has also written film, TV and radio adaptations of his plays, as well as several pieces of non-fiction on the role of theatre and the artist

John Godber, 1956–
British

PLAYS BY JOHN GODBER INCLUDE

Blood Sweat and Tears • Bouncers • Dracula (adapted from Bram Stoker's novel, Dracula, with Jane Thornton) • April in Paris • Gym and Tonic • Happy Families • Happy Jack • It Started with a Kiss • Lucky Sods • Office Party (The) • On a Night Like This • On the Piste • Passion Killers • Salt of the Earth • September in the Rain • Shakers (with Jane Thornton) • Shakers Re-stirred (with Jane Thornton) • Teechers • Up 'n' Under

THE LIFE AND WORKS OF JOHN GODBER

- John (Harry) Godber was born on 15th May, 1956, in Upton, West Yorkshire, into a family of miners
- He attended Minsthorpe High School
- At the age of 16, he wrote short stories for Radio Sheffield
- He trained as a drama teacher at Bretton Hall College and did his postgraduate work at the University of Leeds
- Before turning professional, Godber was appointed Head of Drama at his old school, Minsthorpe High School
- In 1984, he joined The Hull Truck Theatre Company as Artistic Director

- In 2004, John Godber was made Professor of Popular Theatre at Liverpool Hope University
- He is married with two daughters

AND FINALLY

- John has also written for television, including for *Brookside*, *Crown Court* and *Grange Hill*
- He successfully auditioned for a part in the film *The Full Monty*, but turned it down

Trevor Griffiths, 1935–
British

PLAYS BY TREVOR GRIFFITHS INCLUDE

All Good Men • Apricots • Camel Station • Cherry Orchard (The) [A new English version of Chekhov's play] • Comedians • Deeds [with David Hare, Howard Brenton and Ken Campbell] • Gulf Between Us (The) • Occupations • Oi for England • Party (The) • Piano [After Chekhov and based on the original film, unfinished piece for mechanical piano by N. Mikhalov & A. Adabashyan] • Real Dreams [based on a story by Jeremy Pikser] • Sam Sam • Thatcher's Children • Thermidor • Wages of Thin (The) • Who Shall Be Happy?

THE LIFE AND WORKS OF TREVOR GRIFFITHS

- Trevor Griffiths was born on 4th April, 1935, in Manchester
- His father was a chemical process worker
- In 1945, he won a scholarship to St Bede's College, Manchester
- Griffiths went to Manchester University to read English in 1952

- After his National Service, which he served in the Army, he became a teacher
- In 1960, he married Janice Elaine Stansfield, with whom he had a son and two daughters before she died in 1977
- He taught for eight years in Oldham and was a lecturer in Liberal Studies at Stockport College
- From 1965, and for a period of seven years, he was Further Education Officer for the BBC in Leeds
- In 1968, he wrote a stage play entitled *Occupations*, which brought him to the attention of Kenneth Tynan, then the artistic director of The National Theatre. As a result of this, Tynan then commissioned Griffiths to write the play that became *The Party*
- In 1972, he left his job at the BBC in order to write full-time
- From the 1980s onwards, Griffiths began to direct his own work, both in theatre and on film
- In 1992, he married Gillian Cliff

AND FINALLY

- Griffiths has frequently chosen to work in television rather than theatre in order to achieve the widest possible audience. His screen list is highly impressive:

For Television:
Absolute Beginners
Adam Smith
All Good Men
Bill Brand
Country
Food for Ravens
Hope in the Year Two
Last Place on Earth (The)
Silver Mask (The)
Sons and Lovers
Through the Night

Theatre Plays also Produced on Television:
Cherry Orchard (The)
Comedians
Occupations
Oi for England
Party (The)

For the Big Screen:
Fatherland
Reds

• The play for which he is most well known is *Comedians*, which is a study of the nature of comedy

Christopher Hampton, 1946–
British

PLAYS BY CHRISTOPHER HAMPTON INCLUDE

After Mercer • Les Liaisons Dangereuses (from Choderlos de Laclos) • Philanthropist (The) • Portage to San Cristobal of A.H. (The) (from George Steiner) • Savages • Sunset Boulevard (book of the musical) • Tales from Hollywood • Talking Cure (The) • Total Eclipse • Treats • When Did You Last See Your Mother?

THE LIFE AND WORKS OF CHRISTOPHER HAMPTON

• Christopher James Hampton was born on January 26th, 1946, in Portugal
• As a child, he lived in Egypt and Zanzibar
• He was educated at Lancing College and later went on to New College, Oxford, to read German and French, from where he graduated with a First Class Honours degree
• Hampton's first play, *When Did You Last See Your Mother?*, written when he was 18, was staged by Oxford University Dramatic Society. It was taken up by the Royal Court while Hampton was still an undergraduate
• He was the first Resident Dramatist at The Royal Court
• In 1971, he married Laura d' Holesch, with whom he went on to have two children

AND FINALLY

• One of Hampton's most commercially successful plays, *The Philanthropist*, was written when he was Resident Dramatist at the Royal Court

David Hare, 1947–
British

PLAYS BY DAVID HARE INCLUDE

Absence of War (The) • *Amy's View* • *Bay at Nice (The)* • *Blue Room (The)* • *Brassneck* • *Breath of Life (The)* • *Deeds* • *Fanshen* • *Great Exhibition (The)* • *Judas Kiss (The)* • *Knuckle* • *Lay By* • *Map of the World (A)* • *Murmuring Judges* • *My Zinc Bed* • *Permanent Way (The)* • *Plenty* • *Pravda (with Howard Brenton)* • *Racing Demon* • *Secret Rapture (The)* • *Skylight* • *Slag* • *Stuff Happens* • *Teeth 'n' Smiles* • *Vertical Hour (The)* • *Via Dolorosa*

THE LIFE AND WORKS OF DAVID HARE

- David Hare was born on 5th June, 1947, in Bexhill, Sussex
- He was educated at Lancing College and later at Jesus College, Cambridge
- Hare co-founded the Portable Theatre Company with Nick Bicât
- He has held two Resident Dramatist positions: one at the Royal Court (1970–1971) and the other at Nottingham Playhouse (1973)
- He was responsible for founding the Joint Stock Theatre Group with David Aukin and Max Stafford-Clark
- In 1984, Hare was appointed Associate Director of The National Theatre, London
- In 1993, his papers were acquired by the Harry Ransom Humanities Research Center at the University of Texas
- In 1997, the French government honoured David Hare as an *Officier de l'Ordre des Arts et Lettres*
- In 1998, David Hare was knighted and became Sir David Hare

AND FINALLY

- David Hare writes not only for the stage but is prolific in all areas of entertainment such as adaptations, screenplays, films for TV, books and opera libretti:

Film Works Include:
Paris by Night
Plenty
Strapless
Wetherby

Books Include:
Obedience, Struggle and Revolt

Mike Leigh, 1943–
British

PLAYS BY MIKE LEIGH INCLUDE

Abigail's Party • Babies Grow Old • Bleak Moments • Box Play (The) • Ecstasy • Goose-Pimples • Greek Tragedy • It's a Great Big Shame! • Jaws of Death (The) • Smelling a Rat • Two Thousand Years • Wholesome Glory

THE LIFE AND WORKS OF MIKE LEIGH

- Mike Leigh was born in Salford, Lancashire, on 20th February, 1943
- His father was a doctor
- He was educated at Salford Grammar School
- He trained as an actor at the Royal Academy of Dramatic Art, followed by a Foundation Course at Camberwell School of Arts and Crafts; Theatre Design at the Central School of Art and Design and also the London Film School
- In 1973, he married the actress, Alison Steadman, with whom he had two sons. They are now divorced
- Steadman has appeared in many of Leigh's works
- Mike Leigh's most famous stage play is *Abigail's Party*
- He writes and directs not only for the stage, but also for film and television
- His 1999 feature film, *Topsy-Turvy*, was about Gilbert and Sullivan and their original production of *The Mikado* at the Savoy Theatre in 1885

AND FINALLY

- Mike Leigh is well known for his unique method of creating a play through discussion, improvisation and rehearsal. While the long preparatory period this requires is fluid and exploratory, the final play is always precisely structured and scripted

David Mamet, 1947–
American

PLAYS BY DAVID MAMET INCLUDE

American Buffalo • Bobby Gould in Hell • Cryptogram (The) • Duck Variations • Edmond • Frog Prince (The) • Glengarry Glen Ross • Lakeboat • Life in Theatre (A)

• *Oleanna* • *Prairie du Chien* • *Reunion* • *Sexual Perversity in Chicago* • *Shawl (The)* • *Sketches of War* • *Speed-the-Plow* • *Vermont Sketches* • *Water Engine (The)* • *Where Were You When It Went Down* • *Woods (The)*

THE LIFE AND WORKS OF DAVID MAMET

• David Alan Mamet was born into a Jewish family on 30th November, 1947, in Chicago
• He graduated from Goddard College, Plainfield, Vermont in 1969 with a BA degree
• Some of his early plays were produced at Goddard College
• After graduation, he worked at various factory jobs as well as at a real estate agency and as a taxi driver – these experiences all proved useful for his future writing
• He has taught drama at various American colleges and Universities
• In 1973, he co-founded a theatre company in Chicago
• In 1977, he married the actress, Lindsay Crouse, and they went on to have two children before they divorced in 1990
• In 1991, he married the singer/songwriter, Rebecca Pidgeon, with whom he had another two children
• His signature style is his sparse, clipped dialogue; his pieces often feature strong male characters and he is also known for his use of profanity within the dialogue
• He has also written plays for children, fiction, screenplays and poetry

AND FINALLY

• It is said that he will not use a computer for his writing, preferring an old-fashioned typewriter

Somerset W. Maugham, 1874–1965
British

PLAYS BY SOMERSET MAUGHAM INCLUDE

Bread Winner (The) • *Caesar's Wife* • *Circle (The)* • *Constant Wife (The)* • *East of Suez* • *For Services Rendered* • *Home and Beauty* • *Letter (The)* • *Man of Honour (A)* • *Our Betters* • *Penelope* • *Sacred Flame (The)* • *Sheppey*

THE LIFE AND WORKS OF SOMERSET MAUGHAM

- William Somerset Maugham was born in the British Embassy in Paris on 25th January, 1874
- His father, Robert Ormond Maugham, was a wealthy solicitor and worked for the Embassy in France
- Sadly, he was an orphan by the age of 10 and was then brought up by his Uncle, the Rev. Henry Maugham, in Whitstable, Kent
- He was educated at The King's School, Canterbury, and Heidelberg University in Germany
- In 1897, he qualified as a doctor from St Thomas' Medical School
- It was his experiences in medicine which inspired his first novel, *Lisa of Lambeth*
- In 1908, he enjoyed four of his plays running at the same time in London, success which also brought him financial security
- In 1928, he bought a villa in the South of France; this then became his permanent home
- William Somerset Maugham died in 1965

AND FINALLY

- Somerset Maugham's greatest comedy, *The Circle*, was booed at its premiere
- During World War One, he worked as a secret agent

Arthur Miller, 1915–2005
American

PLAYS BY ARTHUR MILLER INCLUDE

After the Fall • All My Sons • American Clock (The) • Archbishop's Ceiling (The) • Broken Glass • Creation of the World and Other Business (The) • Crucible (The) • Danger: Memory • Death of a Salesman • Fame • Incident at Vichy • Last Yankee (The) • Man Who Had All the Luck (The) • Memory of Two Mondays (A) • Mr Peter's Connection • Price (The) • Ride Down Mount Morgan (The) • Two-Way Mirror • Up from Paradise • View from the Bridge (A)

THE LIFE AND WORKS OF ARTHUR MILLER

- Arthur Aster Miller was born in New York on 17th October, 1915
- His father, Isidore Miller, was a ladies' wear manufacturer who was ruined in the Great Depression

- In 1933, Miller graduated from Abraham Lincoln High School and worked in an automobile parts warehouse
- In 1934, he began his studies in journalism at the University of Michigan where he became a reporter and night editor on the student paper, *The Michigan Daily*
- Miller was exempted from draft (military call up), due to a football injury
- In 1940, Arthur Miller married Mary Slattery, with whom he went on to have two children
- In 1956, Miller was awarded an honourary degree at the University of Michigan. In the same year, he married Marilyn Monroe – they divorced in 1961, the year before she died
- A year after his divorce from Marilyn Monroe, Miller married the Austrian photographer, Inge Morath
- Arthur Miller died of heart failure, aged 89 years, at his home in Roxbury, Connecticut, on 10th February, 2005

AND FINALLY

- It is said that Dostoevsky's novel, *The Brothers Karamazov*, was Miller's inspiration to become a writer
- He was politically active throughout his life, at one point being called before The House Un-American Activities Committee – though Miller denied that he was a Communist

John Mortimer, 1923–2009
British

PLAYS BY JOHN MORTIMER INCLUDE

Bells of Hell • *Collaborators* • *Dock Brief (The)* • *Edwin* • *Fear of Heaven (The)* • *Hock and Soda Water* • *Judge (The)* • *Lunch Hour* • *Naked Justice* • *Two Stars for Comfort* • *Voyage Round My Father (A)* • *What Shall We Tell Caroline* • *Wrong Side of the Park (The)*

THE LIFE AND WORKS OF JOHN MORTIMER

- John Clifford Mortimer was born on 21st April, 1923, in London
- He was educated at Harrow Public School and Brasenose College, Oxford, where he studied law
- John Mortimer was called to the Bar in 1948

- He married Penelope Fletcher in 1949 and they went on to have a son and a daughter
- Mortimer was made a Queen's Counsel in 1966
- In 1972, John Mortimer, now divorced from Penelope Fletcher, married another Penelope, Penelope Gollop, with whom he went on to have two daughters
- In 1986, he was awarded a CBE
- John Mortimer was knighted for services to the arts in 1998
- He would frequently start writing at 5am and, up until his death, was producing more than one book a year and touring his one-man show around the country
- John Mortimer died on 16th January, 2009, aged 85 years

AND FINALLY

- John Mortimer referred to his work as a barrister as his 'day job' – he wrote in his spare time
- His authorised biography is aptly titled, *A Voyage Round John Mortimer*, and was written by Valerie Grove
- He is probably most famous for the television series, *Rumpole of the Bailey*

Peter Nichols, 1927–
British

PLAYS BY PETER NICHOLS INCLUDE

Blue Murder • Born in the Gardens • Chez Nous • Day in the Death of Joe Egg (A) • Forget-Me-Not-Lane • Freeway (The) • Harding's Luck • National Health (The) • Passion Play • Piece of My Mind (A) • Poppy • Privates on Parade • So Long Life

THE LIFE AND WORKS OF PETER NICHOLS

- Peter Nichols was born in Bristol on 31st July, 1927
- He was educated at Bristol Grammar School
- Nichols served his National Service with the RAF as a clerk in Calcutta and, after that, in the Combined Services Entertainment Unit in Singapore, where he entertained the troops. These experiences provided crucial material for his future work, *Privates on Parade*, which was set in a song and dance unit in Malaya
- Nichols is known as an 'autobiographical writer' in that his own experiences feed his work

- He trained as an actor at The Bristol Old Vic
- In 1961, Peter Nichols won an Arts Council Bursary
- Frustrated by the difficulties in mounting new plays, he took some time out of playwriting during the 1980s and turned to writing fiction instead
- In 1987, he returned to writing for the stage with his play *A Piece of My Mind*
- Peter Nichols is a Fellow of The Royal Society of Literature and his papers were acquired by the British Library in 1999

AND FINALLY

- He drew upon his own experiences with his disabled daughter for his most famous stage play, *A Day in the Death of Joe Egg*
- As well writing for the theatre, Nichols has also written extensively for radio, TV and film
- His books include *Feeling Your Behind* (*A Memoir*, 1984) and a selection of his *Diaries* (2000)

Sean O'Casey, 1880–1964
Irish

PLAYS BY SEAN O'CASEY INCLUDE

Bedtime Story • *Bishops Bonfire (The)* • *Cock-a-Doodle Dandy* • *Drums of Father Ned (The)* • *Juno and the Paycock* • *Plough and the Stars (The)* • *Purple Dust* • *Red Roses for Me* • *Shadow of a Gunman (The)* • *Silver Tassie (The)* • *Star Turns Red (The)* • *Within the Gates*

THE LIFE AND WORKS OF SEAN O'CASEY

- He was born John Casey on 30th March, 1880, in North Dublin into a Protestant family, where he was the youngest of 13 children
- His father, Michael Casey, was a clerk and died when O'Casey was six years old, leaving his wife Susan to bring up the children alone and in near poverty
- As a result of ill health, O'Casey had only three years of formal schooling and educated himself by reading
- At 14, he started work in the stockroom of a hardware shop and, from there, went from job to job
- As a man, he was an idealist with a great sense of justice, which is evident in his work

- In 1902, O'Casey joined the Gaelic League, learnt the Irish language and changed his name to Sean O'Cathasaigh, which he later changed again to the simpler Sean O'Casey
- The political unrest in Ireland, and the poverty and squalor of the Dublin slums, were a great influence on the attitude and writings of Sean O'Casey. For example the Easter Rising of 1916 became the background to his play *The Plough and the Stars* and the Irish Civil War of 1922–1923 became the background to *Juno and the Paycock*. These, along with *The Shadow of the Gunman*, were all tragi-comedies set in the Dublin slums in a time of war and revolution
- In 1926, O'Casey travelled to England where he met the actress Eileen Carey
- In 1927, and relatively late in life, he married Eileen; together they had three children and made their home in England
- He moved his family to Devon in 1938
- In 1957, his youngest son Niall, died of Leukaemia, aged just 21 years
- Sean O'Casey died of a heart attack on 18th September, 1964

AND FINALLY

- O'Casey never enjoyed good health and suffered numerous eye problems which, as well as causing him immense pain, left him almost totally blind by middle age.
- O'Casey's autobiography runs into a mammoth six volumes

Eugene O'Neill, 1888–1953
American

PLAYS BY EUGENE O'NEILL INCLUDE

Ah! Wilderness • All God's Chillun Got Wings • Anna Christie • Beyond the Horizon • Desire Under the Elms • Emperor Jones (The) • Great God Brown (The) • Hairy Ape (The) • Iceman Cometh (The) • Lazarus Laughed • Long Day's Journey into Night • Marco Millions • Moon for the Misbegotten (A) • More Stately Mansions • Mourning Becomes Electra • Strange Interlude • Touch of the Poet (A) • Welded

THE LIFE AND WORKS OF EUGENE O'NEILL

- He was born Eugene Gladstone O'Neill in New York on 16th October, 1888

- He was, as they say, 'born in a trunk'; in other words he was born into the theatre, the second son of James O'Neill, an actor, and Ella, his wife, who dutifully followed her husband around the country whilst touring the theatres. It was an unsettling lifestyle for all the family
- As a child, O'Neill was educated at boarding schools
- He attended Princeton University for one year (1906–07)
- After leaving Princeton, he hit the bottom; he lived rough, drank heavily and attempted suicide
- A bout of Tuberculosis made him re-evaluate his life and he started to write plays
- His early, unsettled life continued to haunt him throughout adulthood and his tragic view of life spilt over into his relationships
- He was married three times, first was to Kathleen Jenkins, whom he divorced; he then married Agnes Boulton, whom he also divorced; his third wife, Carlotta Monterey, outlived him
- He had three children – all surrounded by tragedy too. His eldest son Eugene, by Kathleen, committed suicide aged 40; his next son Shane, by Agnes, suffered from emotional instability and he cut off his daughter, Oona, when she married Charlie Chaplin (who was the same age as O'Neill)
- In his final years, he was unable to work and died a tragic and broken man

AND FINALLY

- O'Neill was born in a hotel
- His masterpiece, *Long Day's Journey into Night* was produced posthumously and was a disturbingly autobiographical play

Joe Orton, 1933–1967
British

PLAYS BY JOE ORTON INCLUDE

Entertaining Mr Sloan • Erpingham Camp (The) • Funeral Games • Good and Faithful Servant (The) • Loot • Ruffian on the Stair (The) • Up Against It • What the Butler Saw

JOE ORTON THE MAN

- Joe Orton was born John Kingsley Orton on 1st January, 1933 in Leicester. The eldest of four children, he had one brother, Douglas, and two sisters, Marilyn and Leonie
- His parents were William, a gardener and Elsie, a machinist
- When he left school, he had a few menial and mundane clerical jobs, which he hated. He escaped this world by joining amateur dramatic groups
- To get rid of his thick working class accent, Orton took elocution lessons
- In 1951, he began an acting course at RADA where he met Kenneth Halliwell; he moved in with Halliwell in the same year
- After graduating from RADA, Orton secured a job as an ASM at Ipswich whilst Halliwell took an acting job in Llandudno, North Wales. Soon, they both decided that their destiny was to write rather than perform
- As well as collaborating with each other, the pair also wrote independently, Orton using various pseudonyms
- It was only after 10 years of failure that Orton had his first success with *The Boy Hairdresser* which was accepted by the BBC Third programme
- Failures and successes followed, as did the ups and downs which seems to be the natural precursors to becoming established and recognised. Then, the life of this talented young man was so tragically and needlessly cut short
- On 9th August, 1967, police were called to the home of Joe Orton where they found his body on the bed. He had been killed by numerous hammer blows to the head by Kenneth Halliwell whose body was on the floor; he had taken an overdose. Nearby was Halliwell's blood-soaked pyjama top
- Had Orton been allowed to live, who knows what literary mountains he would have climbed?

AND FINALLY

- He failed his eleven plus exam

John Osborne, 1929–1994
British

PLAYS BY JOHN OSBORNE INCLUDE

Déjàvu • *End of Me Old Cigar (The)* • *Entertainer (The)* • *Hotel in Amsterdam (The)* • *Inadmissible Evidence* • *Look Back in Anger* • *Luther* • *Patriot for Me* • *Sense of Detachment* • *Subject of Scandal and Concern (A)* • *Time Present* • *Under Plain Cover* • *Watch it Come Down* • *West of Suez* • *World of Paul Slickey (The)*

COLLABORATIVE PLAYS BY JOHN OSBORNE INCLUDE

Devil Inside Him (The) [with Sheila Linden] • *Epitaph for George Dillon [with Anthony Creighton]* • *Personal Enemy [with Anthony Creighton]*

THE LIFE AND WORKS OF JOHN OSBORNE

- John James Osborne was born on 12th December, 1929, the son of Thomas Godfrey Osborne, a commercial artist and Nellie Beatrice, a barmaid
- He went to Belmont College, a boarding school in Devon
- He was introduced to the theatre after he took a job tutoring young actors
- Early in his career he worked in the provinces as an actor-manager for various repertory companies, whilst at the same time trying his hand at writing
- Osborne was married five times; his first marriage to Pamela Lane ended in divorce, as did his second to Mary Ure, his third to Penelope Gilliatt and his fourth to Jill Bennett. It was his death that ended his fifth marriage to Helen Dawson, which was also his longest marriage
- In 1956, Osborne made his debut as a London actor. In the same year, *Look Back in Anger* was produced by The English Stage Company
- Osborne belonged to a group of playwrights called The Angry Young Men
- Suffering from complications brought on by diabetes, John Osborne died of heart failure on 24th December, 1994, in Shropshire, England

AND FINALLY

- He left his boarding school after hitting the headmaster
- His play, *Look Back in Anger*, was largely autobiographical
- Although primarily a playwright, Osborne also made significant contributions to TV and film

Autobiography
Almost a Gentleman
Better Class of Person

Films and TV
Entertainment (The)
Gift of Friendship (The)
Hedda Gabler [Adaptation]
Look Back in Anger
Picture of Dorian Gray (The) [Adaptation of Oscar Wilde's novel of the same name]

Place Calling Itself Rome (A) [Adaptation of Shakespeare's Coriolanus]
Right Prospectus (The)
Tom Jones
Very Like a Whale

Luigi Pirandello, 1867–1936
Italian

PLAYS BY LUIGI PIRANDELLO INCLUDE:

Cap and Bells • Diana and Tuda • Each in His Own Way • Henry IV • Lazarus • Man and Beast and Virtue • Mountain Giants (The) • Mrs Morli, One and Two • New Colony (The) • Pleasure of Honesty (The) • Right You Are (If You Think You Are) • Six Characters in Search of an Author • Life I Gave You (The) • To Clothe the Naked • To Find Oneself • Tonight We Improvise • When Somebody is Somebody

THE LIFE AND WORKS OF LUIGI PIRANDELLO

- On 28th June, 1867, Luigi Pirandello was born into a wealthy family in Sicily, Italy
- He studied philology at the Universities of Rome and Bonn
- In 1884, he married Antonietta Portulano, a woman from a wealthy background
- In 1897, he was made Professor of Aesthetics and Stylistics at the *Real Istituto di Magistere Femminile* in Rome, a position he held for 25 years
- Pirandello wrote a collection of novellas under the title *Novelle per un anno*; he also wrote six novels
- In 1919, his wife, who suffered from a mental disorder, was taken into a mental institution
- His wife's problems influenced Pirandello's writings, which focused on the changeable nature of the human personality
- Mussolini was a supporter of Pirandello's writings
- In 1934, Luigi Pirandello won the Nobel Prize for Literature
- Luigi Pirandello died on December 10th, 1936, in Rome

AND FINALLY ...

- He wrote over 50 plays

Alan Plater, 1935–
British

PLAYS BY ALAN PLATER INCLUDE

All Credit to the Lads • And a Little Love Besides • Blonde Bombshells of 1943 • Close the Coalhouse Door [music by Alex Glasgow] • Going Home • I Thought I Heard a Rustling • Last Days of the Empire [music by John Dankworth] • On Your Way Riley • Peggy for You • See the Pretty Lights • Simon Says • Sweet Sorrow • Tales from the Backyard • Ted's Cathedral • Trinity Tales [music by Alex Glasgow]

THE LIFE AND WORKS OF ALAN PLATER

- Alan Plater was born on 15th April, 1935, in Jarrow-on-Tyne, England
- He was brought up in Hull and initially trained as an architect in Newcastle
- In 1958, he married Shirley Johnson, with whom he went on to have three children. They divorced in 1985
- In 1961, Alan Plater became a professional writer
- He received an Honorary degree from the University of Hull in 1985
- In 1986, he married Shirley Rubenstein
- In 1991, Plater was appointed President of the Writers' Guild of Great Britain, a position he held until 1995
- In 1997, he was awarded an Honorary degree from the University of Northumbria in Newcastle
- In 2005, Alan Plater was awarded a CBE in the Queen's New Year's Honours List for his services to drama

AND FINALLY

- When all of Alan's work is put together – theatre, television, film, radio, novels, journalistic articles – the sum total of his artistic credits exceed 200

J.B. (John Boynton) Priestley, 1894–1984
British

PLAYS BY J.B. PRIESTLEY INCLUDE

An Inspector Calls • Dangerous Corner Desert Highway • Eden End • Glass Cage (The) • Good Companions (The) [with Edward Knoblock, from his own novel] •

I Have Been Here Before • Johnson Over Jordan • Linden Tree (The) • Music at Night • Scandalous Affair of Mr Kettle and Mrs Moon (The) • Summer Day's Dream • They Came to a City • Time and the Conways • When We Are Married

THE LIFE AND WORKS OF J.B. PRIESTLEY

- Jonathan Priestley was born on 13th September, 1894, in Bradford, in the North of England – he was known as Jack, as was often the case with 'Johns' born at that time
- His father was Jonathan Priestley and his mother, Emma Holt
- In 1896, his mother died at just 31 years of age
- In 1910, Priestley left school to work for a wool firm; it was at this time that he started writing and adopted the name John Boynton Priestley
- In 1914, World War One broke out and Priestley enlisted in the army, seeing active service in France
- Priestley went up to Cambridge on an officer's grant in 1919
- In 1921, he married Pat Tempest
- 1922 was the year in which Priestley moved to London as a freelance writer, also the year in which his two daughters were born
- Priestley's father died in 1924
- Priestley married Jane Wyndham-Lewis in 1926 after Pat's death and they went on to have two daughters and one son together
- In 1933, Priestley formed his own theatrical production company and there followed a very active period of writing, producing and broadcasting
- In 1953, Priestley divorced his second wife and married Jacquetta Hawkes, with whom he wrote *Dragon's Mouth*
- In 1957, he helped to form the Campaign for Nuclear Disarmament (C.N.D.)
- He was granted the Freedom of the City of Bradford in 1973
- In 1977, he was awarded the Order of Merit
- John Boynton Priestley died on 14th August,1984

AND FINALLY

- J.B. Priestley wasn't just a playwright, he was also a scriptwriter, broadcaster, novelist and essayist

Terence Rattigan, 1911–1977
British

PLAYS BY TERENCE RATTIGAN INCLUDE

Adventure Story • After the Dance • Cause Célèbre • Deep Blue Sea (The) • Flare Path • French Without Tears • Love in Idleness • Ross: A Dramatic Portrait • Separate Tables • Sleeping Prince (The) • Variations on a Theme • While the Sun Shines • Who is Sylvia • Winslow Boy (The)

THE LIFE AND WORKS OF TERENCE RATTIGAN

- Terence Rattigan was born on 10th June, 1911, in London; he had one brother, Brian
- His father, Frank, was a qualified Arabic speaker
- During Rattigan's early years, the family were constantly travelling from one country to another – Egypt, Gibraltar, Malta, Marseilles and Morocco
- He attended Sandroyd, a preparatory boarding school in Surrey, where he developed an all-consuming interest in theatre
- In 1925 he continued his education at Harrow Public School
- In 1930 he went up to Trinity College, Oxford, where he was able to mix with others just as passionate about theatre as he
- He wrote his first play, entitled *First Episode*, in 1933
- His 1936 play, *French Without Tears*, brought Rattigan success and also considerable wealth
- In 1940, when Britain was at war with Germany, he joined the Royal Air Force
- In 1942, he wrote a play about his experiences in the services entitled *Flare Path*
- In 1947, his play *The Winslow Boy*, which was later to become synonymous with the name Terence Rattigan, won The Ellen Terry Best Play Award
- In 1952, his father, Frank, died of a stroke and so he bought his country house in Sunningdale, which backed onto Rattigan's favourite golf course
- In 1957, his play, *Variation on a Theme*, was the first play in which he openly addressed his homosexuality, thus allowing him to become more open and truthful about his personal life
- Rattigan was diagnosed with Leukaemia and later decided to leave England for Bermuda
- In 1971, Terence Rattigan was knighted for services to theatre
- He died on 30th November, 1977, in Hamilton, Bermuda

AND FINALLY

- Terence Rattigan was a renowned craftsman in the art of playwriting at a time when such a craftsmanship was not appreciated; sadly, as a result, he was often to be left out in the critical cold
- His father disapproved of his theatrical leanings but agreed to give him £200 a year for two years whilst he tried to make a success of writing, but only on the understanding that if after two years he failed, he would find a more secure profession. After a few months, however, Terence was a success
- He had several screenplays to his credit including film versions of *The Winslow Boy* and *Separate Tables*; he also wrote the screenplays for *The Yellow Rolls Royce* and *Goodbye, Mr Chips* (1969)

Willy Russell, 1947–
British

PLAYS BY WILLY RUSSELL INCLUDE

Blood Brothers [musical] • *Breezeblock Park* • *Educating Rita* • *John, Paul, George, Ringo and … Bert* • *Keep Your Eyes Down* • *One for the Road* • *Our Day Out [musical play]* • *Sam O'Shanker* • *Shirley Valentine* • *Stags and Hens* • *Tam Lin*

THE LIFE AND WORKS OF WILLY RUSSELL

- Willy Russell was born in Liverpool in 1947
- He left school – where he was in the D stream – with only one 'O' Level to his name
- He became a hairdresser, later returning to college in order to become a teacher
- Initially, Willy Russell wrote songs
- His first play, *Keep Your Eyes Down*, was produced in 1971
- *John, Paul, George, Ringo and … Bert* was his 'big break', initially commissioned by the Everyman Theatre Liverpool and later transferring to the West End of London
- Willy Russell wrote the music, book and lyrics for his musical, *Blood Brothers* – which is quite unusual, there being usually at least one collaborator in such works
- His first novel was published in the year 2000

AND FINALLY

- Russell has appeared in his own production of *Blood Brothers*, playing the part of the 'Narrator'

George Bernard Shaw, 1856–1950
Anglo/Irish

PLAYS BY GEORGE BERNARD SHAW INCLUDE

Androcles and the Lion • Apple Cart (The) • Arms and the Man • Back to Methuselah • Buoyant Billions • Caesar and Cleopatra • Candida • Captain Brassbound's Conversion • Cymbeline Refinished • Dark Lady of the Sonnets (The) • Devil's Disciple (The) • Doctor's Dilemma (The) • Fanny's First Play • Farfetched Fables • Fascinating Foundling (The) • Geneva • Getting Married • Great Catherine • Heartbreak House • In Good King Charles's Golden Days • John Bull's Other Island • Major Barbara • Man and Superman • Man of Destiny (The) • Millionairess (The) • Misalliance • Mrs Warren's Profession • Music Cure (The) • O'Flaherty VC • On the Rocks • Overruled • Philanderer (The) • Press Cuttings • Pygmalion • Saint Joan • Shewing-up of Blanco Posnet • Simpletons of the Unexpected Isles • Too True to be Good • Village Wooing • Why She Would Not • Widowers' Houses • You Never Can Tell

THE LIFE AND WORKS OF GEORGE BERNARD SHAW

- George Bernard Shaw was born in Dublin on 26th July, 1856, the son of George Carr Shaw and Lucinda Elizabeth Gurly
- In 1885, Shaw's father died and it was his father's previously unhealthy relationship with alcohol that prompted George into his clean living attitude to life; he neither smoked nor drank and was a vegetarian
- In 1873, Shaw's mother left Ireland for London, taking with her his sister, Lucy
- He worked for a land agent's office from the age of 15 until 1876, when he joined his mother and sister in London
- In London, he became a theatre and music critic as well as a prominent member of The Fabian Society (a political society which is left-of-centre)
- He began his writing career by writing music, drama critiques and novels
- In 1898, Shaw married the wealthy Charlotte Payne-Townshend
- In 1906, they moved to village of Ayot St. Lawrence in Hertfordshire, where they lived until Charlotte's death
- George Bernard Shaw was a great orator and a champion of the ordinary man; he supported many causes, the abolition of private property and a change in the voting system being just two of them
- He died on 2nd November, 1950

AND FINALLY

- Shaw's complete works fill no less than 36 volumes
- Initially an enthusiastic cyclist, after the Turn of the Century he turned instead to motoring
- After accepting the Nobel Prize for Literature in 1926, he put all the prize money into a Trust Fund for the translation of Swedish writing

Sam Shepard, 1943– American

PLAYS BY SAM SHEPARD INCLUDE

Buried Children • Cowboys • Curse of the Starving Class • Fool for Love • God of Hell (The) • Kicking a Dead Horse • La Turista • Late Henry Moss (The) • Lie of the Mind (A) • Rock Garden (The) • Seduced • Simpatico • States of Shock • Suicide in B-Flat • Tooth of Crime (The) • True West

THE LIFE AND WORKS OF SAM SHEPARD

- The eldest of three children, he was born Samuel Shepard Rogers on 5th Nov, 1943, in Ft Sheridan, Illinois
- Much of his childhood was spent in multi-cultural Duarte, California
- Shepard started acting and writing in high school
- He studied agriculture at Mount Antonio Junior College for just one year
- Shepard then joined the Bishop's Company Repertory Players touring with them during the years 1962–1963, later moving to New York
- *La Turista* was Shepard's first full-length play
- In 1969, Shepard married O-Lan Jones, with whom he had one son; they divorced in 1984
- From 1974 until 1984, Shepard was the playwright in residence for the Magic Theatre in San Francisco
- In 1986, he was inducted into the American Academy of Arts and Letters and, in 1994, he was inducted into the Theatre Hall of Fame
- Shepard has lived with Jessica Lange since the early 1980s; they have one son and a daughter

AND FINALLY

- Sam Shepard has also appeared in approximately 50 films and numerous stage plays, in what can only be described as an extensive and successful acting career
- As well as writing for the stage, Shepard has also written for the big screen and directed for both

Film Works Include:
Don't Come Knocking
Far North
Fool for Love
Me and My Brother [co-writers Robert Frank, Allen Ginsberg and Peter Orlovsky]
Paris, Texas
Renaldo and Clara [co-writer Bob Dylan]
Savage/Love
Silent Tongue
Tongues

Books Include:
Cruising Paradise
Great Dream of Heaven
Hawk Moon
Motel Chronicles
Rolling Thunder Logbook

R.C. Sherriff, 1896–1975
British

PLAYS BY R.C. SHERRIFF INCLUDE

Badgers Green • *Home at Seven* • *Journey's End* • *Long Sunset (The)* • *Miss Mabel St Helena (in collaboration with Jeanne de Casalls)* • *White Carnation (The)* • *Windfall*

THE LIFE AND WORKS OF R.C. SHERRIFF

- R.C. Sherriff was born Robert Cedric Sherriff on 6th June, 1896
- He was educated at Kingston Grammar School and later at New College, Oxford
- He served as an Army Captain in the East Surrey Regiment during the First World War
- After the war, Sherriff joined his father's insurance business – where he had temporarily worked before the outbreak of war. He stayed with the business working as a claims adjuster for 10 years
- Sherriff was interested in amateur dramatics and it was this interest that encouraged him to try his hand at writing
- He wrote short plays for Kingston Rowing Club – to raise money for a new boat

- Written in 1928 and published in 1929, *Journey's End* was his seventh play and, based on his experiences in the war, it was the stage play which was to bring him the most recognition
- *Journey's End* was first performed by the Incorporated Stage Society at the Apollo Theatre, with 21-year-old Laurence Olivier in the lead role of Stanhope; it was given just one Sunday evening performance
- *Journey's End* then went on to run for two years at the Savoy Theatre, London; its success enabled Sherriff to become a full-time writer
- His autobiography, *No Leading Lady*, was published in 1969
- 1972 saw a successful London revival of *Journey's End*
- Sherriff lived in a house called 'Rosebriars' in Esher, Surrey, until his death on 13th November, 1975

AND FINALLY

- R.C. Sherriff also wrote many screenplays, including:

Dam Busters (The)
Four Feathers (The)
Goodbye, Mr Chips (1939)
Invisible Man (The)
Lady Hamilton
No Highway
Odd Man Out
Quartet

Neil Simon, 1927– American

PLAYS BY NEIL SIMON INCLUDE

Barefoot in the Park • *Biloxi Blues* • *Brighton Beach Memoirs* • *Broadway Bound* • *California Suite* • *Chapter Two* • *Dinner Party (The)* • *Fools* • *45 Seconds from Broadway* • *Gingerbread Lady (The)* • *God's Favourite* • *Good Doctor (The)* • *I Ought to Be in Pictures* • *Jake's Women* • *Last of the Red Hot Lovers (The)* • *Laughter on the 23rd Floor* • *Little Me [musical]* • *London Suite* • *Lost in Yonkers* • *Odd Couple (The)* • *Plaza Suite* • *Prisoner of Second Avenue (The)* • *Promises, Promises [musical]* • *Proposals* • *Rumours* • *Star-Spangled Girl (The)* • *Sunshine Boys (The)* • *Sweet Charity [musical]* • *They're Playing Our Song*

COLLABORATIVE PLAYS BY NEIL SIMON INCLUDE

Come Blow Your Horn [with Danny Simon]

THE LIFE AND WORKS OF NEIL SIMON

- Marvin Neil Simon was born on 4th July, 1927, the second son of Irving Simon, a salesman, and his wife, Mamie
- He was born in Manhattan and raised in the Bronx
- He studied at New York University and the University of Denver
- Simon began his writing career in the 1950s as a television sketch writer
- By the 1960s, Simon was writing for Broadway
- He married Joan, a dancer, in 1953 with whom he had two daughters; Joan died 20 years later
- His second marriage to Marsha Mason inspired his play, *Chapter Two*, which dramatises the grief of a newly married man attempting to restart his life after the death of his previous wife
- After his divorce from Marshall he went on to marry his third wife, Diane Lander, whom he later divorced before remarrying her
- He adopted Diane's daughter, Bryn
- His fifth – and wife to date – is Elaine Joyce
- Simon has continually drawn upon his own life experiences to create his master-pieces

AND FINALLY

- It was Simon's older brother, Danny, who was the inspiration for one of his most successful plays – *The Odd Couple*. After his divorce, Danny moved in with another divorced man and began writing the story himself, eventually handing it over to his brother to make it into the smash hit it later became, as a stage play, a film and a TV series
- Simon is hailed by many as one of – and by some as 'the' – most successful American playwrights of the Twentieth/Twenty-First Centuries

Peter Terson, 1932–
British

PLAYS BY PETER TERSON INCLUDE

Apprentices (The) • *Ballad of Artificial Mash (The)* • *But Fred, Freud is Dead* • *Cul de Sac* • *1861 Whitby Lifeboat Disaster (The)* • *Fuzz* • *Man Who Changed Places*

(The) • *Mighty Reservoy (The)* • *Mooney and his Caravans* • *Most Cheerful Man (The)* • *Night to Make the Angels Weep (A)* • *Pied Piper (The) [from the poem by Robert Browning and with music by Jeff Parton]* • *Prisoners of the War* • *Rattling the Railings* • *Spring-heeled Jack* • *Strippers* • *Zigger Zagger*

THE LIFE AND WORKS OF PETER TERSON

- Peter Terson was actually born Peter Patterson on 16th February, 1932, in Newcastle-upon-Tyne
- He worked as a teacher for ten years before getting his first break
- From 1966, he was Writer in Residence at The Victoria Theatre in Stoke-on-Trent
- More then 20 of his plays have premiered at The Victoria Theatre

AND FINALLY

- Peter Terson is closely associated with The National Youth Theatre

Plays for Television Include:
Fishing Party (The)
Shakespeare or Bust
Three for the Fancy

Radio Plays Include:
Madam Main Course
Mumper (The)
Poole Harbour
Top Soil of Imberley

Ben Travers, 1886–1980
British

PLAYS BY BEN TRAVERS INCLUDE

After You with the Milk • *Banana Ridge* • *Bed Before Yesterday (The)* • *Bit of a Test (A)* • *Chastity, My Brother* • *Corkers End* • *Cuckoo in the Nest (A)* • *Cup of Kindness (A)* • *Dippers (The)* • *Dirty Work* • *Malacca Linda* • *Mischief* • *Night Like This (A)* • *Nun's Veiling* • *O Mistress Mine* • *Outrageous Fortune* • *Plunder* • *Rookery Nook* • *Runaway Victory* • *She Follows Me about* • *Spotted Dick* • *Thark* • *Thekla* • *Three Graces (The) [libretto]* • *Turkey Time* • *Wild Horses*

THE LIFE AND WORKS OF BEN TRAVERS

- Ben Travers was born on the 12th November, 1886, in Hendon, London
- He was educated at Charterhouse, Godalming, Surrey
- After leaving Charterhouse – apparently by mutual consent – he spent several years working in commerce
- In 1911, he joined the publishing firm of John Lane – founder of Bodley Head
- During the First World War, Travers was a Squadron Commander in the RNAS and the RAF
- In 1925, he became the 'House Dramatist' for the Aldwych Theatre London, a position he held until 1933
- At the start of the Second World War, he rejoined the RAF as a Squadron Leader
- In addition to his successful stage plays, he also wrote five novels, two volumes of his autobiography and a book on cricket
- In 1976, Ben Travers received the CBE in the Queen's Birthday Honours
- On 18th December, 1980, Ben Travers died in London

AND FINALLY

- Like many other thespians, Ben Travers had a life-long love affair with cricket and was Vice President of Somerset County Cricket Club. After his death, at the age of 94, the title of his book on cricket was changed from, *94 Not Out* to *94 Declared!*
- Charterhouse, where Travers was educated, now has a theatre named after him
- His screenplays include *Foreign Affairs, Lady in Danger, Pot Luck* and *Uncle Silas*; most of his 1930s and 1940s farces were also filmed

Arnold Wesker, 1932–
British

PLAYS BY ARNOLD WESKER INCLUDE

Annie Wobbler • Blood Libel • Caritas [a play and an opera with music by Robert Saxton] • Chicken Soup with Barley • Chips with Everything • Circles of Perception • Denial • Four Portraits of – Mothers • Four Seasons (The) • Friends (The) • Groupie • I'm Talking about Jerusalem • Journalists (The) • Kitchen (The) • Lady Othello • Letter to a Daughter [a play for six songs with music by Benjamin Till] • Longitude • Love Letters on Blue Paper • Menace • Men Die Women Survive • Mistress (The) • Nottingham Captain (The) • Old Ones (The) • One More Ride on the Merry-Go-Round • Phoenix Phoenix Burning Bright • Roots • Shylock • Sullied Hands • Their Very Own and Golden City • Whatever Happened to Betty Lemon • When God Wanted a Son • Wild Spring • Yardsale

THE LIFE AND WORKS OF ARNOLD WESKER

- Arnold Wesker was born on 24th May, 1932, in Stepney, in the East End of London
- His father was a Russian-Jewish tailor and his mother was of Hungarian-Jewish extraction
- During the war, Wesker was evacuated a number of times, always nagging to return to London where he experienced the worst of the Blitz
- In 1948, he was offered a place at the Royal Academy of Dramatic Art (RADA) but, unable to secure a financial grant, was forced to turn down the offer and, instead, take on a variety of jobs, including kitchen porter and pastry cook
- Wesker served his compulsory 18-months National Service in the RAF, an experience he recreated in his play, *Chips with Everything*
- In 1952, Wesker met his future wife, Doreen (Dusty) Bicker, whilst working in The Bell Hotel in Norwich where she was a waitress
- After working for eight months in Paris, he was able to pay for a six-month course at The London School of Film Technique
- His first performed play was *Chicken Soup with Barley* which opened at The Belgrade Theatre in Coventry in 1958, before transferring to The Royal Court in London and for which he was awarded a bursary from the Arts Council of Great Britain
- In 1961, Wesker played a leading role in the Committee of 100's demonstrations against the use of nuclear weapons; together with Bertrand Russell and others, he was sentenced to a month in prison
- He was the artistic director of Centre 42, a cultural movement for popularising the arts, which he co-founded with other artists
- In 1989, Wesker received an Honorary Degree (D. Lit.) from the University of East Anglia
- In 1992, BBC TV broadcast a new production of *Roots* in honour of Wesker's 60th birthday
- In 1995, he received his second Honorary Degree, this time from Queen Mary and Westfield College, London
- In 1997, he was honoured for a third time as a Doctor of Humane Letters from Denison University, Ohio
- In 1999, Texas University purchased Arnold Wesker's vast archives of 100 boxes
- In 2006, he received a knighthood

AND FINALLY

- At the age of 13 he wrote, directed and acted in a school play
- He has written more than 40 plays, four volumes of short stories, two volumes of essays, a book on journalism, a children's book, scripts for TV, radio and film, journalistic pieces and poetry, in addition to other writing

- As a teenager, he learnt book-keeping, typing and shorthand
- He is most well known as the author of *The Trilogy* which includes *Chicken Soup with Barley, Roots* and *I'm Talking About Jerusalem*, of which *Roots* remains the most celebrated – however, it is his play, *The Kitchen*, which is the most performed

Thornton Wilder, 1897–1975
American

PLAYS BY THORNTON WILDER INCLUDE

Angel That Troubled the Waters (The) • *Childhood* • *Happy Journey to Trenton and Camden (The)* • *Infancy* • *Long Christmas Dinner (The)* • *Love and How to Cure It* • *Merchant of Yonkers (The)* • *Our Town* • *Pullman Car Hiawatha* • *Queens of France* • *Russian Princess (The)* • *Skin of our Teeth (The)* • *Someone from Assisi* • *Such Things Happen Only in Books* • *Trumpet Shall Sound (The)*

THE LIFE AND WORKS OF THORNTON WILDER

- Thornton Niven Wilder was born in Madison, Wisconsin on 17th April, 1897, the son of Amos Parker Wilder and Isabella Niven Wilder
- His twin brother having died at birth, he was the second child in a family of five children
- He had an older brother, Amos, and three younger sisters, Charlotte, Isabel and Janet
- The Wilder family were a multi-talented and intellectual family and Thornton began writing when he was just a child
- He was educated at Yale and Princeton Universities
- After University, he studied archaeology in Rome
- From 1930 until 1937, he taught dramatic literature and then classics at the University of Chicago
- From 1942 until 1945, he served with the Army Air Force Intelligence in North Africa and Italy
- In 1957, he was awarded the German Peace Prize
- In 1963, he was awarded the Presidential Medal of Freedom
- Thornton Wilder died on 7th December, 1975, at his home in Hamden, Connecticut

AND FINALLY

• Thornton Wilder was awarded the Pulitzer Prize in both fiction and drama

Books Include:
Bridge of San Luis Rey (The)
Cabala (The)
Eighth Day (The)
Heaven's My Destination
Ides of March (The)
Theophilus North
Woman of Andros (The)

Tennessee Williams, 1911–1983
American

PLAYS BY TENNESSEE WILLIAMS INCLUDE

Battle of Angels • *Camino Real* • *Cat on a Hot Tin Roof* • *Clothes for a Summer Hotel* • *Glass Menagerie (The)* • *Gnädiges Fräulein (The)* • *Kingdom of the Earth* • *Lovely Sunday for Creve Coeur (A)* • *Milk Train Doesn't Stop Here Anymore (The)* • *Night of the Iguana* • *Orpheus Descending* • *Outcry* • *Period of Adjustment* • *Red Devil Battery Sign (The)* • *Rose Tattoo (The)* • *Small Craft Warnings* • *Something Cloudy, Something Clear* • *Streetcar Named Desire (A)* • *Suddenly Last Summer* • *Summer and Smoke* • *Sweet Bird of Youth* • *27 Wagons Full of Cotton* • *Vieux Carré*

THE LIFE AND WORKS OF TENNESSEE WILLIAMS

• He was born Thomas Lanier Williams III on 26th March, 1911, in Columbus, Mississippi, one of three children born to Cornelius Williams, a salesman, and Edwina Dakin Williams, the daughter of a minister. He had an older sister and younger brother
• Williams suffered ill health as a child and, as result, became very close to his sister, Rose, and their nurse, Ozzie
• He was aged 16 when he won third prize and received $5 for an essay he wrote called, 'Can a Good Wife Be a Good Sport?' which was published in *Smart Set*
• Before embarking on his successful writing career, he worked at the International Shoe Company
• He graduated form the University of Iowa in 1938

151

- He adopted the name Tennessee as his pen name – taken from the state where his father was born and from his own college nickname
- In 1943, his beloved sister Rose had a prefrontal lobotomy; doctors believed this would cure her of dementia, the consequence being that Williams suffered a lifetime of guilt at having not prevented the surgery
- His first play, *Cairo, Shanghai, Bombay* was initially produced in Memphis, heralding the true start of his writing career
- During the late 1950s and 1960s, Williams was beset with heartache; the death of his father in 1957 sent him into psychoanalysis and he became dependent on alcohol and drugs. Then the death of his long-time companion, Frank Merlo, in the early 1960s, sent him spiralling into depression and, sadly, he spent some months confined to a mental hospital – but he never stopped writing
- Tennessee Williams died on 5th February, 1983, at the Hotel Elysée, New York

AND FINALLY

- The cause of Tennessee Williams' death is said to be the fact that he choked on the cap of a medicine bottle
- Prolific in the extreme, Tennessee Williams wrote 25 full-length plays, numerous short plays and screenplays, two novels, a novella, 60 short stories, over 100 poems and an autobiography

August Wilson, 1945–2005
American

PLAYS BY AUGUST WILSON INCLUDE

Fences • Gem of the Ocean • Jitney • Joe Turner's Come and Gone • King Hedley II • Ma Rainey's Black Bottom • Piano Lesson (The) • Radio Golf • Seven Guitars • Two Trains Running

THE LIFE AND WORKS OF AUGUST WILSON

- In 1945, Wilson was born Frederick August Kittel in Pittsburgh, Pennsylvania, the fourth of seven children
- His father was Frederick August Kittel, his mother Daisy Wilson
- He grew up in poverty in the Hill district of Pittsburgh; this neighbourhood later became the setting for most of his plays

- In 1960, Wilson dropped out of school when a teacher accused him of plagiarising a paper on Napoleon
- He then became self-educated by visiting Carnegie Library
- He enlisted in the army for three years, but left after one and then had a series of casual jobs: short-order cook, porter, gardener and dishwasher
- In the late 1960s, he joined the Black Aesthetic movement
- August Wilson became the co-founder, with Rob Penny, of Black Horizons Theatre in Pittsburgh
- In 1984, *Ma Rainey's Black Bottom* opened on Broadway to critical acclaim and financial success
- A victim of racial abuse himself, Wilson left us a literary legacy of a 10-play cycle with each play is set in a different decade in the Twentieth Century and each depicting the African–American experience, these plays became known as *The Pittsburgh Cycle*
- August Wilson died of liver cancer in 2005

AND FINALLY

- Shortly after his death, the Virginia Theatre on Broadway was renamed the August Wilson Theatre in his honour
- Wilson once told the *Star Tribune* that he has one simple goal:

To put up on stage, in all them big lights, the majesty and nobility of black people, ordinary people, who everybody thinks of as low or worth nothing.

[reproduced by kind permission from an article by
Rohan Preston in the *Minneapolis-St. Paul Star Tribune*]

Chapter Four

The Bard

ASK ANYONE whether they have ever heard of a man called William Shakespeare and the answer will almost be certainly 'Yes', with the majority having studied him to a greater or lesser degree at school. Now, exactly how much 'sank in' at school would be dependent upon the enthusiasm and inspiration with which he was taught. So – in case you weren't listening in class – here is a brief background to the man who continues to live centuries after his death.

Life in the time of William Shakespeare

Whatever our age, we have all been subjected, by our parents, to the phrase, 'in my day it was so different'. We know, of course, that the times in which we live influence the creative output and so, to understand literature, we must have a basic knowledge and understanding of the period in which the playwright lived, together with a basic knowledge and understanding of the period featured in the actual writings. And this was never more important than in the case of William Shakespeare, the most renowned writer of all time.

ELIZABETHAN ENGLAND

So what was life like in Elizabethan England? Well, to start with, everything was smaller. The towns were smaller; the villages were smaller, so too were buildings and even the people. There was less money and only limited opportunities to travel and discover new ways of life, for there were no railroads, motorways or modes of personal transport except for the more wealthy. This meant that many people lived and died in the same place, having never ventured further that the second field on the right.

TRAVEL

Anyone who wanted to travel around England at this time had to have a licence to be allowed to do so and travelling to another country could only be done with permission from the reigning monarch. This was to prevent the spread of disease, especially the feared Bubonic Plague. Anyone who preferred to spend their life travelling – such as peddlers and **actors** – were considered untrustworthy and the most likely of society to commit a crime. At the very least, they were scathingly looked on as potential carriers of the Bubonic Plague, otherwise known as the Black Death.

THE LAW, CRIME AND PUNISHMENT

Many crimes in this era were the result of poverty and the desperation of the poor. Begging was a crime and those caught begging could be beaten, sent to prison or even hanged for their crime.

ENTERTAINMENT

Rather than going to the theatre, theatre generally came to the people, especially in the provinces where professional troupes of actors visited the towns with their entertainments. Aside from that, families made their own entertainment and board games were popular; in addition, the men would play ball games or maybe even skittles whilst the women joined together in the traditional crafts of spinning and sewing.

EDUCATION

From the age of five to seven years, boys were sent to petty school (also known as Dame Schools – as they were run by the ladies of the town); children of noble birth were generally taught at home by tutors from the age of seven to 14 years. Those of a lower class went to Grammar Schools where they were taught the basics of Latin and English Grammar; they would also study the works of the classical writers such as Plautus, Virgil and Seneca. The school days were longer and the holidays shorter; children learnt by rote and their progress was constantly monitored by never-ending examinations. School was tough and corporal punishment was considered normal.

SHAKESPEARE'S LONDON

London in Shakespeare's day was very different to the London we know today. There was no London Underground or London Eye; no busy Oxford Street to negotiate in search of the latest fashions. But London, nevertheless, was a vibrant and lively city, the home of painters, writers and actors; theatre too was becoming an integral part of life in the city where play-going was a regular part of life for all walks of society.

THEATRE IN LONDON

Around the year 1588, William Shakespeare began working in London, just at the time when theatre was thriving; in fact, between 1567 and 1622, nine new outdoor playhouses were built. As far as actors were concerned, there were the Boy Companies and the Adult Companies; William Shakespeare was a part of The Lord Chamberlain's Men, later called The King's Men.

Theatrical performances at this time were very different, and many would say rather more entertaining. In Elizabethan times, the actors and the audience always interacted; try that today as a member of an audience and you would probably be asked to leave the theatre!

The first proper theatre as we would know it was 'The Theatre', built in Shoreditch in 1576 and the owner was James Burbage. The most famous Elizabethan playhouse at this time was The Globe Theatre, which was built by the company in which Shakespeare had a stake and which could hold several thousand people. Women were not permitted to act as it was not considered to be a credible profession and women who went to see a play often wore a mask as a disguise.

ELIZABETHAN AUDIENCES

Unlike today, performances took place during the day because, of course, there was no electric stage lighting for the Elizabethans.

The poorer members of the audience were referred to as groundlings and would pay one penny to stand in the pit of the Globe Theatre; the gentry, however, would pay to sit in the galleries – on cushions – while the rich nobles would actually have a chair and sit on the stage itself. Money to watch a performance was collected in a series of boxes and so evolved the term 'Box Office' where we pay for and collect our tickets to watch a theatre performance today.

BUBONIC PLAGUE

The Elizabethans lived under the constant shadow of the Bubonic Plague and fear of contracting this deadly disease mentally terrorised almost everyone. Crowded environments, such as theatres, were a breeding ground for the Plaque and, therefore, posed a constant threat to Elizabethan theatre-goers.

THE LIFE OF WILLIAM SHAKESPEARE

Let's now take a look at some of the events of the world in which William Shakespeare lived; the world that was his influence and, in turn, the world upon which he was later to become an influence himself.

1564	William Shakespeare was born in the same year as Galileo, the Italian astronomer, mathematician and philosopher
1572	John Donne, possibly the greatest of the Metaphysical poets, was born
1576	The first theatre opened. It was built by James Burbage and called, quite simply, 'The Theatre'. It was dismantled after Burbage's death and the materials from it used to build the first Globe Theatre
1587	Mary Queen of Scots was beheaded
1588	Defeat of the Spanish Armada by the British
1599	The first Globe Theatre opened
1603	Queen Elizabeth I, recognised as one of the greatest advocates of the arts, expecially theatre and literature, died and King James VI of Scotland also became King James I of England
1605	The Gunpowder Plot – an attempt to blow up Parliament – was hatched
1606	Rembrandt was born
1611	The first version of the King James Bible was published
1616	William Shakespeare died

THE BIRTH OF WILLIAM SHAKESPEARE

We cannot say with absolute certainty the actual birth date of William Shakespeare because no one knows that for certain. Accurate recording of events was, in fact, not always accurate. However, what we do know is that he was born in Stratford-upon-Avon and was baptised in Holy Trinity Church on 26th April, 1564, and so, traditionally, his birthday is celebrated three days earlier on 23rd April, 1564 – St George's Day.

WILLIAM SHAKESPEARE'S PARENTS

Shakespeare's father, John Shakespeare, was a glove maker, a tanner, a wool dealer, a local property owner and a prominent figure in the town, even being elected as Mayor in 1568.

Shakespeare's mother, Mary Arden, was the daughter of a well-to-do farmer, Robert Arden, who had left her some land. Sadly, in 1576, John experienced severe financial difficulties and was forced to mortgage his wife's inheritance.

Together, they had eight children; four sons, of whom William was the eldest, and four daughters, of whom only one survived.

EDUCATION

Again, this is an area in which we can only make educated assumptions. We 'assume' he went to one of Stratford's junior schools and, from there, to the King's New School (probably around the age of about seven), where we assume he would have received a good grounding in Latin. He would probably have left school at the age of 14 or 15.

MARRIAGE AND CHILDREN

Shakespeare married Anne Hathaway in 1582, when he was 18 years old. (I suppose we could say he was her 'toy-boy' for, at the time of their marriage, she was 26, making her William's senior by eight years.) In 1583, their first child was born, a daughter whom they called Susanna and then, two years later, they had twins, Hamnet and Judith.

CAREER

We are uncertain of William's life between the birth of his twins and the early 1590s. By then, however, we do know that he was in London and that he was writing, having become a professional actor and dramatist. During his years in London, Shakespeare also became a founding member, shareholder, playwright and actor in The Lord Chamberlain's Men. The company was later renamed The King's Men and performed at court more often than any other company. Shakespeare's career in the theatre made him a very wealthy man and, later in his life, he was able to buy New Place, one of the largest properties in his home town of Stratford; this was followed by further purchases of property and land. Thus, the actor and dramatist also became a man of property.

EARLY INFLUENCES ON WILLIAM SHAKESPEARE

When Shakespeare was a child and a young man, he would have seen travelling troupes of actors visit his home town of Stratford and who knows what impressions they made upon him, or in what way they influenced his future interest in, and writings for, the theatre. Certainly, his early life in the countryside was to infiltrate his works, which are littered with references to wild flowers, animals, birds, country customs and country characters.

FAMILY HISTORY – DESCENDANTS

In 1607, Shakespeare daughter, Susanna, married a physician by the name of John Hall and they had one daughter, Elizabeth, born in 1608. His second daughter, Judith, married a vintner (a wine merchant), called Thomas Quinney in the year 1616; they had three sons: Shakespeare Quinney, who died in infancy, Richard (1618–1639) and Thomas (1620–1639). Judith's twin brother, Hamnet, died at the age of 11.

Having returned to Stratford, it was here, on 23rd April, 1616 (his presumed birthday), that William Shakespeare died, aged 52. He was buried two days later at Holy Trinity Church in Stratford.

Shakespeare 's widow, Anne, died seven years later in 1623 and was buried beside her husband. Sadly, Shakespeare's family line came to an end with the death of his granddaughter, Elizabeth, in 1670.

Shakespeare's Plays

DATE	GENRE	SYNOPSIS
All's Well That Ends Well	Comedy	Take two young people from different backgrounds and it does not bode well for a romantically happy future but, in this comedy, 'all ends well'.
		Major Characters Bertram Helena
Antony and Cleopatra	Tragedy	This is the story of the passionate and tragic love affair between a Roman General, Antony, and an Egyptian Queen, Cleopatra which, ultimately, ends in their deaths.
		Major Characters Cleopatra Mark Antony
As You Like It	Comedy	Rosalind, the daughter of a banished Duke, falls in love with Orlando, the disinherited son of one of the Duke's friends. In true Shakespearean fashion, Rosalind is forced to assume the guise of a man before the course of true love runs smoothly and the two lovers are united in marriage.
		Major Characters Orlando Rosalind
Comedy of Errors (The)	Comedy	The plot centres around twin boys, *both* confusingly called Antipholus, and their twin servants, who, again confusingly, *both* share the name of Dromio. Both sets of twins were separated in a shipwreck and a farcical play ensues when all the estranged parties find themselves in the same town.
		Major Characters Antipholus 1 Antipholus 2 Dromio 1 Dromio 2

DATE	GENRE	SYNOPSIS
Coriolanus	Tragedy	A tale of the problems caused by class distinction, problems that are only solved by the intervention of a mother, a wife and a son – but, alas, too late. **Major Characters** Aufidius Coriolanus
Cymbeline	History	A complicated story of true love. Imogen is the daughter of Cymbeline, the King of England. She marries a poor man, whom her father then banishes to Rome. But she remains true to her husband, despite plots to prove otherwise, and the pair are eventually reunited. **Major Characters** Cymbeline Imogen Posthumus
Edward III	History	England and France clash over the French Throne. King Edward believes that he is the rightful heir to the throne; the French dispute this as his claim is made through his mother's line of inheritance and they claim that inheritance can only pass through a male line. **Major Characters** Artois Countess of Salisbury King Edward III Prince Edward (The Black Prince)
Hamlet	Tragedy	The King of Denmark is dead and has been succeeded by his brother, Claudius, who has also married his brother's widow, Gertrude. Hamlet, Gertrude's son, is visited by the ghost of his dead father who tells him that he was murdered by Claudius. Hamlet plots to revenge his father's death and, to help him achieve this, he feigns madness. In pursuit of his aim, a total of six people die, including Hamlet, so I guess it deserves to be classed as a tragedy! The following characters meet their death in the course of the play: Polonius (Lord Chamberlain & Ophelia's father) Ophelia (who loves Hamlet) Laertes (Polonius' son)

DATE	GENRE	SYNOPSIS

Gertrude (Hamlet's mother)
Claudius (Gertrude's husband; Hamlet's stepfather)
Hamlet

Major Characters
Claudius
Ghost of Hamlet's Father
Hamlet
Ophelia

| *Henry IV* Part I | History | After deposing King Richard II, Henry Bolingbroke ascends the throne as King Henry IV, but his guilt, and opposition from others, threaten his reign. Added to this is his concern about his wayward son, Prince Hal, who is frequenting dubious taverns with Sir John Falstaff. When the rebellion comes, Hal comes to his senses and takes his place by his father's side. |

Major Characters
Prince Hal
Sir John Falstaff

| *Henry IV* Part II | History | As the threat of civil war hangs over the country, King Henry becomes sick; he is also afraid that his son, Hal, has returned to his wayward life with Falstaff. The rebels are finally defeated and the King, on his deathbed, is reunited with his son. Hal denounces his former life and becomes Henry V. |

Major Characters
King Henry IV
Prince Henry
Sir John Falstaff

| *Henry V* | History | England and France are at war and, after the Battle of Agincourt, the French King surrenders. He then offers Henry the hand of his daughter, Katherine de Valois, in marriage and unites England and France. Peace reigns and together Katherine and Henry have a son. |

Major Characters
Henry V
Katherine

| *Henry VI* Part I | History | Henry V is dead and his young son, Henry VI, becomes King whilst, at the same time, Joan of Arc is leading the French against the English. Eventually, the |

DATE	GENRE	SYNOPSIS
		English capture Joan, along with Margaret of Anjou; Joan is burnt as a witch and King Henry marries Margaret.
		Major Characters Henry VI Joan La Pucelle (Joan of Arc)
Henry VI Part II	History	The young King returns victorious from France with his bride; behind the scenes, though, a devious Suffolk, who has influence not just at the court but over the new queen, is at work.
		Major Characters Duke of Gloucester Duke of York King Henry VI Queen Margaret
Henry VI Part III	History	The Yorkists confront the Lancastrians. Henry agrees to York's demand that he disinherits his son, Edward, Prince of Wales. Margaret vows to destroy York. There is much bloodshed before the War of the Roses finally appears to be over.
		Major Characters Henry VI Queen Margaret
Henry VIII	History	Most people know the story of Henry VIII and his wives and here Shakespeare tells the story of Katherine of Aragon and Henry's 'move' from her to Anne Boleyn.
		Major Characters Anne Boleyn Cardinal Wolsey Henry VIII Queen Katherine of Aragon
Julius Caesar	Tragedy	Brutus believes that Rome would be better off without the ambitious Julius Caesar and so plots to have him assassinated, a decision which will plunge the country into civil war.
		Major Characters Brutus Julius Caesar Mark Antony

DATE	GENRE	SYNOPSIS
King John	History	Richard the Lionheart is dead and his weak brother, John, is now King, supported by Queen Elinor, his domineering mother. There is, however, a rival claim to the throne in the form of Arthur, the son of John's dead brother, Geoffrey.

Major Characters
Constance
King John
Queen Elinor

King Lear	Tragedy	Another play of many deaths. King Lear decides to abdicate and divide his Kingdom between his three daughters. His eldest daughters are evil but fool the old man into thinking they care. His youngest is the loyal and true Cordelia, but Lear doesn't see this and disowns her. Stripped of his powers, Lear is treated badly by his elder daughters and is eventually reconciled with Cordelia.

Major Characters
Cordelia
Goneril
King Lear
Regan

Love's Labours Lost	Comedy	Four men decide that they will live for three years without worldly pleasures – including women. Based on a decision which is obviously doomed from the start, this play is, needless to say, a comedy as any situation in which even just one man made such a vow would be comedic.

Major Characters
Ferdinand, the King of Navarre
Princess of France

Macbeth	Tragedy	A chance meeting between Macbeth and three witches leads to murder and suicide as Macbeth, driven by his ambitious wife, strives to make their 'prophecies' come true.

Major Characters
Lady Macbeth
Macbeth
Three Witches (The)

DATE	GENRE	SYNOPSIS
Measure for Measure	Comedy	Vienna has fallen into immoral and corrupt ways and Claudio is sentenced to death for making his girlfriend pregnant. Claudio's sister, Isabella, tries to save her brother's life but everything in Vienna has a sexual undertone and Isabella is a novice nun.

Major Characters
Angelo
Claudio
Duke Vincentio
Isabella
Juliet

Merchant of Venice	Comedy	The greedy money-lender, Shylock, unable to retrieve money he has lent to the good man, Antonio, demands instead a pound of Antonio's flesh (as they agreed, should the need arise). Antonio's life is saved by Portia, his best friend's lover, when she says that, of course, Shylock can have the agreed pound of flesh — but not a drop of blood, as that was not in the contract — of course, this is impossible to achieve and so Antonio's life is spared.

Major Characters
Antonio
Portia
Shylock

Merry Wives of Windsor (The)	Comedy	Sir John Falstaff wreaks havoc with his insincere ways and interest in money; but eventually he gets his comeuppance when the tables are turned.

Major Characters
Mistress Ford
Mistress Page
Sir John Falstaff

Midsummer Night's Dream (A)	Comedy	Take a magic forest inhabited by fairies — one of whom, Puck, is very mischievous — put into it four lovers; add the quarrelsome King and Queen of the Fairies, stir with a magic love potion and you have a fun, Shakespearean farce.

Major Characters
Bottom
Demetrius
Helena
Hermia
Lysander

DATE	GENRE	SYNOPSIS

Oberon (King of the Fairies)
Puck
Titania (Queen of the Fairies)

Much Ado About Nothing — Comedy

This is the story of two very different sets of lovers, Benedick and Beatrice, and Hero and Claudio. Benedick and Beatrice think that they hate each other, when it is really love that is binding them together, whilst many obstacles get in the way of the true love of Hero and Claudio.

Major Characters
Beatrice
Benedick
Claudio
Hero

Othello — Tragedy

Othello is married to Desdemona, whom he loves very much. Yet, despite this, he falls victim to seeds of jealousy planted by Iago, who has a grudge against him. The result is that Desdemona dies at the hands of Othello, who then kills himself when he discovers the truth.

Major Characters
Desdemona
Iago
Othello

Pericles — History

To win the hand of the daughter of the King of Antiochus, prospective suitors must first solve a riddle set by the King; failure to do so means death. Pericles solves this riddle but it holds a terrible secret which he cannot tell and so, in fear of his life, he flees. He later marries, Thaisa, and has a daughter, Marina. But tragedy strikes and he is separated from both and is only reunited with his beautiful daughter many years later.

Major Characters
King Antiochus
Pericles
Thaisa

Richard II — History

Richard II is an intelligent but weak man who nevertheless banishes those who are a threat to him. After Richard confiscates the property of John of Gaunt – after his death – many nobles rebel. Richard

DATE	GENRE	SYNOPSIS
		signs a confession and is sent to the Tower. After the coronation of Henry IV, Richard is transferred to Pomfret Castle where he is killed.

Major Characters
Henry Bolingbroke
John of Gaunt
Richard II

Richard III	History	This is the story of Richard the hunchback, Duke of Gloucester, who becomes King Richard III by murder, killing not only his enemies but his friends and even his wife. His evil acts are finally brought to an end by the Duke of Richmond – who became Henry VII.

Major Characters
Duke of Richmond
Lady Anne
Richard III

Romeo and Juliet	Tragedy	Romeo is a Montague, whilst Juliet is a Capulet and that is the heart of the problem, for their two families are bitter enemies. When Romeo and Juliet fall in love, it is a love that is doomed from the start and ends in various deaths, including the deaths of the two young lovers.

Major Characters
Juliet Capulet
Nurse (The)
Romeo Montague

Taming of the Shrew (The)	Comedy	Everyone loves Bianca and there is no shortage of men wanting to marry her. However, her father will not let her marry until her less popular sister, Katherine, is betrothed. So Bianca's suitors pay Petruchio to court Katherine. Attracted by her large dowry, Petruchio agrees, marries her and resolves to tame her. This he does by denying her food and sleep and by constantly browbeating her. As a consequence, Katherine becomes a dutiful and respectful wife.

Major Characters
Katherine
Petruchio

DATE	GENRE	SYNOPSIS
Tempest (The)	Comedy	Prospero, the Duke of Milan, is usurped by his brother, Antonio. Together with his daughter, Miranda, Prospero is put to sea in a rotten boat, eventually landing on a far off island.
		Major Characters Aerial Alonso Caliban Miranda Prospero
Timon of Athens	Tragedy	The Athenian, Timon, is well known for his generosity but when his purse is empty and he needs help, all of his so-called friends turn their back on him and he leaves Athens, poor and disillusioned, to live as a recluse.
		Major Characters Apemantus General Alcibiades Timon
Titus Andronicus	Tragedy	Titus Andronicus returns from war with his captives. What follows is a bloody tale of revenge sought through countless murders, rape, acts of mutilation and threats of human sacrifice; this is one of Shakespeare's more bloodthirsty and disturbing plays.
		Major Characters Saturninus Titus Andronicus
Troilus and Cressida	Tragedy	Set against the background of the Trojan War, Troilus, a brother of Paris (who abducted the beautiful Helen from her Greek husband), falls in love with Cressida who eventually betrays him.
		Major Characters Cressida Priam Troilus
Twelfth Night	Comedy	Viola and her twin brother, Sebastian, are shipwrecked off the coast of Illyria, each believing the other to have drowned. Viola disguises herself as a boy – called Cesario – and enters the service of Duke Orsino, who then sends him (her) off to woo

DATE	GENRE	SYNOPSIS
		the lady Olivia on his behalf, but Olivia falls in love with the 'boy'. Viola's twin, Sebastian, arrives on the scene and so follows a series of mistaken identities, in this farcical tale until, finally, all is revealed and love triumphs.

Major Characters
Orsino
Sir Toby Belch
Viola

Two Gentlemen of Verona	Comedy	Valentine and Proteus – two gentlemen of Verona – travel to Milan to see the world, where they both fall in love with the same woman, Sylvia. But she loves Valentine and not Proteus, who has actually left behind Julia, to whom he promised to be faithful. Julia pursues Proteus and, eventually, each girl is with the right man.

Major Characters
Julia
Proteus
Sylvia
Valentine

Two Noble Kinsmen	Comedy	Palamon and Arcite ignore their hatred of the tyrannous Creon to fight for Thebes, but the battle is lost. Whilst in prison, the two cousins fall in love with Emilia. Arcite is set free and Palamon escapes; it is decided that the two will fight for Emilia and the loser will be beheaded. Arcite wins but, before the death sentence is carried out, Palamon is thrown from his horse and dies; with his last breath, he bequeaths Emilia to Palamon.

Major Characters
Arcite
Palamon

Winter's Tale (The)	Comedy	King Leontes is mistakenly convinced that his Queen, Hermione, is having an affair with the Polixenes, the King of Bohemia and that the child she is carrying is Polixenes' and not his. Hermione gives birth to a daughter, Perdita, whilst in prison. Leontes orders the baby to be taken away and abandoned in the wilderness; their young son then dies and so too Hermione. Meantime, Perdita is rescued and raised by a shepherd. It is 16 years before Leontes sees his daughter again, only to find that she is in love with Polixenes' son.

Major Characters
King Leontes
Perdita

Shakespeare's World of Words

There were some interesting and basic differences in the Tudor/Elizabethan alphabet to ours, one being that, instead of 26 letters as in our alphabet, the Tudor/Elizabethans only had 24:

- The letters 'u' and 'v' were actually the same letter, the 'u' being used only in the middle of a word and the 'v' at the beginning
- The letters 'i' and 'j' were also the same, with the letter 'j' usually being used as the capital 'I'
- There was another letter which was similar to our letter 'y' and was pronounced 'th'. That explains why 'the' looked like 'ye'
- Many words had an additional 'e' on the end

William Shakespeare was, without a doubt, a 'Wordsmith Extraordinaire'. Not only did he know how to use words in an unequalled, poetic way, but he also invented many new words that are still in use throughout the English speaking world today. In fact, more than 1700 words in common usage today are directly attributed to William Shakespeare. Of course, it is difficult to say with absolute certainty that any given individual actually invented any given word because words were often not written down until long after they were coined – and then, especially during the Renaissance period, not with a great deal of accuracy either. Few words are plucked from thin air, of course, and the roots of many can be found in the classical languages. Shakespeare's actual genius though was in his manipulation of existing words. This is how he did it. He:

i)   changed nouns into verbs
ii)   verbs into nouns
iii)   verbs into adjectives
iv)   adjectives into nouns
v)   added prefixes and suffixes
vi)   shortened words
vii)   made words from proper nouns
viii) gave new meanings to old words
ix)   changed the spellings of existing words
x)   joined two words together to make one word

Here, you will find just some of the words credited to Shakespeare, together with the Shakespearean source, so you can look it up for yourself.

INVENTED WORD	PLAY	INVENTED WORD	PLAY
A		**B**	
accused	*Richard II*	backing	*Henry IV* Part I
assassination	*Macbeth*	bedroom	*A Midsummer Night's Dream*
advertising	*Measure for Measure*	bet	*Henry IV* Part II
addiction	*Henry V*	bloodstained	*Titus Andronicus*
amazement	*King John*	birthplace	*Coriolanus*
C		**D**	
champion	*Macbeth*	dawn	*Henry V*
circumstantial	*As You Like It*	deafening	*Henry IV* Part II
compromise	*The Merchant of Venice*	dickens	*The Merry Wives of Windsor*
critic	*Love's Labour's Lost*	dislocate	*King Lear*
cater	*As You Like It*	domineering	*Love's Labour's Lost*
E		**F**	
elbow	*King Lear*	fashionable	*Troilus and Cressida*
employer	*Much Ado About Nothing*	film	*Hamlet*
engagement	*Julius Caesar*	fixture	*The Merry Wives of Windsor*
excitement	*Hamlet*	flawed	*King Lear*
eyeball	*A Midsummer Night's Dream*	frugal	*The Merry Wives of Windsor*
G		**H**	
generous	*Love's Labour's Lost*	hint	*Othello*
gossip	*The Comedy of Errors*	hobnob	*Twelfth Night*
green-eyed	*The Merchant of Venice*	humour	*Love's Labour's Lost*
grovel	*Henry VI* Part II	hurry	*The Comedy of Errors*
gust	*Titus Andronicus*	hush	*Hamlet*
I		**J**	
immediacy	*King Lear*	jaded	*Henry VI* Part II
importantly	*Cymbeline*	jet	*Titus Andronicus*
inaudible	*All's Well That Ends Well*	jig	*Love's Labour's Lost*
instinctively	*The Tempest*	judgement-day	*Henry VI* Part I
investment	*Henry IV* Part II	juiced	*Romeo and Juliet*
K		**L**	
kissing	*Love's Labour's Lost*	label	*Twelfth Night*
		lapse	*Twelfth Night*
		laughable	*The Merchant of Venice*
		lonely	*Coriolanus*
		luggage	*Henry IV* Part I
M		**N**	
madcap	*The Taming of the Shrew*	negotiate	*Much Ado About Nothing*
majestic	*Julius Caesar*	nervy	*Coriolanus*

WORD		WORD	
manager	*Love's Labour's Lost*	noiseless	*All's Well That Ends Well*
marketable	*As You Like It*	never-ending	*The Rape of Lucrece* (poem)
mimic	*A Midsummer Night's Dream*	numb	*Venus and Adonis* (poem)

O

obscene	*Love's Labour's Lost*		
obsequiously	*Richard III*		
ode	*Love's Labour's Lost*		
Olympian	*Henry VI* Part III		
outbreak	*Hamlet*		

P

pageantry	*Pericles*
partner	*Cymbeline*
pedant	*The Taming of the Shrew*
perusal	*Hamlet*
puke	*As You Like It*

Q

quarrelsome	*The Taming of the Shrew*
questioning	*As You Like It*

R

radiance	*All's Well That Ends Well*
rant	*Hamlet*
retirement	*Henry IV* Part I
rival	*A Midsummer Night's Dream*
rumination	*As You Like It*

S

sacrificial	*Timon of Athens*
scuffle	*Antony and Cleopatra*
shudder	*Timon of Athens*
skim milk	*Henry IV* Part I
swagger	*A Midsummer Night's Dream*

T

tardiness	*King Lear*
threateningly	*All's Well That Ends Well*
tightly	*The Merry Wives of Windsor*
torture	*Henry VI* Part II
traditional	*Richard III*

U

unclog	*Coriolanus*
undervalue	*The Merchant of Venice*
undress	*The Taming of the Shrew*
unmitigated	*Much Ado About Nothing*
unreal	*Macbeth*

V

varied	*Titus Andronicus*
vaulting	*Henry VI* Part II
viewless	*Measure for Measure*

W

watchdog	*The Tempest*
well-behaved	*The Merry Wives of Windsor*
widen	*Coriolanus*
wild-goose chase	*Romeo and Juliet*
worthless	*Henry VI* Part III

X

xantippe	*The Taming of the Shrew*

Y

yelping	*Henry VI* Part I

Z

zany	*Love's Labour's Lost*

171

Famous Quotes from the Works of Shakespeare

There are some sayings which are known and used by us all at some time or another and which have become an intrinsic part of the English language but, in fact, began their life as part of a Shakespearean play. Here are just some of those sayings; you will be amazed at how often you have been quoting Shakespeare, probably without even knowing it!

QUOTE	SOURCE
A horse, a horse! My kingdom for a horse!	*Richard III* Act V: Sc VI
…All that glitters is not gold.…	*The Merchant of Venice* Act II: Sc VII
All the world's a stage, And all the men and women merely players.…	*As You Like It* Act II: Sc VII
as good luck would have it.…	*The Merry Wives of Windsor* Act III: Sc V
…as merry as the day is long.	*Much Ado About Nothing* Act II: Sc I
…as merry as the day is long;.…	*King John* Act IV: Sc I

…be not afraid of greatness.
  Some are born great, some achieve greatness, and some
  have greatness thrust upon 'em.…
	Twelfth Night Act II: Sc V

Beware the ides of March	*Julius Caesar* Act I: Sc II
But, for my own part, it was Greek to me.…	*Julius Caesar* Act I: Sc II
…can one desire too much of a good thing?…	*As You Like It* Act IV: Sc I
Cowards die many times before their deaths;.…	*Julius Caesar* Act II: Sc II
…delays have dangerous ends.…	*Henry VI* Part I Act III: Sc III
Et tu, Brute?…	*Julius Caesar* Act III: Sc I
For ever and a day.	*As You Like It* Act IV: Sc I
Friends, Romans, Countrymen, lend me your ears; I come to bury Caesar, not to praise him…	*Julius Caesar* Act III: Sc II
Get thee to a nunnery…	*Hamlet* Act III: Sc I
Good night, Good night! Parting is such sweet sorrow	*Romeo and Juliet* Act II: Sc I

Have more than thou showest,
  Speak less than thou knowest,
  Lend less than thou owest,
	King Lear Act I: Sc IV

…He hath eaten me out of house and home.…	*Henry IV* Part II Act II: Sc I
…he will give the devil his due.	*Henry IV* Part I Act I: Sc II
…I am a man More sinned against than sinning.	*King Lear* Act III: Sc II
I cannot tell what the dickens his name is.…	*The Merry Wives of Windsor* Act III: Sc II
I will wear my heart upon my sleeve.…	*Othello* Act I: Sc I

QUOTE	SOURCE
If music be the food of love, play on,	*Twelfth Night* Act I: Sc I
In my mind's eye....	*Hamlet* Act I: Sc II
...Is this a dagger which I see before me, The handle toward my hand?	*Macbeth* Act II: Sc I
...It is a wise father that knows his own child....	*The Merchant of Venice* Act II: Sc II
...It is the green-eyed monster,....	*Othello* Act III: Sc III
...Love looks not with the eyes, but with the mind....	*A Midsummer Night's Dream* Act I: Sc I
...Neither a borrower nor a lender be....	*Hamlet* Act I: Sc III
Nothing will come of nothing....	*King Lear* Act I: Sc I
...not that I loved Caesar less, but that I loved Rome more....	*Julius Caesar* Act III: Sc II
Now is the winter of our discontent....	*Richard III* Act I: Sc I
O Romeo, Romeo, wherefore art thou Romeo?	*Romeo and Juliet* Act II: Sc I
...Off with his head....	*Richard III* Act III: Sc IV
Once more unto the breach, dear friends, once more....	*Henry V* Act III Sc I
Out, damned spot:	*Macbeth* Act V: Sc I
...The better part of valour is discretion....	*Henry IV* Part I Act V: Sc IV
...The course of true love never did run smooth....	*A Midsummer Night's Dream* Act I: Sc I
The first thing we do, let's kill all the lawyers	*Henry VI* Part II Act IV: Sc II
...The fool doth think he is wise, but the wise man knows himself to be a fool....	*As You Like It* Act V: Sc I
The lady protests too much, methinks.	*Hamlet* Act III: Sc II
...The Play's the thing Wherein I'll catch the conscience of a king	*Hamlet* Act II: Sc II
The quality of mercy is not strained....	*The Merchant of Venice* Act IV: Sc I
...This above all – to thine own self be true....	*Hamlet* Act I: Sc III
...This is the short and the long of it....	*The Merry Wives of Windsor* Act II: Sc II
This was the noblest Roman of them all....	*Julius Caesar* Act V: Sc V
Though this be madness, yet there is method in 't....	*Hamlet* Act II: Sc II
'Tis neither here nor there	*Othello* Act IV: Sc III
To be, or not to be: that is the question:....	*Hamlet* Act III: Sc I
...Tomorrow, and tomorrow, and tomorrow....	*Macbeth* Act V: Sc V
True is it that we have seen better days....	*As You Like It* Act II: Sc VII
...We are such stuff As dreams are made on...	*The Tempest* Act IV: Sc I
...We have seen better days	*Timon of Athens* Act IV: Sc II

QUOTE	SOURCE
…What light through yonder window breaks?	*Romeo and Juliet* Act II: Sc I
…What's done is done.	*Macbeth* Act III: Sc II
…What's in a name? That which we call a rose By any other name would smell as sweet….	*Romeo and Juliet* Act II: Sc I
When shall we three meet again, In thunder, lightning, or in rain?	*Macbeth* Act I: Sc I
Why, then, the world's mine oyster….	*The Merry Wives of Windsor* Act II: Sc II

Other Works by Shakespeare

William Shakespeare is recognised the world over as a literary genius, which is all the more remarkable when one realises that his parents were probably illiterate and he himself never went to university. In general, he is known for his plays and yet he also wrote poetry – a more reputable genre at the time – and sonnets. In that period, it was far more fashionable to write poetry, and his poetry gave him a credibility which his plays could not. How ironic is that?

Poems Attributed to William Shakespeare, include
1. *Lover's Complaint (A)*
2. *Phoenix and the Turtle*
3. *Rape of Lucrece (The)*
4. *Venus and Adonis*

Sonnets attributed to William Shakespeare
Sonnets are lyric poems, 14 lines in length, traditionally written in iambic pentameter – that is, in lines 10 syllables long, with accents falling on every second syllable. 154 sonnets are attributed to Shakespeare with probably Sonnet No. 18 being the most famous:

> *Shall I compare thee to a summer's day?*
> *Thou art more lovely and more temperate:*
> *Rough winds do shake the darling buds of May,*
> *And summer's lease hath all too short a date:*
> *Sometime too hot the eye of heaven shines,*
> *And often is his gold complexion dimm'd;*
> *And every fair from fair sometime declines,*
> *By chance or nature's changing course untrimm'd;*
> *But thy eternal summer shall not fade*
> *Nor lose possession of that fair thou owest;*

Nor shall Death brag thou wander'st in his shade,
When in eternal lines to time thou growest:
So long as men can breathe or eyes can see,
So long lives this and this gives life to thee.

A complete list of sonnets attributed to William Shakespeare (by first line):
1. *From fairest creatures we desire increase,*
2. *When forty winters shall besiege thy brow,*
3. *Look in thy glass, and tell the face thou viewest*
4. *Unthrifty loveliness, why dost thou spend*
5. *Those hours that with gentle work did frame*
6. *Then let not winter's ragged hand deface*
7. *Lo! in the orient when the gracious light*
8. *Music to hear, why hear'st thou music sadly?*
9. *Is it for fear to wet a widow's eye*
10. *For shame! deny that thou bear'st love to any,*

11. *As fast as thou shalt wane, so fast thou grow'st*
12. *When do I count the clock that tells the time*
13. *O that you were yourself! but, love, you are*
14. *Not from the stars do I my judgment pluck,*
15. *When I consider every thing that grows*
16. *But wherefore do not you a mightier way*
17. *Who will believe my verse in time to come,*
18. *Shall I compare thee to a summer's day?*
19. *Devouring Time, blunt thou the lion's paws,*
20. *A woman's face, with Nature's own hand painted,*

21. *So is it not with me as with that Muse*
22. *My glass shall not persuade me I am old*
23. *As an unperfect actor on the stage*
24. *Mine eye hath play'd the painter and hath stell'd*
25. *Let those who are in favour with their stars*
26. *Lord of my love, to whom in vassalage*
27. *Weary with toil, I haste me to my bed,*
28. *How can I then return in happy plight*
29. *When in disgrace with fortune and men's eyes*
30. *When to the sessions of sweet silent thought*

31. *Thy bosom is endeared with all hearts*
32. *If thou survive my well- contented day*
33. *Full many a glorious morning I have seen*
34. *Why didst thou promise such a beauteous day,*

35. *No more be griev'd at that which thou hast done:*
36. *Let me confess that we two must be twain,*
37. *As a decrepit father takes delight*
38. *How can my Muse want subject to invent,*
39. *O, how thy worth with manners may I sing,*
40. *Take all my loves, my love, yea take them all*

41. *Those pretty wrongs that liberty commits*
42. *That thou hast her it is not all my grief*
43. *When most I wink, then do mine eyes best see,*
44. *If the dull substance of my flesh were thought,*
45. *The other two, slight air and purging fire,*
46. *Mine eye and heart are at a mortal war*
47. *Betwixt mine eye and heart a league is took,*
48. *How careful was I when I took my way,*
49. *Against that time, if ever that time come,*
50. *How heavy do I journey on the way*
51. *Thus can my love excuse the slow offence*
52. *So am I as the rich whose blessed key*
53. *What is your substance, whereof are you made,*
54. *O, how much more doth beauty beauteous seem*
55. *Not marble nor the gilded monuments,*
56. *Sweet love, renew thy force; be it not said*
57. *Being your slave, what should I do but tend*
58. *That god forbid that made me first your slave*
59. *If there be nothing new, but that which is*
60. *Like as the waves make towards the pebbled shore,*

61. *Is it thy will thy image should keep open*
62. *Sin of self-love possesseth all mine eye,*
63. *Against my love shall be as I am now,*
64. *When I have seen by Time's fell hand defaced*
65. *Since brass, nor stone, nor earth, nor boundless sea,*
66. *Tir'd with all these for restful death I cry:*
67. *Ah! wherefore with infection should he live*
68. *Thus is his cheek the map of days outworn*
69. *Those parts of thee that the world's eye doth view*
70. *That thou art blam'd shall not be thy defect,*

71. *No longer mourn for me when I am dead*
72. *O, lest the world should task you to recite*
73. *That time of year thou mayst in me behold*
74. *But be contented. When that fell arrest*

75. So are you to my thoughts as food to life,
76. Why is my verse so barren of new pride?
77. Thy glass will show thee how thy beauties wear,
78. So oft have I invok'd thee for my Muse,
79. Whilst I alone did call upon thy aid,
80. O, how I faint when I of you do write,

81. Or I shall live your epitaph to make
82. I grant thou wert not married to my Muse,
83. I never saw that you did painting need,
84. Who is it that says most? which can say more
85. My tongue-tied Muse in manners holds her still,
86. Was it the proud full sail of his great verse,
87. Farewell! thou art too dear for my possessing
88. When thou shalt be dispos'd to set me light,
89. Say that thou didst forsake me for some fault,
90. Then hate me when thou wilt; if ever, now;
91. Some glory in their birth, some in their skill,
92. But do thy worst to steal thyself away,
93. So shall I live, supposing thou art true,
94. They that have power to hurt, and will do none,
95. How sweet and lovely dost thou make the shame
96. Some say thy fault is youth, some wantonness;
97. How like a winter hath my absence been
98. From you I have been absent in the spring
99. The forward violet thus did I chide:
100. Where art thou, Muse, that thou forget'st so long

101. O truant Muse, what shall be thy amends
102. My love is strength'ned, though more weak in seeming;
103. Alack, what poverty my Muse brings forth
104. To me, fair friend, you never can be old
105. Let not my love be call'd idolatry,
106. When in the chronicle of wasted time
107. Not mine own fears, nor the prophetic soul
108. What's in the brain that ink may character
109. O, never say that I was false of heart
110. Alas, 'tis true I have gone here and there

111. O for my sake do you with Fortune chide,
112. Your love and pity doth th' impression fill
113. Since I left you, mine eye is in my mind;
114. Or whether doth my mind, being crown'd with you,

115. *Those lines that I before have writ do lie;*
116. *Let me not to the marriage of true minds*
117. *Accuse me thus: that I have scanted all*
118. *Like as to make our appetites more keen*
119. *What potions have I drunk of Siren tears,*
120. *That you were once unkind befriends me now,*

121. *'Tis better to be vile than vile esteemed,*
122. *Thy gift, thy tables, are within my brain*
123. *No, Time, thou shalt not boast that I do change,*
124. *If my dear love were but the child of state,*
125. *Were't aught to me I bore the canopy,*
126. *O thou, my lovely boy, who in thy power*
127. *In the old age black was not counted fair,*
128. *How oft, when thou, my music, music play'st*
129. *Th' expense of spirit in a waste of shame*
130. *My mistress' eyes are nothing like the sun;*

131. *Thou art as tyrannous, so as thou art*
132. *Thine eyes I love, and they, as pitying me.*
133. *Beshrew that heart that makes mine heart to groan*
134. *So, now I have confess'd that he is thine*
135. *Whoever hath her wish, thou hast thy Will,*
136. *If thy soul check thee that I come so near,*
137. *Thou blind fool, Love, what does thou to mine eyes*
138. *When my love swears that she is made of truth,*
139. *O, call not me to justify the wrong*
140. *Be wise as thou art cruel; do not press*

141. *In faith, I do not love thee with mine eyes,*
142. *Love is my sin, and thy dear virtue hate,*
143. *Lo as a careful huswife runs to catch*
144. *Two loves I have, of comfort and despair,*
145. *Those lips that Love's own hand did make*
146. *Poor soul, the centre of my sinful earth,*
147. *My love is as a fever, longing still*
148. *O me, what eyes hath love put in my head*
149. *Canst thou, O cruel, say I love thee not*
150. *O, from what power hast thou this powerful might*

151. *Love is too young to know what conscience is;*
152. *In loving thee thou know'st I am forsworn,*
153. *Cupid laid by his brand, and fell asleep.*
154. *The little love-god, lying once asleep,*

Chapter Five

The World of the Playwright

A Day in the Life of a Playwright

Ask a doctor what he does all day, or a teacher, a shop assistant, or a car mechanic for that matter, and they will be able to describe, in a fair amount of detail, the format of their day; ask any writer, be they a playwright or novelist, and they will probably struggle to tell you!

A teacher's day or a car mechanic's day will, in essence, bear striking similarities, in that they will have a structure; a time to start and a time to finish, with lunch and tea breaks in between; they will also have a set of tasks to complete before their day is done, this being the case of most jobs and professions. A writer's day, however, is more unpredictable. Although I do know many writers who try to add structure to their day, I know many more who struggle on this score. So, let's look at the hurdles, the joys and sorrows of being a writer and, more specifically, of a playwright before any of you decide to give up the day job.

SELF-DISCIPLINE

Any writer, be they a writer of plays, books, articles, or whatever, must have an abundance of self-discipline, for there is no one to answer to but themselves. If the sun is shining or there is something interesting on daytime television, then there is also the temptation to do absolutely nothing at all, safe in the knowledge that there is no one to rebuke you.

Imagine a Monday morning in July; the sun is shining and the weather forecast has promised temperatures will reach at least 80^0. There is no boss to question why you are not working, so why should you? Because it is a job and you need the money; but of course you could just do twice the work tomorrow when the sun might not shine. That's the problem you face on warm sunny days whereas on cold days you just want to stay in bed!

Once you have acknowledged the need to start work, then another set of problems present themselves. What time should you start? You have no contract of employment, so no one cares; maybe you could leave it until the afternoon and just work later into the evening? Interestingly though, after a time, most writers do find a rhythm and tend to start around the same time each day, finishing around the same time too – until, of course, the dreaded deadline rears its ugly head, when they can find themselves working around the clock in order to – catch up!

TOOLS OF THE JOB

What about office stationery? When you work for someone else, then it is their responsibility to supply you with the tools you need for the job. When you work for yourself then you have to leave the house (and leave the work behind) to go out and buy your own tools – out of your own money, which you won't earn unless you exercise that self-discipline.

EVERYBODY'S SERVANT

There is the added problem of all the domestic chores too, because the world and its dog seem to think that, as you are at home all day, just 'sticking on' the dishwasher, putting the joint in the oven – oh, and picking up the kids from school would hardly eat into your day. They don't understand about interrupting the creative flow, and don't try to explain to them because you will be greeted with blank stares.

RESEARCH

Of course, you need to get out and about too; you need to do research; you need to meet or observe people who might just form the basis for a character in your next play. You know that you are 'people watching' but, to mortals, you are being downright rude! And if you did attempt to explain you would be told that the 'people watching' could so easily be done whilst you are running back and forth to the shops for various members of the family, picking up the kids from school, putting the joint in the oven, weeding the garden etc, etc, etc. And don't try to tell them that you couldn't absorb the subtleties of human nature whilst arguing over the price of lamb or tying little Johnny's shoelaces because that will only bring more blank stares.

THE WRITER'S OFFICE

Now this is a real bone of contention in many of my friends' homes. Most agree that they need somewhere that is theirs – and theirs alone – where they can retreat to let the creative juices flow. In family homes, however, all the spare rooms seem to be taken up with children and their toys; and the air seems to be filled with the constant noise of those children. So, enter the garden shed – many, many writers now work in a little wooden hut at the bottom of the garden, ranging in size from a simple garden shed to an elaborate summer house. Be warned though, that as pleasant as this idyllic retreat might be in the summer months, in the winter it will be very, very cold.

INCOME

This is the most difficult part because there is no regular income at the end of each month. In fact, there is no guaranteed income at all, for the money a writer makes is dependent upon many factors, some outside their control. These include:

i)   producing enough saleable work
ii)   producing work of a good standard
iii) producing work the public want to see
iv)   LOTS AND LOTS OF LUCK!

Now, let's assume that you have written your theatrical masterpiece; your next problem is to get it …

From Page to Stage

This is a complicated process, a sort of artistic Grand National with a long, arduous course stretching out in front. Each jump must be carefully negotiated before the course can be completed; each horse merely completing the course is a winner in his own right, for many stumble and fall at the early fences. The winner is, of course, heralded a champion, and all associated with the journey are also heralded champions, for it is a team victory.

The analogy may seem strange, but keep it in mind as you read on and you will see the comparisons can be fascinatingly close.

Course …   The journey from page to stage.
Horse …   This is the play itself, only as good as all those in control of it.
Rider …   This is the playwright who must negotiate all the jumps,
                (hurdles), and take his 'horse' to the finishing post.
Jumps …   These are all the obstacles any playwright will encounter along the
                way, from writer's block to finding an interested producer.
Trainer …   Now this can be anyone, in any capacity. We all have emotional
                support in our lives and, if we are lucky, perhaps even an artistic
                mentor too, and it is that support that keeps us going whenever

we want to give in. Just as a trainer knows how hard and how far to push his horse, so your family/friends/mentor know exactly how to 'encourage' you.

Punters … In the theatrical world they are called 'angels'; they are the investors who gamble their money on financing a production, in the hope that they have 'backed a winner'.

Winner … The playwright whose work is staged to critical acclaim.

All completing Playwrights who manage to negotiate all the obstacles and reach
the Course … the finishing post will inevitably go on to greater things, for they have the stamina to succeed and do well.

A PLAY

A play is a dramatic work written to be performed by actors/actresses on a stage, screen, radio or any other public or private place where an audience can watch the action.

A PLAYWRIGHT

A playwright is the person who not only puts the story into words and onto the paper, but who breathes into the finished work the fire in their heart and the truth in their soul, which will fuel the director's eventual artistic direction.

Now, the most interesting thing is that anyone can be a playwright – to a lesser or greater degree, of course – because anyone can write down a story and ask others to act it out for them – or, indeed, act it out themselves if they feel so inclined. Most of us played the game of 'Let's Pretend' as children and most of us took part in improvisation classes at school which were, in fact, the seeds of play-writing given us at various points in out lives; whether or not we chose to plant them would decide whether or not we became a playwright.

Now, suppose you planted the seeds and started to write, then, as with all things, there are degrees of ambition and consequent successes. Maybe you just wanted to write for yourself as a sort of cathartic expression or for your school friends, or perhaps you set your sights much higher. Well, you know what, I am a great believer in having a go if that's what interests you; think of it as a ladder to climb and, as with all ladders, you have to start at the bottom – but with this one, you never know what you might find when you reach the top. The sky is your limit.

The Ladder to Success

STEP 1
Amateur Playwright – Digging the Foundations

It goes without saying that, before you write for theatre, you must love theatre and go to the theatre as often as possible in order to experience every style of writing. Watch carefully: watch the scenery, watch the light, watch the sets and the set changes, and watch the audience reaction. Listen to the dialogue, and to the pacing of the dialogue. Watch the characters: observe their body 'language'. Be prepared to work a long time on these basics for you need to understand it before you can be a part of it. When you understand theatre, then and only then are you ready to start on the theatrical 'course'. It is my opinion that a good way to begin is by writing stories – a good playwright has to be a good storyteller; a good playwright is also a good observer of people and situations which he can then incorporate into his stories, so always keep your eyes and ears open. Remember, everyone you ever encounter could become a small part of a character you will one day create.

STEP 2
Amateur Playwright – Ready to Write

So, now you have written a good story with great characters which means the time has come to craft your story into a play by segmenting the storyline into scenes and turning the narrative into dialogue. This is quite a task so, as well as going to see plays, **read** them too; learn how the professionals make their dialogue live and take note of the layout of scripts.

STEP 3
Amateur Playwright – The Read Through

Your play is now ready, but what works on the page doesn't necessarily 'read' well and so ask some friends to read through your piece with you and act out the parts too; you will soon find any flaws this way.

STEP 4
Amateur Playwright – Work into Practice
After a successful read through, and as a consequence of the inevitable rewrites, you are now ready to see your work on stage and in action. At this point, why not try approaching a local amateur dramatic society with your work, maybe they will be interested in staging your piece, especially when you demand no fee.

STEP 5
The Missing Link No 1
Think of this as a huge chasm to cross, or as a river with no bridge. This is the first of two very difficult hurdles which, until you manage to cross them, indicate that there is no going forward. This first hurdle involves submitting your masterpiece to agents/producers/theatres in the hope that they will show some interest in both you and your piece, and then sitting back and waiting for the rejection slips to drop through your letter box – and, believe me, they will! The day that one of these elusive butterflies says yes to your work then, and only then, may you cross to the next step.

STEP 6
First Professional Production
This step will probably be the most satisfying and exhilarating of all the steps you will ever take for this is the first time you will see an audience pay for the 'privilege' of watching your work. But one word of warning – at this point in your career be prepared to let go of your baby. Leave the more experienced professionals to make it a success; it won't always be like this, though.

STEP 7
Turning Fully 'Pro'
This is the momentous time when you decide to give up the day job and devote yourself to writing full-time. You may only move on to STEP 8 when you earn enough money to live without the help of a part-time bar job. A word of caution – very few move past STEP 7.

> **STEP 8**
> **Professional Playwright**
> This is where you and your work are in demand by all the right people in all the right places.

> **STEP 9**
> **The Missing Link No 2**
> Another chasm or river to cross and once more the bridge is missing. This time, only the elitist few will discover the bridge and be 'allowed' to cross over to the other side where the pastures are so green. These elitist few may graze and those who do are recognised with awards and rewarded with international acclaim for they are now at the top of the ladder; they have not only crossed the finishing line but have crossed it ahead of all the other competitors and they are …

> **STEP 10**
> **THE GRAND MASTER PLAYWRIGHTS**
> These are the best and most celebrated playwrights in the world. (See pp 33–70).

A Successful Production

A successful production relies on more than just an excellent playwright and play; it relies on a producer willing to gamble his reputation on what he thinks is a good piece of work; it relies on 'angels' wanting to risk their money by backing the production; it relies on a director with the same vision as the writers and one who breathe life into the work. Then, of course, there are the rest of the production team, all important and all necessary to a successful stage production. There are the set, light, sound and costume designers, as well as the technical stage crew and the front of house staff. But, for now, we will take a closer look at two key contributors, the producer and the director.

THE PRODUCER

The producer is the individual who lifts the playwright's work from the page and who is responsible for not only raising the money for the production, but for gathering together the most suitable artistic team who will do justice to the work in question. In the UK, we have some excellent producers – and generally it would seem that they tend to stick to one of two genres, i.e. musical or straight drama. However, there are some who cross back and forth, producing for both mediums, including Bill Kenwright.

Producers

Bill Kenwright, 1945–

NON-MUSICAL WORKS PRODUCED BY BILL KENWRIGHT INCLUDE

Absurd Person Singular • All's Well That Ends Well • Brief Encounter • Cat on a Hot Tin Roof • Caught in the Net • Constant Wife (The) • Dangerous Corner • Design for Living • Elmina's Kitchen • Festen • Few Good Men (A) • Ghosts • Gift of the Gorgon (The) • Glass Menagerie (The) • Hamlet and an Absolute Turkey • Hay Fever • Lady Windermere's Fan • Letter Treats (The) • Long Day's Journey into Night • Lysistrata • Major Barbara • Miss Julie • RSC Jacobean Season • Secret Rapture (The) • Separate Tables • She Stoops to Conquer • Sleuth • Tamer Tamed (The) • Taming of the Shrew (The) • Vortex (The) • Waiting for Godot • We Happy Few

THE LIFE OF BILL KENWRIGHT

- Bill Kenwright was born on 4th Sept, 1945, in Liverpool, England
- Kenwright has produced extensively for Broadway, as well as for the West End and the Provincial theatre circuit
- In addition to the stage, he has produced for the cinema and co-produced an arena tour
- He was awarded an Honorary Fellowship from Liverpool's John Moore's University
- He is an Honorary Professor of Thames Valley University
- In 2001, he was awarded a CBE in The Queen's New Year's Honours

- In 2002, Kenwright received the Variety Club Bernard Delfont Award for his contribution to the entertainment industry
- He is both Chairman of, and a major shareholder in, Everton Football Club – oh and a huge fan too!

AND FINALLY ...

- He once appeared in Coronation Street as the character, Gordon Clegg

Sonia Friedman, 1965–

Female producers, by comparison, are a bit thin on the ground and so we must take great pride in our very successful homegrown female producer, Sonia Friedman who, like Bill Kenwright, jumps back and forth between the musical and straight play divide.

NON-MUSICAL WORKS PRODUCED BY SONIA FRIEDMAN INCLUDE

Absolutely! [Perhaps] • *Afterplay* • *As You Like It* • *Bent* • *Boeing-Boeing* • *Calico* • *Day in the Death of Joe Egg (A)* • *Dealer's Choice* • *Donkey's Years* • *Dumb Waiter* • *Eh Joe* • *Endgame* • *Faith Healer* • *Guantánamo* • *Hergé's Adventures of Tintin* • *Hitchcock Blonde* • *Home Place (The)* • *In Celebration* • *In Flame* • *Jumpers* • *Last Dance at Dum Dum* • *Late Middle Classes (The)* • *Lobby Hero* • *Love Song* • *Macbeth* • *Mystery of Charles Dickens (The)* • *Noises Off* • *On an Average Day* • *On the Third* • *Otherwise Engaged* • *Port Authority* • *Rock 'n' Roll* • *See You Next Tuesday* • *Sexual Perversity in Chicago* • *Shoot the Crow* • *Shopping and F**king* • *Speed-the-Plow* • *Spoonface Steinberg* • *Steward of Christendom (The)* • *That Face* • *Under the Blue Sky* • *Up for Grabs* • *What the Night Is For* • *Whose Life Is It Anyway?*

THE LIFE AND WORK OF SONIA FRIEDMAN

- Sonia Friedman was born in London on 19th April, 1965, to Leonard and Claire Friedman, the youngest child in a family of performers
- In 1977, she started her secondary education at St Christopher's School, Letchworth
- Friedman's professional training was in stage management at the Central School of Speech and Drama
- In the late 1980s, she successfully organised several benefits for Shop Assistants for AIDS Awareness. She also started bucket collections in theatres across the UK for World AIDS Day which continues to this day – a precursor to her producing career
- In 1989, Friedman joined The National Theatre as a producer, specialising in touring productions and theatre for young people, where she stayed until 1993
- In 1993, Friedman co-founded Out of Joint Theatre Company with Max Stafford-Clark. This is now the UK's most successful touring company specialising in new writing
- In 1998, Friedman joined the Ambassador Theatre Group as a producer
- In 2002, she formed Sonia Friedman Productions (SFP)
- In 2007, she was listed in *The Evening Standard* as one of London's 1,000 most influential people
- Friedman has also produced extensively on Broadway, as well as for the West End and the Provincial theatre circuit

AND FINALLY ...

- Since 1990, Sonia has produced over 75 new productions

DIRECTOR

The playwright has finished his work and it is now in pre-production. That then means it is in the hands of the director. Now, there is only one thing a writer can do in this situation and that is to 'Let the Baby Run'! Many new, inexperienced writers find it so hard to let go of their work and allow the director to take over, but that's what they must do if the piece is to grow and develop.

If a work is well-written, then the director can only enhance and improve it, for when they enter the equation, then it is simply a case of adding another dimension. Of course, there are directors who couldn't direct traffic but, equally, there are visionaries who can open the otherwise closed eyes of an audience, allow them to experience depths of previously untapped emotions and maybe even question theories that had hitherto seemed unquestionable; these directors use the medium of theatre for the social, political and artistic benefit of the audience. Two men of such genius are Sir Peter Hall and Nicholas Hytner.

Sir Peter Hall, 1930–

PLAYS DIRECTED BY SIR PETER HALL INCLUDE

Amadeus • *As You Like It* • *Bacchai (The)* • *Bedroom Farce* • *Betrayal* • *Coriolanus* • *Hay Fever* • *Homecoming (The)* • *Ideal Husband (An)* • *John Gabriel Borkman* • *Lesson (The)* • *Measure for Measure* • *Merchant of Venice (The)* • *No Man's Land* • *Old Times* • *Oresteia (The)* • *Orpheus Descending* • *Pygmalion* • *Tamburlaine* • *Tantalus* • *Uncle Vanya* • *Waiting for Godot* • *Wars of The Roses (The)*

THE LIFE AND WORK OF PETER HALL

- On 22nd November, 1930, Peter Reginald Frederick Hall was born in Bury St. Edmunds, Suffolk
- Coming from a working class family, his academic life was encouraged by his parents who valued education and the arts; soon he realised that he loved the theatre and music
- In 1953, Peter Hall graduated from St Catharine's College, Cambridge. Having successfully directed a number of plays as an undergraduate, he was determined to become a theatre director
- In 1954, he was appointed Assistant Director at the Arts Theatre, London, eventually becoming its director. It was while in this post that he was sent *Waiting for Godot,* which he then staged in its English speaking premiere
- From 1960–1968, he was the Founder/Director of the Royal Shakespeare Company
- In 1963, Peter Hall was awarded the CBE
- He became an Honorary Fellow of St Catharine's College, Cambridge in 1964
- In 1973, Hall succeeded Lord Olivier as Director of The National Theatre, remaining in the post for 15 years and moving the company into the theatres on the South Bank
- He was knighted in 1977, becoming Sir Peter Hall

- In 1988, he founded the Peter Hall Theatre Company which, to date, has staged some 60 productions
- In 2003, Sir Peter Hall became Director of The Rose Theatre, a newly built theatre in Kingston upon Thames which opened in January 2008 with Sir Peter's production of *Uncle Vanya*

AND FINALLY...

- In a career spanning more than 50 years, Sir Peter Hall has directed over 300 productions
- In addition to his work in the theatre, he is also an internationally renowned opera director working in many of the world's leading opera houses. He was Artistic Director of Glyndebourne Festival Opera 1984–90

Opera Productions Include:
Albert Herring
Don Giovanni
La Calisto
La Cenerentola
Marriage of Figaro (The)
Midsummer Night's Dream (A)
Moses and Aaron
Othello
Ring Cycle (The)

Directed Films for Cinema and Television Including:
Akenfield
Camomile Lawn (The)
Final Passage (The)
Homecoming (The)
Never Talk to Strangers
Perfect Friday
Three Into Two Won't Go

Books Include:
Exposed by the Mask
Making an Exhibition of Myself (autobiography)
Necessary Theatre (The)
Peter Hall Diaries (The)
Shakespeare's Advice to the Players

Nicholas Hytner, 1956–

PLAYS DIRECTED BY NICHOLAS HYTNER INCLUDE

As You Like It • Carousel • Country Wife (The) • Cressida • Cripple of Inishmaan (The) • Don Carlos • Edward II • Ghetto • Henry IV, Parts I and II • Henry V • His Dark Materials • History Boys (The) • Importance of Being Earnest (The) • Lady in the Van (The) • Madness of George III (The) • Mother Clap's Molly House • Mumbo Jumbo • Orpheus Descending • Recruiting Officer (The) • Southwark Fair • Stuff Happens • Sweet Smell of Success (The) • Twelfth Night • Volpone • Wind in the Willows (The) • Winter's Tale (The)

THE LIFE AND WORK OF NICHOLAS HYTNER

- Nicholas Hytner was born in Manchester on 7th May, 1956, the son of Benet Hytner QC
- He was educated at Manchester Grammar School and later at Trinity Hall, Cambridge, where he read English
- After Cambridge, he directed a series of productions at Leeds Playhouse
- In 1985, Hytner became an Associate Director of the Royal Exchange Theatre, Manchester
- He directed *Measure for Measure* for the RSC in 1987
- In 1988, he directed *The Tempest*, again for the RSC, followed by *King Lear* in 1990
- In 1990, he also became Associate Director of The National Theatre
- In 1994, Hytner's first feature film, *The Madness of King George*, was released
- In 2000, he was appointed Visiting Professor of Theatre at Oxford University
- Hytner became Director of The National Theatre in 2003

AND FINALLY ...

- He is an Associate Director of the Lincoln Centre Theatre, New York
- He also directs musicals and opera, his biggest commercial success in the world of musicals being *Miss Saigon*

The Playwright's Home is His 'Palace'

To say that 'theatre is theatre' is about as accurate as saying one person is the same as the next! There are so many different types of theatre, each catering for the needs of a cross section of people and answering those needs as their tastes grow, develop or change. Some people enjoy commercial theatre and want to go along, be entertained and then go home, having had a good night out, and forget about it – and there is nothing at all wrong with that. Others see theatre as a form of education; they want their own beliefs to be challenged, stimulating them to question themselves and society.

There is a theatrical form for everyone. The only time I get angry is when one 'form' of theatre looks down contemptuously on another 'form' of theatre. Whatever our choice of theatre – and I mean that both in terms of what is playing upon the stage and in terms of the building itself – I do firmly believe that going to the theatre should be an 'experience'. In other words, I believe that the building, ambience, facilities, amenities and, indeed the audience itself, all actually contribute to the overall production and performance. For those old enough to remember the folk clubs of the 1960s, just cast your mind back for a moment. Weren't the best clubs the ones in dimly lit – and now, ironically, smoky – cellars? Didn't it seem that they played the best music? I'm sure they didn't as I, for one, distinctly remember some of the artistes touring the clubs at that time! No, I am sure it was just the general ambience which created that impression. So, you see, the actual theatre itself has a huge part to play in the theatrical experience.

First, however, we do need to make sure that 'everyone' is aware of the joys of theatre before they are able to make choices about what to see and where to see it. So we must capture that interest early on, and one of the best ways to do that is through:

Children's Theatre

The continuing survival of theatre is not in the hands of the writers or the actors, nor is it in the hands of the producers or, indeed, the audience; no, it is quite firmly in the hands of our children, the future generation of theatre-goers. If a child loves theatre when they are five, nine, 11 or whatever age, then the chances are that they will love theatre for the rest of their life. But, as with any love, it has to be carefully nurtured and encouraged to develop; left alone, then it could quite possibly die.

As a small child, I was often taken to the theatre by my mother and so was very fortunate in that I was exposed to many different forms of theatre from a very early age. As a result, I developed a passion for Gilbert and Sullivan; this was at a time when the D'Oyly Carte still toured. I can remember, on one particular occasion, when they visited my home town of York, my mother, bless her, decided that, instead of buying herself and me tickets to go twice, she would buy me tickets for four performances; in the early-1960s, it wasn't a financial option for us both to go four times. So there I sat, all alone, in the front row of the Dress Circle, at the age of about 13, absolutely enthralled by the Gilbert and Sullivan operettas, all thanks to my mother's encouragement and self-sacrifice. My Uncle Tommy, who loved music, followed this by giving me his own set of G & S LPs (quaint name now, isn't it!). So my early interest in theatre was nurtured into a lifelong passion that has given me not only years of enjoyment, but a career and many like-minded friends too. Thank you, Mum!

Since that time, the realisation that we have to catch and captivate young audiences early on if we are to secure a future generation of theatre lovers has grown to such an extent that many schools now have their own thriving theatre companies and visiting professionals. We also have specialist Children's Theatre Companies, and even a Theatre dedicated to children: the wonderful Polka Theatre in Wimbledon.

Polka Theatre – Where Theatre Begins

HISTORY OF THE POLKA THEATRE

Polka Theatre began as a touring company in 1967 under the Artistic Directorship of Richard Gill who, with a passion for puppetry, took the company's work out to many of Britain's major theatres. However, Gill dreamt of a permanent home for his own theatre, a dream that was realised in 1979 when 'Polka – The Children's Theatre' opened its doors for the first time, thus becoming the first theatre in the UK dedicated exclusively to children. Since that date all those years ago, it is estimated that over 2000,000 people have walked over the Polka threshold and this is without counting the massive audiences when it takes a show out on the road.

External photo of the theatre

AMENITIES

Polka Theatre has a 300-seat Main Auditorium and a 90-seat studio known as, 'The Adventure Theatre'. The Adventure Theatre is used exclusively for theatre work with the under-fives and so is quite unique in this respect – I did say we need to capture them young didn't I! In addition, there is a café, a playground, a toyshop and an exhibition and gallery space. It is not just 'child friendly', it has been designed specifically for children.

Polka thrived; then a second Artistic Director joined the company, by the name of Vicky Ireland, and the diversity and quality just grew and grew. One of the most remarkable productions at this time was *Off the Wall*, which took works of art by the likes of René Magritte, Henry Moore and Francis Bacon and brought them to life on stage, thus artistically exposing and educating children in the widest sense of the word 'art'. Over the years, Polka has worked with some of the UK's leading writers, such as Alan Ayckbourn and Philip Pullman, ensuring that children are always exposed to 'quality theatre' of the very best kind.

In 1994, Polka won the Vivian Duffield Theatre Award to begin the pioneering audience development initiative, 'Curtain-Up!' This scheme, which is still running today, offers free theatre tickets to disadvantaged schools whose pupils would not otherwise have the opportunity to experience theatre due to financial or other difficulties. This is supplemented by money to cover transport costs and a free post-show drama workshop to support the visits. It is estimated that 30,000 school children have now been introduced to the magic of theatre through this innovative scheme.

In 2003/04, Polka extended its target audience both downwards and upwards when the Adventure Theatre played host to recent developments in theatre for babies and toddlers and the first 'Polka Teens' show, Abi Bown's poetic *Hey There, Boy with the Bebop* went into production. This is theatre at its very best and those fortunate enough to live near Polka in Wimbledon can be sure that their children

Interior photo of
Polka audience

can enjoy theatre before they even reach their first birthday. Those who don't should at least make one journey to this powerhouse of theatrical experiences. My own daughter's introduction to theatre came when she was just six weeks old, when she sat in her baby bouncer in the orchestra pit of a theatre whilst her father – an MD (Musical Director) – conducted a show. Even at that age, she was mesmerised and, as a consequence, theatre has been her life ever since.

Once the young theatre-goer has grown, they will find an abundance of choices and a diversity of theatres. They should try them all, for each has something to offer that, perhaps, others do not and, eventually, they will discover a type of theatre for themselves.

'Catch them young; keep them forever.'

The Royal Court Theatre

The Royal Court Theatre is a leading national company renowned around the world as the home of new writers. *The New York Times* once described it as 'the most important theater in Europe'; it also stages productions in New York, Sydney, Brussels, Toronto and Dublin and has inspired confidence in new work throughout the theatrical world. Many theatre producers are afraid to give new writers the opportunity to stage their work because they fear great financial losses whilst, at The Royal Court, it is their 'policy' to stage new work and so that fear never enters the equation.

At the grassroots of this ground-breaking theatre are always the artistic directors; those with vision, artistic wisdom and courage.

THE ROYAL COURT AND ITS ARTISTIC DIRECTORS

1956   The English Stage Company moved into the Royal Court under the Artistic Directorship of George Devine and Tony Richardson.

1956   George Devine went where other angels feared to tread and staged John Osborne's *Look Back in Anger*, and continued to believe in this angry young man when all others doubted; George Devine thus pointed the way for The Royal Court and it has been a well-trodden path ever since.

1965–72 William Gaskill was appointed Artistic Director.

1969   Gaskill was joined by Lindsay Anderson and Anthony Page.

1969   The Theatre Upstairs opened.

1972–75 Oscar Lewenstein was appointed Artistic Director.

1975–77 Robert Kidd and Nicholas Wright took over from Oscar Lewenstein.

1977–79 Stuart Burge was appointed Artistic Director.

1979–92 Max Stafford-Clark was appointed Artistic Director; his name was destined to become synonymous both with 'The Court' and new writing.

1992–98 Stephen Daldry took over from Max Stafford-Clark.

1998–06 Ian Rickson was appointed Artistic Director.

2007– Dominic Cooke took over from Ian Rickson.

ARTISTIC BACKGROUND

The Royal Court has always stuck firm to its belief that it is a writer's theatre and, as such, has always encouraged its playwrights to push boundaries even further; I suppose one could say it is a 'thinking man's theatre'. In the 1960s, The Royal Court regularly came into conflict with the Lord Chamberlain's Office, (then the official censors of the London stage) and, as a result, three plays were refused a licence to be performed at all (John Osborne: *A Patriot for Me*, Edward Bond: *Saved* and *Early Morning*). It was the subsequent battle over these plays which eventually led to the abolition of stage censorship under the 1968 Theatres Act.

The Royal Court can proudly say that it has had a hand in launching the careers of such renowned writers as Howard Brenton, David Edgar, Athol Fugard, Peter Gill, Christopher Hampton, David Hare, Ann Jellicoe, Mary O'Malley, Joe Orton, Sam Shepard, Wole Soyinka and David Storey. Throughout the decades, it has proudly held out against the commercial musicals and straightforward comedies and staged plays that challenged and questioned, thus giving a voice to the socially vocal playwrights of the times.

PAST PRODUCTIONS AT THE ROYAL COURT INCLUDE:

Ashes to Ashes – Harold Pinter
Blasted – Sarah Kane
East is East – Ayub Khan-Din
Far Away – Caryl Churchill
Hitchcock Blonde – Terry Johnson
Mojo – Jez Butterworth
Number (A) – Caryl Churchill
Saved – Edward Bond
Shopping & F***ing – Mark Ravenhill
Top Girls – Caryl Churchill
Weir (The) – Conor McPherson

AMENITIES

The Royal Court realises that 'going to the theatre' is an experience far wider than merely sitting in a seat and watching a play, and so contributes to this experience in the most magnificent way. The lively, artisan ambience of this theatre brings with it the feeling of 'belonging'. This is carried through to – what can only be described as – the splendid eaterie, where, as one would expect, you will find only the very best and most imaginative food. Yes, even here commercialism is 'out' and innovation 'in'!

The bookshop within The Royal Court offers a diverse selection of contemporary plays and publications on the theory and practice of modern drama, along with many Royal Court play-texts from past productions. Uniquely, too, the staff here can offer help to those seeking out suitable audition pieces; it is a haven for the drama student.

The Royal National Theatre

Then there is that other national institution, The National Theatre, which too often pushes the boundaries when it stages new works. Here, though, one is also more likely to find the classics and the work from more recognised and established writers than at the Royal Court. It is every young actor's dream to play The National and every writer's goal to have their work staged on those hallowed boards. The National Theatre sits majestically on the South Bank, a monument to all that is good and great in British theatre.

THE HISTORICAL STRUGGLE

The National Theatre is such an accepted part of our lives now that it is sometimes hard to appreciate just how long it took us actually to get to this point. But, in fact, the struggle began way back in 1848.

1848	The first proposal for a National Theatre was made by London publisher, Effingham Wilson. For the next 50 plus years, various public figures added weight to the call for a National Theatre.
1909	60 years later and the first substantial financial donation of £70,000 was received from Carl Meyer, the son of a Hamburg banker.
1914–18	The First World War put The National on the back burner.
1918	Geoffrey Whitworth, a young publisher, became one of the most vigorous campaigners for the NT.
1939	Another World War – the Second World War – and another delay to plans.

1942	The South Bank site was decided upon as the home for The National.
1946	The Joint Council of The National Theatre and the Old Vic was set up and they entered into an agreement for the promotion and building of a National Theatre.
1955	Almost 10 years elapsed and still no theatre.
1960	Costs of the proposed building had been escalating daily and, at this point in time, they hit £2.3 million, with annual running costs estimated at £500,000.
1962	The Governors of the Old Vic agreed to offer their theatre as a temporary home for The National Theatre. The initial lease was for five years; Laurence Olivier, The National's first Director, was appointed and he, in turn, appointed Kenneth Tynan as the first Literary Manager. Finally, progress had been made.

*   *   *

1963	The inaugural production of The National Theatre at The Old Vic was *Hamlet* by William Shakespeare.
1965	The National visited Russia and East Germany with productions of *Othello*, *Hobson's Choice* and *Love for Love*. **But, still, the estimated building costs kept rising until, in 1967, the figure hit £7.5 million.**
1967	The National took a gamble on an untried playwright by the name of Tom Stoppard, and his play *Rosencrantz and Guildenstern Are Dead*. The gamble paid off.
1970	Olivier became the first actor to be offered a life peerage.
1973	Lord Olivier resigned and was succeeded by Peter Hall. **The building cost had now risen to £16 million.**
1976	The National opened theatre-by-theatre with The Lyttelton Theatre the first to open in March of this year with a production of *Hamlet*, directed by Peter Hall. Although it was still unfinished, the Queen officially opened The National Theatre in the same year.
1977	The Cottesloe Theatre finally opened. The National Theatre was complete.
1988	The National Theatre was granted the title 'Royal', though it rarely uses this to describe itself.

After a struggle lasting over one hundred years, Great Britain had a 'Great' National Theatre of which it could be justifiably proud and, since that time, from within its portals we have seen the greatest actors, directed by the greatest directors, in the greatest plays, written by the greatest playwrights.

THE NATIONAL THEATRE TODAY

Well, it took a long time to get there, so was it worth it? Is The National for the nation or is it for the artistic elite? I believe it is a very special place and caters for all stages of 'artistic needs and development'. Some think it is not for them, but I would suggest that it is – it is for everyone, it is the National for the Nation.

So, if it is your first trip to The National, what can you expect to find? The answer is everything for everybody; it is a true theatrical 'experience'. But let's start with the obvious – the theatres. There are three theatres within The National:

The Olivier Theatre is the largest of the three theatres and was named after Laurence Olivier, The National's first Artistic Director. It has an open stage and fan-shaped auditorium with seating for approximately 1,120. One very special feature of The Olivier is the 'drum revolve'. Explained simply, this is a giant rotating stage, measuring four stories high and 15 metres across, which 'lives' deep underneath the actual stage of the Olivier theatre and which can produce – from the bowels of the theatre – an entire piece of three-dimensional scenery in just seconds. In this, the main theatre, comfort, sight-lines and acoustics are first class.

The Lyttelton Theatre was named after Oliver Lyttelton, Viscount Chandos who was the first Chairman of The National Theatre. With an auditorium seating an audience of 890, it is a conventional proscenium arch-style theatre. However, the Lyttelton does differ in style to other similar theatres in that it has an adjustable proscenium and can be made into an open-end stage, or to which a forestage can be added; another variation on the basic design is that an orchestra pit for 20 musicians can also be created. As in the Olivier Theatre, comfort, sight-lines and acoustics are first class in the Lyttelton.

The Cottesloe Theatre is the smallest of the three theatres with space for just 300 people. It was named after Lord Cottesloe, Chairman of the South Bank (the body responsible for the construction of The National). This small black box theatre is often used for new and experimental pieces; the space is flexible and the performance space can be turned and used in any manner, the only fixed seating being the galleries which overlook the space. Seating in this theatre is not as comfortable as in the two larger theatres and sight lines not as clear. But, in an experimental theatre space, none of this ever seems to matter; it's part of the fun, part of the theatrical experience.

A TRUE THEATRICAL EXPERIENCE

Each day, The National conducts backstage tours for the public, taking in the three theatres, scenic workshops and the backstage areas, as well as Front of House. Each year, these tours are enjoyed by over 20,000 people from all over the world.

The National also has its own bookshop with an impressive collection of books on theatre and boasts that, if it doesn't stock the book you are seeking, it will do everything in its power to get it for you; ah, the Harrods approach to theatre! One word of advice though, don't go in there just before the start of a show (as one particular person, not far removed from this page, did) for you will be in danger of becoming so engrossed in the books that you might just miss the performance!

At The National, there is foyer music to enjoy, exhibitions to browse and outdoor entertainment for all. The National also offers training courses which bring the useful vocal – and other techniques – used by professional actors to 'mortals' from the worlds of business and management in a way that, in turn, will be useful to them in 'their' world; masterclasses, workshops and storytelling sessions, to capture the young and fertile minds, cafés, bars and a restaurant add to the social atmosphere, and alfresco seating enhances the international and artistic feel of the National, offering the full eclectic experience to those who visit this wonderful National treasure that was so well worth the wait.

DIRECTORS OF THE NATIONAL THEATRE

There is an old saying to which I wholly subscribe and that is, 'a ship is only as good as its captain'. And what great captains The National has had in the form of its Directors.

1. Laurence Olivier – 1963–1973
2. Peter Hall – 1973–1988
3. Richard Eyre – 1988–1997
4. Trevor Nunn – 1997–2003
5. Nicholas Hytner – 2003–

Theatres around the World

If an Englishman's home is his castle, then it figures that maybe a playwright's home could be his palace – perhaps that is why so many theatres are actually called The Palace Theatre. In Great Britain, apart from The Palace Theatre in London, in the provinces there are three other Palace Theatres, in Manchester, Newark and Watford.

In keeping with the royalty theme – as in the use of the name Palace – we also find many British theatres with 'Royal' in their name and why not as a nation with one of the most theatrical monarchies in the world? Such theatres can be found in:

- Bacup – Royal Court Theatre
- Bath – Theatre Royal
- Brighton – Theatre Royal
- Bristol – Theatre Royal and Studio
- Bury St Edmunds – Theatre Royal
- Edinburgh – Royal Lyceum Theatre Company
- Glasgow – Theatre Royal
- Lincoln – Theatre Royal
- London – Royal Court
- London – Royal Opera House
- London – Theatre Royal
- London – Theatre Royal, Stratford East
- Manchester – Royal Exchange Theatre
- Margate – Theatre Royal
- Plymouth – Theatre Royal
- Newcastle upon Tyne – Theatre Royal
- Northampton – Royal and Derngate Theatres
- Norwich – Theatre Royal
- Nottingham – Theatre Royal and Royal Concert Hall
- Richmond (North Yorks) – Georgian Theatre Royal
- St Helens – Theatre Royal
- Stratford-upon-Avon – Royal Shakespeare Theatre
- Winchester – Theatre Royal
- Windsor – Theatre Royal
- York – Theatre Royal

Another popular name for theatres is 'Playhouse'; quite sensible as it is, of course, specifically a house of plays; such theatres can be found in:

- Harlow – The Playhouse
- Leeds – West Yorkshire Playhouse
- Liverpool – Everyman and Playhouse Theatre
- London – Greenwich Playhouse
- London – Playhouse
- London – Southwark Playhouse
- Nottingham – Nottingham Playhouse
- Oxford – Oxford Playhouse
- Salisbury – Playhouse
- Sevenoaks – Playhouse

Now, we must remember that, when a playwright has spent many hours lovingly crafting their work before giving birth to the finished masterpiece, it stands to reason that they would care very much about which theatre would be home to their 'baby'. Theatres, just like people, have a personality, a feel to them which would not work for all shows and that's before the producer enters into the equation with talks of seating capacities and profit margins. The theatre is a very important part of a playwright's life and many have their own favourite theatres, some even write with a specific theatre in mind to house their baby; remember Alan Ayckbourn and his affinity with The Stephen Joseph Theatre in the Round in Scarborough, North Yorkshire.

Having taken a look at the names of theatres, some of which are in the provinces, we will now concentrate predominantly on the West End and Broadway, names which are not only synonymous with theatre, but with the very best in theatre. Having said that, however, the following list will feature some theatres which don't fall, geographically speaking, into these two catchment areas (The National being one). Instead, I am going to draw your attention to prominent theatres in London and New York.

PROMINENT LONDON THEATRES

THEATRE	INFORMATION
Adelphi	The first theatre here opened in 1806 under the name the *Sans Pareil* (Without Compare). The current theatre opened in 1930 • Seating capacity – 1,500+ • The theatre has no curves and was designed with straight lines only!
Aldwych	• Opened in 1905 • Seating capacity – 1,190+ • The Aldwych and The Strand theatres were actually built as a pair of theatres on either side of the Waldorf Hotel
Apollo	• Opened in 1901 • Seating capacity – 770+ • The balcony – third tier – is said to be the steepest in London
Apollo Victoria	• Opened in 1930 • Seating capacity – 1,830+ • It was originally built as a cinema, eventually closing in 1975 and reopening as a theatre in 1981
Arts	• Opened in 1927 • Seating capacity – 335+ • It started as a members' club in order to avoid the censorship of the Lord Chamberlain

THEATRE	INFORMATION
Cambridge	• Opened in 1930 • Seating capacity – 1,230+ • This theatre generally tends to house short runs; in 1969, it was used as a cinema
Comedy	• Opened in 1881 • Seating capacity – 795+ • It was originally called The 'Royal' Comedy Theatre
Criterion	• Opened in 1874 • Seating capacity – 580+ • Apart from the box office, the entire theatre is underground
Dominion	• Opened in 1929 • Seating capacity – 2,005+ • This theatre has been used as a cinema and concert hall too; in theatre-land, it is affectionately called 'The Barn' because it has a large and sprawling, open feel to it
Donmar Warehouse	• Opened in 1977 • Seating capacity – 245+ • Prior to its opening as a theatre, the theatre impresario, Donald Albery, bought the old warehouse and converted it into a rehearsal studio for the London Festival Ballet, a company he formed with his friend, Margot Fonteyn; it is the combination of their Christian names which gave the theatre its name
Drury Lane	• Opened in 1812, although there was a theatre on this site way back in 1663 which was destroyed by The Great Fire of London • Seating capacity – 2,235+ • The rake (incline) on this stage is so steep that actors, and especially dancers, live in constant fear that one day they will end up in the pit with the orchestra!
Duchess	• Opened in 1929 • Seating capacity – 475+ • This theatre is one of the smallest proscenium arched theatres in London
Duke of York's	• Opened in 1892 • Seating capacity – 635+ • It has gone through a number of name changes, twice being called 'The Duke of York's Theatre' in the process
Fortune	• Opened in 1924 • Seating capacity – 430+ • The theatre stands next door to a church and the first production it housed was called *Sinners*
Garrick	• Opened in 1889 • Seating capacity – 655+ • A theatre mostly associated with comedies

THEATRE	INFORMATION
Gielgud	• Opened in 1906 • Seating capacity – 885+ • Like many London theatres, this has had more than one name: The Hicks > The Globe > The Gielgud. It is renowned for its beautiful circular Regency staircase
Hammersmith Apollo	• Opened in 1932 • Seating capacity – 3,630+ • This is another theatre which was originally built as a cinema
Haymarket Theatre Royal	• Opened in 1821, although there has been a theatre here since 1720, the first being called 'The Little Theatre in the Haymarket' • Seating capacity – 900+ • In 2004, a chandelier in the auditorium came away from the ceiling – nobody was seriously injured; and all this in a theatre opposite another theatre housing *Phantom of the Opera*
Her Majesty's	• Opened in 1897, the fourth theatre on the site • Seating capacity – 1,205+ • The name of this theatre changes according to whether the reigning Monarch is male or female i.e. 'Her Majesty's' or 'His Majesty's'
London Coliseum	• Opened in 1904 • Seating capacity – 2,355+ • This theatre was designed as 'The People's Palace of Entertainment and Art'. So there goes that word 'Palace' again
London Palladium	• Opened in 1910 • Seating capacity – 2,295+ • This is a theatre which has also been used for television shows, probably the most famous being the 1960s TV show, *Sunday Night at the London Palladium*
Lyceum	• Opened in 1904, although the first theatre on this site dates back to 1770 • Seating capacity – 2,105+ • Try walking up the stairs to the highest seat in the house – and breathing normally afterwards!
Lyric	• Opened in 1888 • Seating capacity – 965+ • This is the oldest surviving theatre of all the theatres on the famous Shaftesbury Avenue
Menier Chocolate Factory	• Opened in 2004 • Seating capacity – 200+ • Originally built in 1870 as a chocolate factory
National	• Opened in 1976 • Seating capacity, three theatres in total – 2,500+ Olivier Lyttelton Cottesloe • The idea of a National Theatre was first suggested in 1848

204

THEATRE	INFORMATION
New Ambassadors	• Opened in 1913 • Seating capacity – 440+ • This theatre has a very small stage – only 6.25 metres deep
New London	• Opened in 1973, although there was a theatre on this site as far back as 1851 • Seating capacity – 1,105+ • In the late 1970s, it was used as a television studio
Noël Coward (formerly Albery)	• Opened in 1903 • Seating capacity – 870+ • Noël Coward made his very own West End debut in this theatre in 1920
Novello (formerly The Strand)	• Opened in 1905 • Seating capacity – 1,065+ • This theatre is the twin of the Aldwych, sitting as it does on the other side of the Waldorf Hotel – it was originally called The Waldorf Theatre. It was given its most recent name in honour of Ivor Novello who lived in a flat above the theatre for years
Old Vic	• Opened in 1818 • Seating capacity – 1,065+ • It was the home of the original National Theatre until it moved to its new home on The South Bank
Palace	• Opened in 1891 • Seating capacity – 1,390+ • Renowned for housing blockbuster musicals
Phoenix	• Opened in 1930 • Seating capacity – 1,010+ • A theatre which has strong links with Noël Coward and, in fact, opened with a production of his play *Private Lives* and went on to be the home for many more of his works. So it was that the foyer bar was renamed 'The Noël Coward Bar' in his honour
Piccadilly	• Opened in 1928 • Seating capacity – 1,230+ • It is said that, if all the bricks used in the building of this theatre were laid in a straight line, they would stretch from London to Paris
Playhouse	• Opened in 1882 • Seating capacity – 780+ • It was once used as a BBC radio studio
Prince of Wales	• Opened in 1884 • Seating capacity – 1,155+ • In the 1930s, it was known as London's *Folies Bergère* when it presented risqué revues
Prince Edward	• Opened in 1930 • Seating capacity – 1,655+

205

THEATRE	INFORMATION
	• It was dark for two years during the Second World War before reopening as the home of the Queensberry All Services Club, where the audience was made up of members of the different forces
Queen's	• Opened in 1907 • Seating capacity – 975+ • During World War Two, a bomb fell on the theatre destroying the front of house and the rear stalls
Royal Court	• Originally opened as a theatre in 1870, it wasn't until 1956 that The Royal Court began producing the innovative theatre for which it is known today • Seating capacity – Jerwood Theatre Downstairs – 390+ Jerwood Theatre Upstairs – 80+ • *Look Back in Anger* was first produced here
Savoy	• Opened in 1929, although the first theatre on the site opened in 1881 • Seating capacity – 1,150+ • It was the first theatre in the world to be lit entirely by electricity
Shaftesbury	• Opened in 1911 • Seating capacity – 1,385+ • In 1973, part of the ceiling fell in, prematurely closing the production of the musical, *Hair*
Shakespeare's Globe Theatre	• Opened in 1997 [the original Globe Theatre, built in 1599, was on a different site] • Seating capacity – 1,380 plus 500 standing • The building of The Globe was initiated by an American who thought that there should be a theatrical monument to the Bard
St Martin's	• Opened in 1916 • Seating capacity 545+ • Agatha Christie's long-running play, *The Mousetrap*, has been housed here since 1974
Trafalgar Studios	• Opened in 1930 • Seating capacity – Studio 1 – 380, Studio 2 – 100 • Formerly 'The Whitehall Theatre' and famous for 'The Whitehall Farces'
Vaudeville	• Opened in 1926; the original theatre on this site opened in 1870 • Seating capacity – 685+ • In keeping with its name, it was mostly revues and vaudeville shows which played this theatre in the early days
Victoria Palace	• Opened in 1911, although there has been a theatre on this site since the 1830s • Seating capacity – 1,515+ • This is the theatre which will forever be remembered by many as the home of the *Black and White Minstrel Show*
Wyndhams	• Opened in 1899 • Seating capacity – 755+ • Following the outbreak of the Second World War and the compulsory closure of theatres in September 1939, Wyndham's was one of the first to reopen

PROMINENT AMERICAN THEATERS INCLUDE

So now we'll travel across the pond to take a look at just a few of the American THEATERS – notice the spelling of the word theatre now that we are referring to America.

NEW YORK THEATERS	INFORMATION
August Wilson	• Opened in 1925 • Seating capacity – 1,270+ • For a while, the theater was used as a radio studio
Eugene O'Neill	• Opened in 1925 • Seating capacity – 1,100+ • Until Neil Simon started to produce his own plays almost exclusively at the O'Neill, the theater went for years without a hit
Gershwin	• Opened in 1972 • Seating capacity – 1,900+ • It was named after George and Ira Gershwin
Majestic	• Opened in 1927 • Seating capacity – 1,640+ • It was always intended that this theater would house musicals
Nederlander	• Opened in 1921 • Seating capacity – 1,230+ • Over the years it has been known as 'The National', 'The Billy Rose' and 'The Trafalgar'
Neil Simon	• Opened in 1927 • Seating capacity – 1,440+ • Originally known as the 'Alvin' it was renamed The Neil Simon Theater in celebration of America's prolific playwright, Neil Simon
Palace	• Opened in 1913 • Seating capacity – 1,740+ • Until the 1960s, the theater was used for Vaudeville and concerts
Richard Rodgers	• Opened in 1924 • Seating capacity – 1,315+ • Here can be found 'The Richard Rodgers Gallery' housing historic memorabilia from Rodgers' legendary career

CALIFORNIAN THEATERS	INFORMATION
El Capitan (Hollywood)	• Opened in 1926 • Seating capacity – 999+ • In recent years, the stage has been restored to its original 1926 dimensions
Kodak (Hollywood)	• Opened in 2001 • Seating capacity – 3,399+ • The Kodak Theater is well known for hosting the Oscars every year
Orpheum (San Francisco)	• Opened in 1926 • Seating capacity – 2,199+ • This theater is recognised as a San Francisco historical landmark and features ornate architecture
Pantages (Los Angeles)	• Opened in 1930 • Seating capacity – 2,690+ • For 10 years it was home to Academy Awards Presentations

PROMINENT AUSTRALIAN THEATRES INCLUDE

Theatre in Australia is a fast-growing medium; Australian thespians need to start thinking what they will call the area where their top shows play, an area which could one day well rival the West End and Broadway and also become synonymous with the very best in theatre.

MELBOURNE THEATRES	INFORMATION
Comedy Theatre	• Opened in 1928 • Seating capacity – 995+ • The exterior is a replica of a Florentine palace
Her Majesty's Theatre	• Opened in 1886 • Seating capacity – 1,699+ • There was a separate entrance to the Grand Circle as it was thought inappropriate for those sitting in the Gods to mingle with those in the more expensive seats!
Regent Theatre	• Opened in 1929 • Seating capacity – 2,160+ • Fire almost destroyed the theatre in 1945 and it was two years before it reopened

SYDNEY THEATRES	INFORMATION
Capitol Theatre	• Opened 1928, though performance buildings on this site date back over a hundred years • Seating capacity – 2,000+ • After a chequered past and extended periods of decay, the Capitol was restored to its former glory and reopened in 1995
Sydney Opera House	• Opened 1973 • Seating capacity: Concert Hall – 2,675+ Drama Theatre – 540+ Opera Theatre – 1,545+ Playhouse – 395+ Studio – 279+ • The forecourt has even been used as an amphitheatre for outdoor events
Theatre Royal	• Opened 1976 – although there has been a theatre here since 1875 • Seating capacity – 1,130+ • It is said that the first Theatre Royal in Sydney was built by the brother of a convict

Excellent, enjoyable and groundbreaking theatre happens everywhere in the world, from a small hut in a country village to a large theatre in the heart of London or New York; such is theatre that it is created by everyone, everywhere and belongs to everyone, everywhere. For that reason, it has only been possible to include a small selection of theatres in this book; this is certainly no reflection on the quality of theatre produced in those countries that are not represented.

Chapter Six

And for an Encore

Prizes and Awards

'And I'd like to thank …' We have all heard, and groaned at, those opening words of the traditional acceptance speech when someone is awarded public recognition for their contribution to the arts. The audience – in part made up of rejected celebrities – sit with fixed smiles, pleased for the recipient whilst, at the same time, trying not to show their own disappointment at being overlooked – again! The public, perhaps watching on TV as the industry pats itself on the back, yet again, just wish that they would get on with it and not reel off a meaningless list of names. But it is actually good to hear a very public face recognise that, without the help of those faceless names, they would not be clutching that coveted award.

Theatre is a complex industry; rather like a jigsaw puzzle where every piece needs to be in place to make the whole complete and so those thank you speeches, boring as they may be, are in fact important to the other pieces of the jigsaw puzzle, for they make the whole.

There are various awards for theatre professionals on both sides of the pond – and indeed around the world – each recognising various pieces of this puzzle. Here you will find the most prestigious of these awards, generally just dealing with the plays and playwrights sections. And so we start with:

THE NOBEL PRIZE FOR LITERATURE

Since 1901, the Nobel Prize has been awarded to individuals in recognition for their outstanding achievements in physics, chemistry, medicine, literature and for work to achieve world peace. Among the great literary figures to be awarded the Nobel Prize for literature are five world famous playwrights:

Year	Playwright	Nationality
1934	Luigi Pirandello	Italian
1936	Eugene O'Neill	American
1969	Samuel Beckett	Irish
1997	Dario Fo	Italian
2005	Harold Pinter	British

THE LAURENCE OLIVIER AWARDS

'The Society of West End Theatre Awards' were established in 1976 and, in 1984, renamed, 'The Laurence Olivier Awards', (now affectionately referred to as 'The Larries'), after the great British actor Laurence Olivier. These awards publicly honour and recognise achievement in London theatre.

YEAR	PLAY	PLAYWRIGHT
THE BBC AWARD FOR BEST NEW PLAY		
1976	Dear Daddy	Denis Cannan
1977	The Fire That Consumes	Henry de Montherlant; English version by Vivian Cox with Bernard Miles
1978	Whose Life is it Anyway	Brian Clark
1979	Betrayal	Harold Pinter
1980	The Life and Adventures of Nicholas Nickleby	Charles Dickens; adapted by David Edgar
1981	Children of a Lesser God	Mark Medoff
1982	Another Country	Julian Mitchell
1983	Glengarry Glen Ross	David Mamet
1984	Benefactors	Michael Frayn
1985	Red Noses	Peter Barnes
1986	Les Liaisons Dangereuses	Christopher Hampton
1987	Serious Money	Caryl Churchill
1988	Our Country's Good	Timberlake Wertenbaker
1989/90	Racing Demon	David Hare
1991	Dancing at Lughnasa	Brian Friel
1992	Death and the Maiden	Ariel Dorfman
1993	Six Degrees of Separation	John Guare
1994	Arcadia	Tom Stoppard
1995	Broken Glass	Arthur Miller
1996	Skylight	David Hare
1997	Stanley	Pam Gems
1998	Closer	Patrick Marber
1999	The Weir	Conor McPherson
2000	Goodnight Children Everywhere	Richard Nelson
2001	Blue/Orange	Joe Penhall
2002	Jitney	August Wilson
2003	Vincent in Brixton	Nicholas Wright
BEST NEW PLAY		
2004	The Pillowman	Martin McDonagh
2005	The History Boys	Alan Bennett
2006	On the Shore of the Wide World	Simon Stephens
2007	Blackbird	David Harrower
2008	Disappearing Number	Simon McBurney
2009	Black Watch	Gregory Burke

YEAR	PLAY	PLAYWRIGHT
BEST COMEDY		
1976	*Donkey's Years*	Michael Frayn
1977	*Privates on Parade*	Peter Nichols
1978	*Filumena*	Eduardo de Filippo; adapted by Keith Waterhouse and Willis Hall
1979	*Middle-Age Spread*	Roger Hall
1980	*Educating Rita*	Willy Russell
1981	*Steaming*	Nell Dunn
1982	*Noises Off*	Michael Frayn
1983	*Daisy Pulls it Off*	Denise Deegan
1984	*Up 'n' Under*	John Godber
1985	*A Chorus of Disapproval*	Alan Ayckbourn
1986	*When We Are Married*	J.B. Priestley
1987	*Three Men on a Horse*	John Cecil Holm & George Abbott
1988	*Shirley Valentine*	Willy Russell
1989/90	*Single Spies*	Alan Bennett
1991	*Out of Order*	Ray Cooney
1992	*La Bête*	David Hirson
1993	*The Rise and Fall of Little Voice*	Jim Cartwright
1994	*Hysteria*	Terry Johnson
1995	*My Night with Reg*	Kevin Elyot
1996	*Mojo*	Jez Butterworth
1997	*Art*	Yasmina Reza
1998	*Popcorn*	Ben Elton
1999	*Cleo, Camping, Emmanuelle and Dick*	Terry Johnson
2000	*The Memory of Water*	Shelagh Stephenson
2001	*Stones in His Pockets*	Marie Jones
2002	*The Play What I Wrote*	Hamish McColl, Sean Foley, Eddie Braben
2003	*The Lieutenant of Inishmore*	Martin McDonagh
BEST NEW COMEDY		
2006	*Heroes*	Gerald Sibleyras; translated by Tom Stoppard
2007	*The 39 Steps*	John Buchan; adapted by Patrick Barlow from an original concept by Simon Corble and Nobby Dimon
2008	*Rafta Rafta*	Ayub Khan-Din; based on *All in Good Time* by Bill Naughton
2009	*God Of Carnage*	Yasmina Reza, translated by Christopher Hampton

EVENING STANDARD AWARDS

The Evening Standard Awards – which are sponsored by *The Evening Standard* newspaper – were established in 1955 and are presented annually for outstanding achievement in London Theatre.

YEAR	CATEGORY	TITLE	PLAYWRIGHT
1955	Best New Play	*Tiger at the Gates*	Jean Giraudoux
	Most Controversial Play	*Waiting for Godot*	Samuel Beckett
1956	Best New Play	*Romanoff and Juliet*	Peter Ustinov
	Most Promising Playwright	*Look Back in Anger*	John Osborne
1957	Best Play	*Summer of the Seventeenth Doll*	Ray Lawler
1958	Best Play	*Cat on a Hot Tin Roof*	Tennessee Williams
	Most Promising Playwright	*Five Finger Exercise*	Peter Shaffer
1959	Best Play	*The Long and the Short and the Tall*	Willis Hall
	Most Promising Playwright (Joint)	a. *Sergeant Musgrave's Dance*	John Arden
		b. *Roots*	Arnold Wesker
1960	Best Play	*The Caretaker*	Harold Pinter
	Most Promising Playwright	*Fairy Tales of New York*	J.P. Donleavy
1961	Best Play	*Beckett*	Jean Anouilh
	Most Promising Playwright (Joint)	a. *The Keep*	Gwyn Thomas
		b. *Stop it Whoever You Are* and *Big Soft Nellie*	Henry Livings
1962	Best Play	*The Caucasian Chalk Circle*	Bertolt Brecht
	Most Promising Playwright	*Afore Night Come*	David Rudkin
1963	Best Play	*Poor Bitos*	Jean Anouilh
	Most Promising Playwright (Joint)	a. *Cockade*	Charles Wood
		b. *Next Time I'll Sing to You*	James Saunders
1964	Best Play	*Who's Afraid of Virginia Woolf*	Edward Albee
1965	Best Play (Joint)	a. *A Patriot for Me*	John Osborne
		b. *The Killing of Sister George*	Frank Marcus
	Most Promising Playwright	*Ride a Cock Horse*	David Mercer
1966	Best Play	*Loot*	Joe Orton
	Most Promising Playwright	*Little Malcolm and His Struggle Against the Eunuchs*	David Halliwell
1967	Best Play	*A Day in the Death of Joe Egg*	Peter Nichols
	Most Promising Playwright (Joint)	a. *Rosencrantz and Guildenstern are Dead*	Tom Stoppard
		b. *The Restoration of Arnold Middleton*	David Storey
1968	Best New Play	*Hotel in Amsterdam*	John Osborne
	Special Award	*Forty Years On*	Alan Bennett
1969	Best Play	*National Health*	Peter Nichols
	Most Promising Playwright	*The Ruling Class*	Peter Barnes
1970	Best Play	*Home*	David Storey
	Most Promising Playwright (Joint)	a. *Slag*	David Hare
		b. *AC/DC*	Heathcoat Williams
1971	Best Play	*Butely*	Simon Gray
	Best Comedy	*Getting On*	Alan Bennett
	Most Promising Playwright	*The Foursome*	E. A. Whitehead
1972	Best Play	*Jumpers*	Tom Stoppard
	Best Comedy	*Veterans*	Charles Wood
	Most Promising Playwright	*Within Two Shadows*	Wilson John Haire
	Special Award (for 10-year World Theatre Season)		Peter Daubeny

YEAR	CATEGORY	TITLE	PLAYWRIGHT
1973	Best Play	*Saturday Sunday Monday*	Eduardo de Filippo
	Best Comedy	*Absurd Person Singular*	Alan Ayckbourn
	Most Promising Playwright	*The Removalists*	David Williamson
	Special Award		Laurence Olivier
1974	Best Play	*Norman Conquests*	Alan Ayckbourn
	Best Comedy	*Travesties*	Tom Stoppard
	Most Promising Playwright	*Play Mas*	Mustapha Matura
1975	Best Play	*Otherwise Engaged*	Simon Gray
	Best Comedy	*Alphabetical Order*	Michael Frayn
	Most Promising Playwright	*Hitting Town and Sugar*	Stephen Poliakoff
	Special Award		Ben Travers
1976	Best Play	*Weapons of Happiness*	Howard Brenton
	Best Comedy	*The Thoughts of Chairman Alf*	Johnny Speight
	Most Promising Playwright	*Spokesong*	Stewart Parker
	Special Award		Peggy Ashcroft
1977	Best Play	*Just Between Ourselves*	Alan Ayckbourn
	Best Comedy	*Privates on Parade*	Peter Nichols
	Most Promising Playwright	a. *Once a Catholic*	Mary O'Malley
	(Joint)	b. *Factory Birds*	James Robson
	Special Award		Hampstead Theatre
1978	Best Play	*Night and Day*	Tom Stoppard
	Best Comedy	*Gloo-Joo*	Michael Hastings
	Most Promising Playwright	a. *Slab Boys*	John Byrne
	(Joint)	b. *Whose Life is it Anyway*	Brian Clark
1979	Best Play	*Amadeus*	Peter Shaffer
	Best Comedy	*A Day in Hollywood/A Night in the Ukraine*	Dick Vosburgh & Frank Lazarus
	Most Promising Playwright	a. *Outside Edge*	Richard Harris
	(Joint)	b. *Talent*	Victoria Wood
	Special 25th Anniversary Award		Peter Hall
1980	Best Play	*The Dresser*	Ronald Harwood
	Best Comedy	*Make and Break*	Michael Frayn
	Most Promising Playwright	*Not Quite Jerusalem*	Paul Kember
	Special Award		Ralph Richardson
1981	Best Play	*Passion Play*	Peter Nichols
	Best Comedy	*Goose-Pimples*	Mike Leigh
	Most Promising Playwright	*Steaming*	Nell Dunn
	Special Award		Royal Shakespeare Company
1982	Best Play	*The Real Thing*	Tom Stoppard
	Best Comedy	*Noises Off*	Michael Frayn
	Most Promising Playwright	*Insignificance*	Terry Johnson
	Special Award		John Gielgud
1983	Best Play	*Master Harold and the Boys*	Athol Fugard
	Best Comedy	*Tales from Hollywood*	Christopher Hampton
	Most Promising Playwright	*Crystal Clear*	Phil Young

YEAR	CATEGORY	TITLE	PLAYWRIGHT
1984	Best Play	*Benefactors*	Michael Frayn
	Best Comedy	*Stepping Out*	Richard Harris
	Most Promising Playwright	*When I Was a Girl I Used to Scream and Shout*	Sharman MacDonald
1985	Best Play	*Pravda*	David Hare & Howard Brenton
	Best Comedy	*A Chorus of Disapproval*	Alan Ayckbourn
	Most Promising Playwright	*Grafters*	Billy Hamon
1986	Best Play	*Les Liaisons Dangereuses*	Christopher Hampton
	Best Comedy	*A Month of Sundays*	Bob Larbey
	Most Promising Playwright	*Observe the Sons of Ulster Marching Towards the Somme*	Frank McGuinness
1987	Best Play	*A Small Family Business*	Alan Ayckbourn
	Best Comedy	*Serious Comedy*	Caryl Churchill
	Most Promising Playwright	*Curtains*	Stephen Bill
1988	Best Play	*Aristocrats*	Brian Friel
	Best Comedy	*Lettice and Lovage*	Peter Shaffer
	Most Promising Playwright	*Our Country's Good*	Timberlake Wertenbaker
	Special Award		National Theatre
1989	Best Play	*Ghetto*	Joshua Sobol
	Best Comedy	*Henceforward*	Alan Ayckbourn
	Most Promising Playwright	*Valued Friends*	Stephen Jeffreys
	Special Award		Stephen Sondheim
1990	Best Play	*Shadowlands*	William Nicholson
	Best Comedy (Joint)	a. *Man of the Moment*	Alan Ayckbourn
		b. *Jeffrey Bernard is Unwell*	Keith Waterhouse
	Most Promising Playwright	*My Heart's a Suitcase*	Clare McIntyre
1991	Best Play	*Dancing at Lughnasa*	Brian Friel
	Best Comedy	*Kvetch*	Steven Berkoff
	Most Promising Playwright	*Bold Girls*	Rona Munro
1992	Best Play	*Angels in America*	Tony Kushner
	Best Comedy	*The Rise and Fall of Little Voice*	Jim Cartwright
	Most Promising Playwright	*The Fastest Clock in the Universe*	Philip Ridley
1993	Best Play	*Arcadia*	Tom Stoppard
	Best Comedy	*Jamais Vu*	Ken Campbell
	Most Promising Playwright (Joint)	a. *The Life of Stuff*	Simon Donald
		b. *Unidentified Human Remains*	Brad Fraser
1994	Best Play	*Three Tall Women*	Edward Albee
	Best Comedy	*My Night with Reg*	Kevin Elyot
	Most Promising Playwright	*Babies*	Jonathan Harvey
	Special Award		Peter Brook
1995	Best Play	*Pentecost*	David Edgar
	Best Comedy	*Dealer's Choice*	Patrick Marber
	Most Promising Playwright	*Mojo*	Jez Butterworth
1996	Best Play	*Stanley*	Pam Gems
	Best Comedy	*Art*	Yasmina Reza
	Most Promising Playwright	*The Beauty of Queen*	Martin McDonagh

YEAR	CATEGORY	TITLE	PLAYWRIGHT
1997	Best Play	*The Invention of Love*	Tom Stoppard
	Best Comedy	*Closer*	Patrick Marber
	Most Promising Playwright	*The Weir*	Conor McPherson
	Special Award		Richard Eyre
	(For his Directorship of the Royal National Theatre)		
1998	Best Play	*Copenhagen*	Michael Frayn
	Most Promising Playwright	*Handbag*	Mark Ravenhill
	Special Award		Nicole Kidman
1999	Most Promising Playwright	*The Glory of Living*	Rebecca Gilman
	Theatrical Event of the Year	*The Lion King*	Book by Roger Allers & Irene Mecchi
2000	Best Play	*Blue/Orange*	Joe Penhall
	Best Comedy	*Stones in His Pocket*	Marie Jones
	The Charles Winter Award for Most Promising Playwright	*The Force of Change*	Gary Mitchell
2001	Best Play	*The Far Side of the Moon*	Robert Lepage
	Best Comedy	*Feelgood*	Alistair Beaton
	The Charles Winter Award for Most Promising Playwright	*Clubland*	Roy Williams
2002	Best Play	*A Number*	Caryl Churchill
	The Charles Winter Award for Most Promising Playwright	*Plasticine*	Vassily Sigarev
	Special Award		Mark Rylance (Shakespeare's Globe)
2003	Best Play	*Democracy*	Michael Frayn
	The Charles Winter Award for Most Promising Playwright	*Elmina's Kitchen*	Kwame Kei Armah
	Special Award		Max Stafford-Clark (Lifetime contribution to theatre and dedication to new writing)
2004	Best Play	*The History Boys*	Alan Bennett
	The Charles Winter Award for Most Promising Playwright	*The Goat, or Who is Sylvia*	Eddie Redmayne
	Special 50th Anniversary Playwright Award		Harold Pinter
2005	Best Play	*The Home Place*	Brian Friel
	The Charles Winter Award for Most Promising Playwright	*Comfort Me with Apples*	Nell Leyshon

YEAR	CATEGORY	TITLE	PLAYWRIGHT
	Special Award		Royal Court Theatre (For fifty years of making and changing theatrical history)
2006	Best Play	*Rock 'n' Roll*	Tom Stoppard
	The Charles Winter Award for Most Promising Playwright	*Rabbit*	Nina Raine
	Special Award		Tricycle Theatre (For its pioneering work in political theatre)
2007	Best Play	*A Disappearing Number*	Simon McBurney (Complicite)
	The Charles Winter Award for Most Promising Playwright	*That Face*	Polly Stenham
	Special Award		Steve Tompkins (For innovative theatre architecture)
2008	Best Play	*The Pitmen Painters*	Lee Hall
	The Charles Winter Award for Most Promising Playwright	*In The Red And Brown Water/ The Brothers Size*	Tarell Alvin McCraney
	Editors Award	*The Histories Cycle*	RSC

And then we cross the Pond for –

THE PULITZER PRIZE FOR DRAMA

A Pulitzer Prize is an American award and generally recognised as the highest national honour in various categories, with drama being one of them, and was established by Joseph Pulitzer, a Hungarian/American journalist who, upon his death, left money to Columbia University, some of which is now used to fund the Pulitzer Prizes.

DATE	PLAY	PLAYWRIGHT
1920	*Beyond the Horizon*	Eugene O'Neill
1921	*Miss Lulu Bett*	Zona Gale
1922	*Anna Christie*	Eugene O'Neill
1923	*Icebound*	Owen Davis
1924	*Hell-Bent fer Heaven*	Hatcher Hughes

DATE	PLAY	PLAYWRIGHT
1925	*They Knew What They Wanted*	Sidney Howard
1926	*Craig's Wife*	George Kelly
1927	*In Abraham's Bosom*	Paul Green
1928	*Strange Interlude*	Eugene O'Neill
1929	*Street Scene*	Elmer L. Rice
1930	*The Green Pastures*	Marc Connelly
1931	*Alison's House*	Susan Glaspell
1932	*Of Thee I Sing*	Music: George Gershwin
		Lyrics: Ira Gershwin
		Book: George S. Kaufman & Morrie Ryskind
1933	*Both Your Houses*	Maxwell Anderson
1934	*Men in White*	Sidney Kingsley
1935	*The Old Maid*	Zoe Akins
1936	*Idiots Delight*	Robert E. Sherwood
1937	*You Can't Take It with You*	Moss Hart & George S. Kaufman
1938	*Our Town*	Thornton Wilder
1939	*Abe Lincoln in Illinois*	Robert E. Sherwood
1940	*The Time of Your Life*	William Saroyan
1941	*There Shall Be No Night*	Robert E. Sherwood
1942	No Award	
1943	*The Skin of Our Teeth*	Thornton Wilder
1944	No Award	
1945	*Harvey*	Mary Chase
1946	*State of the Union*	Russel Crouse & Howard Lindsay
1947	No Award	
1948	*A Streetcar Named Desire*	Tennessee Williams
1949	*Death Of a Salesman*	Arthur Miller
1950	*South Pacific*	Music: Richard Rodgers
		Lyric: Oscar Hammerstein II
		Book: Oscar Hammerstein II & Joshua Logan
1951	No Award	
1952	*The Shrike*	Joseph Kramm
1953	*Picnic*	William Inge
1954	*The Teahouse of the August Moon*	John Patrick
1955	*Cat on a Hot Tin Roof*	Tennessee Williams
1956	*The Diary of Anne Frank*	Albert Hackett & Frances Goodrich
1957	*Long Day's Journey into Night*	Eugene O'Neill
1958	*Look Homeward, Angel*	Ketti Frings
1959	*JB*	Archibald MacLeish
1960	*Fiorello*	Book by: Jerome Weidman & George Abbott
		Music by: Gerry Bock
		Lyrics by: Sheldon Harnick
1961	*All the Way Home*	Tad Mosel
1962	*How to Succeed in Business Without Really Trying*	Frank Loesser & Abe Burrows
1963	No Award	
1964	No Award	
1965	*The Subject Was Roses*	Frank D. Gilroy

DATE	PLAY	PLAYWRIGHT
1966	No Award	
1967	*A Delicate Balance*	Edward Albee
1968	No Award	
1969	*The Great White Hope*	Howard Sackler
1970	*No Place to be Somebody*	Charles Gordone
1971	*The Effect of Gamma Rays on Man-In-The-Moon Marigolds*	Paul Zindel
1972	No Award	
1973	*That Championship Season*	Jason Miller
1974	No Award	
1975	*Seascape*	Edward Albee
1976	*A Chorus Line*	Conceived, choreographed & directed by: Michael Bennett Book by: James Kirkwood & Nicholas Dante Music by: Marvin Hamlisch Lyrics by: Edward Kleban
1977	*The Shadow Box*	Michael Cristofer
1978	*The Gin Game*	Donald L. Coburn
1979	*Buried Child*	Sam Shepard
1980	*Talley's Folley*	Lanford Wilson
1981	*Crimes of the Heart*	Beth Henley
1982	*A Soldier's Play*	Charles Fuller
1983	*Night Mother*	Marsha Norman
1984	*Glengarry Glen Ross*	David Mamet
1985	*Sunday in the Park with George*	Music: Stephen Sondheim Lyrics: Stephen Sondheim Book: James Lapine
1986	No Award	
1987	*Fences*	August Wilson
1988	*Driving Miss Daisy*	Alfred Uhry
1989	*The Heidi Chronicles*	Wendy Wasserstein
1990	*The Piano Lesson*	August Wilson
1991	*Lost in Yonkers*	Neil Simon
1992	*The Kentucky Cycle*	Robert Schenkkan
1993	*Angels in America: Millennium Approaches*	Tony Kushner
1994	*Three Tall Women*	Edward Albee
1995	*The Young Man from Atlanta*	Horton Foote
1996	*Rent*	Jonathan Larson
1997	No Award	
1998	*How I learned to Drive*	Paula Vogen
1999	*Wit*	Margaret Edson
2000	*Dinner with Friends*	Donald Margulies
2001	*Proof*	David Auburn
2002	*Topdog/Underdog*	Suzan-Lori Parks

DATE	PLAY	PLAYWRIGHT
2003	*Anna in the Tropics*	Nilo Cruz
2004	*I am My Own Wife*	Doug Wright
2005	*Doubt, a Parable*	John Patrick Shanley
2006	No Award	
2007	*Rabbit Hole*	David Lindsay-Abaire

TONY AWARDS

The Tony Awards were established in 1947 and named after Antoinette Perry, an American actress, director and producer, to recognise excellence in theatre.

DATE	PLAY	PLAYWRIGHT
1947	*All My Sons*	Arthur Miller
1948	*Mister Roberts*	Thomas Heggen & Joshua Logan: based on the Thomas Heggen novel
1949	*Death of a Salesman*	Arthur Miller
1950	*The Cocktail Party*	T.S. Eliot
1951	*The Rose Tattoo*	Tennessee Williams
1952	*The Four Poster*	Jan de Hartog
1953	*The Crucible*	Arthur Miller
1954	*The Teahouse of August Moon*	John Patrick
1955	*The Desperate Hours*	Joseph Hayes
1956	*The Diary of Anne Frank*	Albert Hackett & Frances Goodrich
1957	*Long Day's Journey into Night*	Eugene O'Neill
1958	*Sunrise at Campobello*	Dore Schary
1959	*JB*	Archibald MacLeish
1960	*The Miracle Worker*	William Gibson
1961	*Beckett*	Jean Anouilh; translated by Lucienne Hill
1962	*A Man for All Seasons*	Robert Bolt
1963	*Who's Afraid of Virginia Woolf*	Edward Albee
1964	*Luther*	John Osborne
1965	*The Subject Was Roses*	Frank D. Gilroy
1966	*Marat/Sade*	Peter Weiss English version by Geoffrey Skelton
1967	*The Homecoming*	Harold Pinter
1968	*Rosencrantz and Guildenstern Are Dead*	Tom Stoppard
1969	*The Great White Hope*	Howard Sackler
1970	*Borstal Boy*	Frank McMahon
1971	*Sleuth*	Anthony Shaffer
1972	*Sticks and Bones*	David Rabe
1973	*That Championship Season*	Jason Miller
1974	*The River Niger*	Joseph A. Walker
1975	*Equus*	Peter Shaffer

DATE	PLAY	PLAYWRIGHT
1976	*Travesties*	Tom Stoppard
1977	*The Shadow Box*	Michael Cristofer
1978	*Da*	Hugh Leonard
1979	*The Elephant Man*	Bernard Pomerance
1980	*Children of a Lesser God*	Mark Medoff
1981	*Amadeus*	Peter Shaffer
1982	*The Life and Adventures of Nicholas Nickleby*	David Edgar
1983	*Torch Song Trilogy*	Harvey Fierstein
1984	*The Real Thing*	Tom Stoppard
1985	*Biloxi Blues*	Neil Simon
1986	*I'm Not Rappaport*	Herb Gardner
1987	*Fences*	August Wilson
1988	*M. Butterfly*	David Henry Hwang
1989	*The Heidi Chronicles*	Wendy Wasserstein
1990	*The Grapes of Wrath*	Frank Galati
1991	*Lost in Yonkers*	Neil Simon
1992	*Dancing at Lughnasa*	Brian Friel
1993	*Angels in America: Millennium Approaches*	Tony Kushner
1994	*Angels in America: Perestroika*	Tony Kushner
1995	*Love! Valour! Compassion!*	Terrence McNally
1996	*Master Class*	Terrence McNally
1997	*The Last Night of Ballyhoo*	Alfred Uhry
1998	*Art*	Yasmina Reza
1999	*Side Man*	Warren Leight
2000	*Copenhagen*	Michael Frayn
2001	*Proof*	David Auburn
2002	*The Goat, or Who is Sylvia?*	Edward Albee
2003	*Take Me Out*	Richard Greenberg
2004	*I Am My Own Wife*	Doug Wright
2005	*Doubt*	John Patrick Shanley
2006	*The History Boys*	Alan Bennett
2007	*The Coast of Utopia*	Tom Stoppard

Theatrical Terms

Just like other professions, theatre has its own language which, to thespians, is a natural and normal way of speaking but, to anyone else, it must seem at best glamorous and at worse just plain confusing. This 'language' is, of course, extensive and, at times, complicated; however, for the time being, here is just a smattering of our interesting 'speak'.

ANGEL   This, in our world, is not a heavenly body but someone who invests money in a production in return for a share of the profits.

APRON	Not a protective piece of clothing but an extension of the stage reaching out beyond the proscenium arch.
ASIDE	A term which is used to denote that a character must speak directly to the audience – the other characters in the cast are ostensibly unable to hear them.
ASM	An abbreviation for the overworked and much maligned Assistant Stage Manager.
BACKLIGHT	This is a light which comes from behind the actors and is used to sculpt and shape their bodies.
BAND PARTS	This is what we call the music for each of the instruments in the band.
BARN DOORS	The words used to describe the external shutters on a lantern which, in turn, control the spread of its beam.
BEGINNERS	1. A term used to describe the actors who are on stage or ready in the wings at the beginning of each act. 2. The warning call given by the DSM five minutes before each act begins.
BLACKS	These are the black clothes that are worn by the crew and stage management team so they cannot be seen by the audience during scene changes.
BLEED THROUGH	The effect of lighting a gauze from behind to make whatever is behind it gradually visible to the audience.
BLOCKING	When the director plots the actors' entrances, exits and movements around the stage, it is called blocking. (This is then recorded in the prompt copy by the DSM).
BOARDS	The stage is generally called the boards. An actor is said to 'tread the boards'.
BOX SET	An enclosed set consisting of three walls and sometimes a ceiling piece. (The proscenium arch is the open fourth wall – through which the audience view the action.)
BUSINESS	Actions performed by an actor during a performance are called business.
CALL	1. The time an actor/musician is required at rehearsal. 2. A tannoy announcement which is made to backstage or front of house. 3. Curtain call – when an actor takes their final bow.

	4. Company call – rehearsal session at which all performers are required.
CANS	Headsets used by stage management and technical departments to communicate with each other during rehearsals in the theatre and during the actual performance.
CLEARANCE	1. Confirmation from the front of house staff that the audience are seated and the performance can begin. 2. The distance between one flying piece and the next.
COME DOWN	'What time does a show come down?' is actually a thespian's way of asking what time the show finishes.
COMPS	Short for 'complimentary', these are free tickets.
CORPSE	When an actor corpses, it means that they are unable to deliver their lines due to 'unscripted' laughter.
CROSSFADE	A crossfade is the movement from one lighting or sound cue to the next, with no gap.
CROSSOVER	This is a route from one side of the stage to the other – usually extreme upstage – which the actors can use without being seen by the audience.
CUE	1. This can be an actor's signal to speak their line or perform some action on stage. 2. A point at which stage lighting or a stage effect takes place.
CUE LIGHT	A light used to give a cue which cannot be given verbally, such as to the conductor to start the show.
CUE TO CUE	Running the entire show but cutting sequences in which there are no technical effects or cues and often done at the technical rehearsal.
DANCE CAPTAIN	A choreographer's assistant responsible for leading dance warm-ups and running clean-up calls once the show has opened.
DARK	A theatre that is temporarily or permanently closed is said to be 'dark'.
DEAD	1. This is the exact position of a flown piece when it is either in view ('in dead') or out of view ('out dead') or when something is no longer required: 'The settee is dead in Act Two'.

DESK	The term given to the lighting board, sound mixing control or the production desk, the latter of which is generally a table where the creative team and board operators sit during the tech and dress rehearsals.
DIRECTOR	The director is the person in overall control of the artistic and creative elements of a show.
DRESS	We 'dress' a set when we add objects to make it look more realistic.
DRESSER	A dresser is a member of the wardrobe department who assists the actors with costume and wig changes during a performance, especially when quick changes are involved.
DRY	This has nothing to do with not being wet, it actually means to forget one's lines.
DSM	An abbreviation for the Deputy Stage Manager who is responsible for recording all elements of the production in the prompt copy and for running the show during the performance.
FEEDBACK	A high-pitched squeal from a microphone is called feedback; sometimes it is called a 'howlround'.
FLIES	In the theatre, this doesn't necessarily have anything to do with wings and neither does it have to do with men's trousers, but is an area above the stage that holds suspended scenery and lighting.
FLOAT MIC	The name given to a microphone fixed at the edge of the stage.
FLOOD	Nothing at all to do with inclement weather or Noah and his ark, this is actually an all over and complete spread of light across a stage.
FLYMAN	Back to the flies again where we find a flyman, who is a specialist crew member operating the flying system.
FOLDBACK	Loudspeakers placed in such a way that they allow the band and cast to hear each other clearly.
FOLLOW SPOT	A lantern that can be moved to follow performers is called a follow spot.
FOH (Front of House)	1. The area in the theatre that is open to the public. 2. The department responsible for all aspects of this area, including the audience.

GAUZE	A stage cloth which is transparent when lit from behind.
GEL	Ever wondered how lights become coloured? Well, it is by a translucent plastic filter which is placed in front of the lantern to colour the light beam.
GET-IN	The process of moving all the equipment for the show into the theatre.
GET-OUT	The opposite of the Get-In.
GOBOS	These are metal or glass filters which are used to break up or shape the beam of light produced by a lantern. These are used to create particular shapes or effects on the stage.
GREEN ROOM	This is the actors' common room, somewhere for them to meet and relax when not on stage.
HALF (THE)	A half-hour call is given 35 minutes before curtain up and is called 'The half'; a ten-minute call is given 15 minutes before the required time. In the theatre, all calls are five minutes out.
HOUSE	This is the name given to both: 1. The auditorium. 2. The audience.
HOUSE TABS	These are heavy curtains separating the stage from the auditorium.
IN THE ROUND	A form of theatre where the audience sit on all four sides of the acting area.
IRON	Nothing to do with laundry, this is a safety curtain used to separate the auditorium from the stage in the event of a fire. The Iron must be lowered and raised at least once during a performance, usually during the interval.
LANTERN	This is a name given to a single stage light of whatever type.
LEGS	These are vertical strips of fabric, usually used for masking.
LUVVIES	Luvvies is an affectionate and, in my opinion, wonderful name for actors.
LX	Electrics.
MARKING	To sing, dance or act in rehearsal with limited energy in order to conserve it for the actual performance.

225

MD	Abbreviation for Musical Director.
PACK	A radio mic transmitter.
PAPER THE HOUSE	Producers are said to 'paper the house' when they give away a large number of complimentary tickets to ensure a full house.
PASS DOOR	This is the door which leads from the back stage area to the auditorium.
PRESET	Anything that is positioned in advance of a performance is preset.
PREVIEW	Public performances held before the official first night are called previews. During such a preview, the production company reserves the right to stop the show should anything 'go wrong' and seats are usually sold at a reduced price for these performances.
PROMPT COPY	Definitive and annotated copy of the score/libretto used by the DSM to run the show.
PROSCENIUM ARCH	This is the traditional form of 'picture frame' theatre.
PYROTECHNICS	Bangs, flashes, fire specials etc, usually fired electronically.
Q	Shorthand form of cue.
QUARTER	The 15-minute call, given 20 minutes before curtain up.
RESIDENT DIRECTOR	The person who takes care of the day-to-day artistic running of the show once the director has left.
RIG	The lanterns, microphones and speakers for a performance.
SEGUE	Musical term meaning to follow on immediately without any break.
SITZPROBE	A rehearsal at which the cast sing along with the orchestra but do not act or dance.
SM	The abbreviation for Stage Manager.
SPEED RUN	This is a very fast run of all the words and blocking, without any of the dramatic pauses, pacing or emotion.
SPILL	When light strays outside the main beam of a spotlight, it is said to 'spill'.
STAGE LEFT	An actor's positioning on the stage, according to him.

(RIGHT)   This means that an actor standing stage right would be on the left when viewing the stage from the audience. A Director working from the auditorium would then have to reverse all that his eyes see when giving directions. Clever, and quick thinking folk, we thespians.

STAND BY   The words 'stand by' is the warning given to an operator or performer that a cue is about to be given.

STRIKE   To remove an item from the stage when it is no longer needed. To take down a set once the show is over.

SWING   A swing is a performer who understudies all chorus roles.

TBA   To be announced.

TBC   To be confirmed.

TOP   The beginning of a song/show/programme.

TREADS   Stairs.

TRUCK   This is a castored platform on which sets, or parts of a set, can be transported (trucked), on and off the stage.

TWIRLIES   The affectionate name by which dancers are called.

UNDERDRESS   Many actors are called upon to underdress when a part involves a lot of quick changes. The term simply means to wear several costumes at once, one over another, to facilitate quick changes.

UNDERSCORING   Music which is played under dialogue.

UV   Ultraviolet light used to give a fluorescent effect on a darkened stage.

WALK THE LIGHTS   To stand on or move around the stage during the focusing or lighting session so that the position of the lanterns can be fixed and focused.

WINGS   1. Space at the side of the stage.
       2. Painted flats/black masking that define the limits of the acting area.

WORKING LIGHTS   These are theatre lights that are independent from the stage lights and are used during rehearsals and fit up.

Theatrical Superstitions

Thespians are well known for their superstitions and, unless a 'newcomer' to the world of theatre is aware of the major ones, they may be accused of bringing the show down around everyone's ears. The major superstitions are:

- Don't whistle in the dressing room
- Never use fresh flowers on the stage
- Never use a real Bible
- Never say 'Macbeth'. Always refer to it as 'The Scottish Play with the Scottish King and the Scottish King's Wife'
- If an actress drops a comb, she must dance over it or she will lose her job
- Never put peacock feathers or a goldfish bowl on the stage
- Never hang pictures in the dressing room until after opening night
- Never wish anyone good luck
- If more than one person washes their hands in the wash basin at the same time, they must make the sign of the cross on the water, or a quarrel will follow
- Some actors refuse to speak the last line of a play in rehearsal, thinking it will mean the play will flop
- Never put shoes on a table
- At the end of a run, do not leave soap in the dressing room as it means you will never work in that theatre again
- Receiving a bouquet of flowers at the stage door BEFORE a performance begins is considered to be an omen of failure, after is fine!
- Knitting on the side of the stage, or on stage, by an actor or actress is considered unlucky
- Never use a real mirror on stage
- Before making a first entrance an actor, or actress, should be pinched for luck
- A good rehearsal is a bad omen
- To trip on entering on the first night is a sign of success
- MAKE UP:
    1. Upsetting a make up box means bad luck is coming
    2. Make up boxes should never be cleaned out, as this is said to bring bad luck
    3. Powder, if dropped, should be danced upon to bring good luck

Deaths on Stage – Or Thereabouts!

There is an old show business saying, 'The show must go on', and it would seem that, in the world of theatre, some are so committed and obsessional about their work that they are actually quite prepared to die on the job!

MOLIÈRE: DIED 1673

Overcome by a coughing fit during a performance of his play, *Le Malade Imaginaire*, (*The Hypochondriac*), Molière was taken home where he later died.

THOMAS HALLAM: DIED 1745

During a quarrel over a wig, Hallam was attacked with a sword-stick – which pierced his eye – in the Green Room of Drury Lane Theatre by the leading actor, Charles Macklin. Hallam died within 24 hours.

EDMUND KEAN: DIED 1833

Kean was appearing in the role of Othello with his son, Charles, as Iago when he collapsed in Act Three. The curtain was lowered and he was later carried to his home in Richmond where he died on May 15th without ever properly recovering.

WILLIAM TERRIS: DIED 1897

Terris was stabbed to death at the stage door of the Adelphi Theatre by a fellow actor.

MARIE LLOYD: DIED 1922

Lloyd, one of the best-loved artistes of all time, collapsed on stage at the Edmonton Empire whilst singing, *One of the Ruins that Cromwell Knocked About a Bit*. She was carried to her home where she died a few days later; her death, at the age of 52, led to a vast outpouring of public grief.

HARRY HOUDINI: DIED 1926

World famous escapologist, Harry Houdini, died as a result of a punch in the abdomen at a theatre in Montreal, Canada. A student asked Houdini if he knew how to sustain blows to his abdomen without injury. Houdini said yes but, before he was able to brace himself, the student struck and Houdini died just over a week later from this injury.

ARTHUR LUCAN – 'OLD MOTHER RILEY': DIED 1954

Lucan died in his dressing room at the Tivoli Theatre, Hull just before the opening performance of a week of variety.

SID JAMES: DIED 1976

James collapsed on the stage of the Sunderland Empire and consequently died of a heart attack.

TOMMY COOPER: DIED 1984

He died during a televised performance of his act when he suffered a heart attack.

ERIC MORECAMBE: DIED 1984

The much-loved comedian, Eric Morecambe, one half of the double act, Morecambe and Wise, suffered a fatal heart attack during a curtain call of a performance in Tewkesbury, Gloucester.

LEONARD ROSSITER: DIED 1984

Rossiter collapsed in his dressing room at the Lyric Theatre, Shaftesbury Avenue, dying two hours later in Middlesex hospital.

And it would seem to be no safer in the audience either...

TWO PLAYGOERS DIED IN AN ACCIDENT: 1587

A device used for shooting an actor during a play went disastrously wrong and swerved into the audience, killing a child and a pregnant woman. The theatre in question was not named.

GALLERY COLLAPSED AT NORWICH: 1699

The gallery at the Angel Theatre, Norwich, collapsed, killing a young woman and wounding a great many more.

15 PEOPLE WERE KILLED AND HUNDREDS MORE INJURED AT THE OVERCROWDED HAYMARKET THEATRE: 1794

The Haymarket Theatre was hosting its first ever Royal Command performance, attracting a huge crowd. Then, more and more people without tickets forced their way past the box office and into the auditorium. A troop of guards, fearing for the safety of His Majesty, King George III, moved in and panic ensued. 15 people were trampled to death and hundreds more were injured.

16 THEATRE-GOERS KILLED AT THE ROYAL VICTORIA THEATRE: 1858

16 people were killed and many more injured in a stampede – the result of a false fire alarm.

186 KILLED IN EXETER THEATRE FIRE: 1887

186 people lost their lives when fire broke out at The Theatre Royal; most of the victims were in the upper gallery where there was only one exit. As a result of the Exeter fire, a whole new range of safety measures were introduced and ever since, the safety record of theatre buildings has been excellent.

*   *   *

'We enter the world as a soloist; we depart as a soloist. The part we play in the intervening years in the theatre of life is entirely up to us, for there are no auditions, no parts to cast; neither is this life a dress rehearsal, it's the real thing and you have but one chance to show just how good you are.'

(Anon)

Permissions

Maureen Hughes is grateful to the following for kindly giving permission to use their images:

Michael Billington – Reproduced with kind permission of Michael Billington
York Mystery – York Festival Trust – www.mysteryplays.co.uk
Chester Mystery Plays – Photographer Geoffrey Newcombe
Oberammergau –- Oberammergau Tourism
Alan Ayckbourn Copyright: Scarborough Theatre Trust/Supplied by The Bob Watson Archive
David Wood (Head Shot) – Lisa Bowerman
David Wood (with rocking horse) – Jill Furmanovsky
Brian Friel – Bobby Hanvey
Trevor Griffiths – Gill Griffiths
Bill Kenwright – Everton Football Club
Sonia Friedman – Dan Wooller
Sir Peter Hall – Kingston University
Nicholas Hytner – Ivan Kync
The Polka Theatre – Simon Jay Price, and also with kind permission of The Polka Theatre

Bibliography

REFERENCE BOOKS

Banham (ed.), M., *The Cambridge Guide to World Theatre* (Cambridge University Press, 1988)

Brown, J.R., *The Oxford Illustrated History of Theatre* (Oxford University Press, 2001)

Bryson, B., *Shakespeare: The World as a Stage* (Harper Perennial, 2008)

Chambers, C., *The Continuum Companion to Twentieth Century Theatre* (Continuum, 2002)

Griffiths, T.R., *The Theatre Guide* (A & C Black Publishers Ltd, 2003)

McQuain, J., Malless, S., *Coined by Shakespeare* (Merriam Webster Inc, 1998)

Nicoll, A., *World Drama from Aeschylus to Present Day* (Harrap, 1949)

Patterson, M., *Oxford Guide to Plays* (Oxford University Press, 2007)

Thompson, J.C., *An Introduction to Fifty British Plays 1660–1900* (Pan Books, 1979)

Trussler, S., *The Cambridge Illustrated History of British Theatre* (Cambridge University Press, 2000)

Welch (ed.), R., *The Oxford Companion to Irish Literature* (Oxford University Press, 1996)

WEBSITES

I would like to thank the creators of the final three sites for their personal help with my research.

www.britannica.com
www.doollee.com
www.historycentral.com
www.brendanbehan.info

Index

237

Fanshen 126
Fantastic Mr Fox 64
Far Away 118, 196
Farfetched Fables 142
Far North 144
Far Side of the Moon (The) 216
Farquhar, George 77, 107
Fascinating Foundling (The) 142
Fastest Clock in the Universe (The) 215
Father (The) 82
Fatherland 125
Faust 79
Faust is Dead 93
Fear of Heaven (The) 130
Feelgood 216
Feeling Your Behind 132
Fen 118
Fences 97, 152, 219, 221
Ferdinand, the King of Navarre 163
Festen 186
Few Good Men (A) 186
Flibberty and the Penguin 65
Fiddlers Three 117
Field Day Theatre Company 122
Fierstein, Harvey 221
Filippo, Eduardo de 212, 214
Filumena 212
Final Passage (The) 190
Fiorello 218
Fire That Consumes 211
First Course 44
First Episode 140
Fishing Party (The) 147
Five Finger Exercise 94, 213
Flare Path 140
FlatSpin 38
Fletcher, John 77
Flowering Cherry (The) 84, 116
Fo, Dario 86, 99, 210
Foley, Sean 212
Folies Bergère 205
Food for Ravens 124
Fool for Love 143, 144
Fools 145

Foote, Horton 219
Footfalls 113
For Services Rendered 128
Force of Change (The) 216
Forc'd Marriage (The) 76
Ford, John 110
Foreign Affairs 148
Foreman, Michael 65
Forest Child 66
Forest of Ostrovsky (The) 44
Forget-Me-Not-Lane 131
Forest (The) 44
Fortune (London Theatre) 203
Fortunes of War 48
Forty Years On 46, 47, 213
Four Degrees Over 70
Four Feathers (The) 145
Four Portraits – of Mothers 148
Four Poster (The) 220
Four Seasons (The) 148
Foursome (The) 213
Fowler, Richard 69
Fragments 113
Frank, Robert 144
Fraser, Brad 215
Frayn, Michael 10, 87, 101, 102, 106, 120, 121, 211, 212, 214, 215, 216, 221
Freedom of the City (The) 121
Freeway (The) 131
French Lieutenant's Woman (The) 55
French Without Tears 140
Friedman, Sonia 187, 188,
Friel, Brian 87, 101, 121, 122, 211, 215, 216, 221
Friendly Fire 87
Friends (The) 148
Fringe Theatre 14
Frings, Ketti 218
Frog Prince (The) 127
Frogs (The) 72
Front Page (The) 103
Fry, Christopher 87, 104
Fugard, Athol 87, 196, 214
Fulgens and Lucrece 74
Full Monty (The) 123
Fuller, Charles 219

Funeral Games 134
Funny Bunny's Magic Show 69
Funny Money 86, 119
Fuzz 146

G
Galati, Frank 221
Gale, Zona 217
Galileo 157
Gallicanus 74
Galsworthy, John 81, 110
Game of Chess (A) 10, 78
Game of Golf (A) 38
GamePlan 38
Garden Fête (A) 38
Gardner, Herb 221
Garrick (London Theatre) 203
Garrick, David 29, 79
Gaskill, William 195
Gaslight 34, 88
Gay, John 79, 99
Gem of the Ocean 152
Gems, Pam 211, 215
General Alcibiades 167
Genet, Jean 87
Geneva 142
Gentle Island (The) 121
Gentle Jack 116
Gershwin (New York Theatre) 207
Gershwin, George 207, 218
Gershwin, Ira 207, 218
Gertrude 160, 161
Getting Married 142
Getting On 213
Ghetto 191, 215
Ghost of Hamlet's Father (The) 161
Ghost Sonata (The) 82
Ghost Trio 113
Ghosts 9, 81, 186
Gibson, William 220
Gielgud (London Theatre) 203
Gielgud, Sir John 214
Gift of Friendship (The) 136
Gift of the Gorgon (The) 186
Gill, Peter 87, 196
Gill, Richard 193

251